Focus Group Interviews: A Reader

2nd Edition

Focus Group Interviews: A Reader
2nd Edition

Thomas J. Hayes
Xavier University

Carol B. Tatham
Qualitative Associates, Inc.

AMERICAN
MARKETING
ASSOCIATION

250 S. Wacker Drive • Chicago, Illinois 60606 • (312) 648-0536

Copyright © 1989, American Marketing Association
Printed in the United States of America
All rights reserved. No part of the material protected by this
copyright notice may be reproduced or utilized in any form or
by any means, electronic or mechanical, including photocopy-
ing, recording, or by any information storage and retrieval system, without the written permission of the copyright owner.

Library of Congress Cataloging-in-Publication Data

Focus Group Interviews: A reader/ [edited by] Thomas J. Hayes,
Carol B. Tatham.—2nd ed.
    p.   cm.
ISBN 0-87757-201-1
1. Interviewing in marketing research.   2. Focused group
 interviewing.   I. Hayes, Thomas J.   II. Tatham, Carol B.
HF5415.2.F63   1989
658.8′3—dc20
89-17500
CIP

TABLE OF CONTENTS

Introduction

SECTION I

The Nature Of Focus Groups

SECTION II

Planning And Preparing Focus Groups

SECTION III

Case Studies And Applications

SECTION IV

Advantages And Limitations

SECTION V

Variations On A Theme

INTRODUCTION

This book is about focus group research. It has been compiled in order to help educate marketing practitioners on how focus groups are used and just as importantly, how they shouldn't be used. The articles presented here range from what focus groups are in their most basic sense to some of their more controversial applications.

Traditionally, the use of focus groups has been lauded by their champions and sharply criticized by their detractors. While one group may feel that the use of focus group interviews allows the researcher to "go beyond counting noses and delve into the complexities of the human soul", the critics of these interview techniques claim they are over used and misapplied. The reality is that both ends of the spectrum are to some extent correct.

Focus group interviewing is merely a research tool. Like any other tool it is only as good as the person using it and is not applicable to all problems. Focus groups may be the source of valuable insights to a marketing organization. Unfortunately, they are easily misinterpreted and many times employed for political purposes. If focus groups are designed and executed properly they will appear as if anyone could lead one. This is far from the case. Additionally, focus groups are by their very nature flexible, giving the impression that virtually any technique can be employed within their two hour time constraint. This is also not true.

Focus groups are an important research technique that require the user to understand their nature. strengths and weaknesses before attempting to use them. Focus groups are not to be employed as an afterthought or in a non-empirical fashion if one wishes to use any of the information they may provide. This text is designed to provide the reader the information and knowledge necessary to design and execute focus group interviews properly. Articles have been selected to that not only present the basic material explaining their use but also challenge the reader to evaluate for themselves some of the more argumentative focus group techniques.

Over eighty articles were examined before choosing those that appear here. Some of the articles that were published in the first edition of this book were reprinted again in this edition. These "classics" were retained because of their quality and continuing applicability.

The reader may notice that the number of sections have been expanded to five. This was done to allow the reader exposure to some some of the newer and more controversial techniques employed in focus groups.

Section I examines the nature of focus groups. It covers the topic of what focus groups are from theoretical to a practical positions.

Section II is devoted to educating the reader in preparing and planning effective focus groups. Articles in this section alert researchers to some of the pitfalls in using focus groups as well how to fine tune the research effort.

Section III introduces the reader to case studies and applications of focus groups. This section allows the reader the opportunity to judge how well focus groups may work in their research environment.

Section IV highlights articles that examine the strengths and limitations of focus group research. This section is meant to inform the reader what focus group interviewing techniques are capable of achieving. Dispelling myths and focusing on realistic expectations are emphasized.

Section V introduces a number of variations of the traditional focus group. A few of these techniques are quite dialectic and their inclusion here is not an endorsement. This section is presented to the reader to provide a full array of present focus group applications. These variations each have their own strengths and limitations that the reader needs to consider.

SECTION I

The Nature Of Focus Groups

A total of six articles were chosen for this section based on their ability to communicate what focus groups are and how they fit into the world of marketing research. Two of these six readings are 'classics' reprinted from the first edition. The first classic 'The Group Depth Interview' by Goldman was originally published in 1962. Although at first glance it may appear theoretical in nature it is very application oriented and easy to read. The reader may even be surprised to find a few of the techniques described by Goldman are the same ones being sold as new and revolutionary today.

The second "classic" is written by Bellenger, Bernhardt and Goldtucker. Their article on Focus Group Techniques does a very good job of addressing such issues as: the dynamics of the moderator, advantages and limitation of focus groups and uses and misuses of this research technique.

"Turning Focus Groups Inside Out" by Cook describes how focus groups work and can be improved by comparing them to another group interaction methodology, synectics.

Tynan and Dsoyten provide a wonderful primer for the first time user of focus groups. Their article is ideal for someone who does not have a strong research or marketing background. It is also extremely well referenced.

Raymond Rowe Johnson draws on survey results of over 100 tapes of focus groups. He identifies four basic types of groups each defined by a significant adaptation of interviewing techniques to answer one of four basic research questions. The purpose of this article is to provide some structure to a field that is generally perceived as being the opposite.

The last article in this section is Calder's "Focus Groups and the Nature of Qualitative Marketing Research." This is an excellent theoretical work applied to practical situations. To some, this article may seem difficult to read, but press on. It's worth it!

The Group Depth Interview

ALFRED E. GOLDMAN

"Discussion panels," "respondent-oriented interviews," "consumer conferences," and "focused group interviews" have enjoyed increasing popularity in attempting to solve marketing problems. This article describes the mechanics of conducting group interviews and also some of its consequences.

The title of the article, "The Group Depth Interview," reflects a situation in which information is sought from a number of interacting individuals at the same time, using a combination of probing and direct-inquiry techniques.

CONSIDERATION of each of the three elements of the name given to the group-interview technique suggests that, while the label may be as serviceable as any other, under certain conditions it is not wholly accurate. A comprehensive review of group methods is beyond the scope of this article; and the interested reader can refer to the voluminous literature on this technique and its application to marketing, education, and psychotherapy.[1]

Instead, the present article explains what is meant by *group, depth,* and *interview* in a group depth interview . . . the mechanics of moderating such interviews . . . and the five requirements of these interviews.

Group

A group is a number of *interacting individuals having a community of interests.* These two criteria of groups must be satisfied in order to derive the benefits of collecting information in a group setting.

Interaction

In the group situation a person is asked an opinion about something—a product, a distribution system, and advertisement, a television program, or perhaps a candidate for office. In contrast to the individual interview in which the flow of information is unidirectional, from the respondent to the interviewer, the group setting causes the opinions of each person to be considered in group discussion. Each individual is exposed to the ideas of the others and submits his ideas for the consideration of the group.

This assumes, of course, that social interaction occurs at some overt level. If the group members do not interact with one another, but each member directs his remarks to the moderator, this is not a group. It might better be described as multiple or serial interviewing, since the advantages of the group setting are precluded. It is the interviewer's responsibility to stimulate the group members to interact with each other rather than with him.

Community of Interest

The establishment of group cohesiveness is dependent in large part on the second criterion of "groupness," namely, *sharing a common interest.*

1 Suggested sources: H. H. Lerner and H. C. Kelman, "Group Methods in Psychotherapy, Social Work, and Adult Education," *Journal of Social Issues*, Vol. 8, Whole issue No. 2, 1952, pp. 1-88; W. Mangold, *Gegenstand und Methode des Gruppendiskussions verfahrens: Aus der Arbeit des Instituts fur Sozialforschung,* (Frankfurt am Main: Europaische Verlagsanstalt), pp. 176.

Reprinted from *Journal of Marketing*, 26 (July 1962), 61-68, published by the American Marketing Association.

This common interest should, of course, be relevant to the topic under discussion. A number of individuals may be very different in national origin, religious beliefs, political persuasion, and the like; but if they share a common identity relevant to the discussion (shoe buyers, drug manufacturers, purchasers of luxury items), a group can form. This involves some risks that can be minimized by thoughtful selection of group members. For example, in a discussion of a home-decorating product, the inclusion of one or two low-income people in a group of wealthy individuals may serve to inhibit the free expression of the attitudes of all.

How may these two characteristics of a group be exploited in eliciting useful information, and in what way is this information different from that produced by individual interviewing?

1. First, the interaction among group members *stimulates new ideas* regarding the topic under discussion that may never be mentioned in individual interviewing. When a group member does bring up a new idea, however tangential, the group as a whole is given the opportunity to react to it in a variety of ways that indicate its interest to the group.

The idea can be readily and enthusiastically taken up by the group and ultimately accepted or rejected. The idea can be discussed without a decision being reached, with considerable confusion expressed in the process. The idea can be discussed briefly and then dropped not to be mentioned again. Sometimes, and most significant of all, it can be studiously ignored and avoided, despite the moderator's reiteration of the idea. This behavior, when accompanied by indications of anxiety, such as lighting cigarettes, shuffling uneasily in seats, clearing throats, and so on, suggests that a particular idea has provoked sufficient psychic discomfort and threat as to require its rigorous avoidance in open discussion.

2. These possible reactions to a new idea may also demonstrate a second value of group interviewing—*the opportunity to observe directly the group process.* In the individual interview, respondents *tell* how they would or did behave in a particular social situation. In the group interview, respondents react to each other, and their behavior is directly *observed.*

For example, a housewife who hesitantly and timidly describes how she cleans her floors suggests the tenuousness with which she herself regards these procedures. In one group, the timid admission by one housewife that she hated washing floors and did so only when forced to by fear of social rejection brought immediate and firm support from other group members. They then verbally "turned on" the two group members who washed floors more frequently and meticulously. Here the attitudes of women toward washing floors was reflected in the

way they behaved toward each other *in the group.*

A purchasing decision is frequently a social act in that the items are considered in the context of what others think of the product, and what others will think of *them* for having purchased it. The group creates or recapitulates the marketing situation, depending upon the point at which the decision process is intercepted. Here the process of the decision is exposed in the sharing of experiences, rumors, and anecdotes that go on in a group discussion about a product, service, person, or event. Here we are concerned with the *process* of the purchasing decision, not just in the static end-result of that process. Effective marketing requires understanding of this decision process.

3. A third advantage of group interviewing is that it *provides some idea of the dynamics of attitudes and opinions.* The flexibility or rigidity with which an opinion is held is better exposed in a group setting than in an individual interview. Within the two hours of the typical group session, an opinion that is stated with finality and apparent deep conviction can be modified a number of times by the social pressures or new information that may be provided by the group. As the discussion proceeds, some group members modify their initial reaction, some defend their positions even more rigorously, some admit confusion. In this way, the group setting offers some idea of the dynamics of opinion—its initiation and modification, and its intensity and resistance to change. This pattern of modification in opinion is often as rewarding with regard to understanding motives as the one initially stated.

4. Discussion in a peer group often *provokes considerably greater spontaneity and candor than can be expected in an individual interview.* This is its fourth advantage. The interviewer is frequently an "outsider," regardless of how skillful he or she may be. In the group setting it is not unusual for group members, after an initial period of orientation, to ignore completely the presence of the moderator. For example, in a group of small-

• ABOUT THE AUTHOR. Alfred E. Goldman is Director of Research Development with National Analysts, Inc., of Philadelphia. Dr. Goldman received his B.S. and M.A. degrees from the City College of New York, and his Ph.D. in clinical psychology from Clark University.

Since 1950 he has been associated with various state and federal clinics and hospitals where he was particularly interested in group psychotherapy and research. He was Assistant Professor of Psychology at Northeastern University and Research Associate in the School of Public Health of Harvard University. In 1956 he was Director of Psychological Research at Norristown State Hospital. He has published various articles in psychological and psychiatric journals.

business managers, several of them admitted blatant acts of petty dishonesty at the expense of their customers. It seems unlikely that this would have been admitted to an individual interviewer.

Because of the demands on their time, physicians are unusually difficult to interview at length. Yet in group discussions with other physicians, two hours does not seem to tax their interest or cooperation. Physicians who appear impatient, constrained, cautious, or curt when interviewed alone, seem considerably more garrulous, frank, and at times argumentative when in a group with other physicians.

Candor is permitted not only because the members of the group understand and feel comfortable with one another, but also because they draw social strength from each other. The group provides support to its members in the expression of anxiety-provoking or socially unpopular ideas.

An example may illustrate this. At the beginning of a 2½ hour session, a group of jobbers individually expressed loyalty to, and appreciation of, their suppliers. After an hour, most of these same group members joined in the expression of a pervasive and deeply felt antagonism toward their manufacturers—attitudes which they had not previously expressed for a variety of reasons, including fears of economic reprisal by the jobber.

In another instance, members of a minority group at first vehemently denied favoritism in buying from members of their own group. Later, following a profound and emotional discussion of racial and religious intolerance, *all* admitted that they preferred to buy from a salesman of their own ethnic group. By virtue of its community of interests, the group permitted exposure of feelings not ordinarily given casual or public expression.

5. A fifth advantage is that the group setting is *emotionally provocative in a way that an individual interview cannot be.* A group composed of housewives ranging in age from 25 to 45 may serve to illustrate how the group can provoke reactions which elicit interesting and useful insights into the motives of its members. This discussion focused on how these women felt about their weight, and what effect this had on their diets. At one point in the discussion, the youngest and most slender woman in the group said, "Weight isn't a problem for me yet, but I imagine that for older women like yourselves it would be." Immediately, perceiving the unintended offense to the other group members, she explained, "Well, as you get older, you get fatter." This attempt at diplomacy fell somewhat short of soothing the injured self-concepts of some of the other women, but it did serve to provoke quite profound feelings toward "getting old" and how these feelings were expressed in their eating habits. Thus, a member of the group confronted the other group members with

anxieties that the moderator could mention only at considerable risk to continued *rapport*.

Thus, by virtue of the interaction and common relevant interests of its members, the group offers more and qualitatively different information than can be obtained from the sum of its individual human parts.

Depth

The use of the word "depth," in the name given this technique, implies seeking information that is more profound than is usually accessible at the level of interpersonal relationships. While a respondent may be the best authority on *what* he did, he is often an unreliable source of information as to *why* he did it. His response reflects what he wants you to believe, and also what he himself wants to believe. Retroactive distortion helps him to maintain a self-concept of a wise, judicious buyer motivated by reason rather than feeling.

Much of our daily behavior is motivated by subliminal stimuli (sensory impressions of which the individual is only minimally aware). Depth interviewing seeks to bring these motives to light. Technically these motives are *preconscious*, and are distinguished from *unconscious* motives by the more profound depth of repression of the latter.

A study of the factors that determine which of several supermarkets were used by shoppers in a particular neighborhood illustrates the definitive and lasting reaction to subliminal stimuli. Some of the women in each of four group sessions were adamant in their intention not to shop in one of the markets, although they did not appear able to express their reasons in a clear or consistent manner. Some mentioned a vague feeling that the market in question was somehow messy or even dirty. Yet, upon further exploration, these same women agreed that the shelves were neatly stacked, the personnel clean, the floors swept, the counters well dusted. They could not point out anything to support their charges of uncleanliness. Further, they readily agreed that the store they did shop in was more messy than the one in which they refused to shop. A casual reference by one of the women to a peculiar odor evoked immediate recognition from the others. This occurred spontaneously in several of the groups and led to the consensus that it was a "bloody" or "meaty" odor. This process of "consensual validation" suggested that this vague impression of untidiness stemmed not from anything that could be seen, but rather from this faint yet pervasive and offensive odor. Later this information served to bring to the attention of the management an ineffective exhaust-and-drainage system in the supermarket's meat room.

In seeking "depth" material we do not make the assumption that we can in some way get the respondent to express unconscious motives *directly*. A thing is repressed, that is, remanded to the care of the unconscious, if it is too threatening to the self-concept to allow into consciousness. Generally there is little that a moderator can do, or ethically should do, to provoke the overt expression of such threatening material. What is usually done is to infer the nature of these impulses from who says what, in what sequence, to whom he says it, and how he says it.

However, there are certain conditions under which the moderator may wish to explore some facets on an unconscious motive. By focusing on the motives of one group member, the others are frequently provoked to react to the repressed motive, even if that motive is never made quite explicit. For example, in a discussion of an easy-to-prepare "instant" food, one woman made the following slip-of-the-tongue: "Especially when I'm in a hurry, I like foods that are time-*consuming*." The context of the preceding discussion, which centered upon the role that food preparation plays in the housewife's concept of herself, made it quite clear that the eagerness with which this woman embraced "instant" foods was not without psychic conflict. In this case, the moderator inquired into the error without interpreting to her the feeling of guilt that this slip may have revealed. It did serve, however, to stimulate other women to discuss this problem more openly.

Probing for unconscious material should be undertaken with extreme caution. The danger, in most cases, is not that any appreciable damage will be done to a reasonably stable personality; the normal protective mechanisms will adequately protect the ego from ill-advised assaults by the moderator. Rather, the danger of unskilled probing is represented by the risk of completely alienating the offended group member, and thereby limiting the cooperation and spontaneity of the whole group. In these situations, the professional psychologist with clinical experience is more likely to avoid such pitfalls.

Interview

The word "interview" has the least precise meaning of the three elements of the term, group depth interview. An interview implies an interviewer, rather than a moderator. The role of moderator requires using the group as the device for eliciting information. The moderator guides the discussion, keeping it within fruitful bounds, but rarely participates in it himself. When he can lead a group member to ask a question of the group, the moderator will not question them himself.

An interviewer, especially with a structured questionnaire, is frequently restricted to a direct question-and-answer approach, while the moderator has the greatest possible flexibility and freedom in pursuing motivational "pay dirt" and may seek to exploit unique characteristics of a particular group in the most effective way by whatever devices at his disposal.

The Mechanics of Moderating

The best way to describe group depth interviewing is in terms of the specific mechanics of moderating the group. Many of the techniques considered here have been suggested by those used in group psychotherapy. Although psychotherapy has a radically different primary goal, it shares with group interviewing the goal of eliciting information which the group member himself finds difficult, or impossible, to produce.

All sessions are tape recorded, with the recorder placed in full view. For training purposes and client observation a one-way vision mirror is used. All group members are paid, to compensate them for the expense of traveling to where the session is conducted, and to attract people other than the merely curious.

Rapport

The most important factor in producing usable information from the group depth interview is the relationship between the moderator and the panel members, and that among the panel members themselves.

The first job of the moderator is to structure the roles of all of the participants. The purpose of the session, how long it will last, and the manner in which it will be conducted are all explained in as comfortable and friendly a way as possible. Good *rapport* is crucial in establishing the candidness needed; and this is facilitated when the language of the moderator is not too discrepant from that of the majority of the group. For example, when the group is composed of young, poorly educated subjects of marginal socio-economic level, "they won't dig you if you bug 'em with a lot of high-falutin' jazz."

Verbal Activity

The verbal activity or passivity of the moderator is determined by the nature of the group and its goals. With alert and articulate people the moderator can assume a more passive role—passive, not inert. In an especially talkative group, or at the other extreme, with a very quiet group, a more active role will be required of the moderator, either to inhibit or provoke more discussion.

Relevancy

One of the most important things that the moderator does is to keep the discussion within relevant limits. Here he must be very careful not to rule out that which is apparently unrelated, but may reveal relevant unconscious motives. A general discussion of grandma and grandpa and the "good old days" may have extensive significance in marketing such things as upholstery fabric or canned foods.

Sensitivity to unconscious processes is, of course, important here and a clinical background is helpful, although not essential.

Projective Questions

The researcher who pursues those motives of the buying decision of which the consumer is unaware must give particular thought to developing various "projective" techniques which expose these motives. The answer to a projective question enables the respondent to express needs which he cannot or does not wish to admit. These, of course, must be individually designed to fit the particular marketing problem. For example, in the selection of kinds of housing materials, material design, or fabric pattern, the following question was found to be very effective: "What kind of family would find this pattern appealing, and why?"

Different reactions to various designs may also be provoked by asking the group what well-known person each pattern suggests to them. In this way, a design that suggests Jayne Mansfield may be qualitatively differentiated from those which suggest Liberace, Eleanor Roosevelt, or Marshall Matt Dillon. Similar material may be provoked by *stereotype photographs and the illustrative cases method*.

Illustrative Case Method

To explore personal habits, the illustrative case method is valuable. Several people are described who differ from each other according to the intensity or consistency of some behavior. Then the group members are asked to describe the other characteristics of the person. For example, Miss A uses underarm deodorant four times a day; Miss B uses one only in the morning—what kind of people are they? Or Mr. A traded his Chevrolet in for a Pontiac; Mr. B traded his Cadillac in for a small foreign car—what kind of people are they? Intensive probing follows their responses in order to clarify what motivates Miss A or B, or Mr. A or B.

Stereotype Photographs

A related type of stimulus is represented by *stereotype photographs*. These are pictures of men and women who typify a particular age, income, or vocational group. Each of these variables, of course, can be independently varied to suit the objectives of the study. The appropriately selected photographs are exposed singly or all together, and a question might be asked, such as: "Which of these women would be most likely to use instant tea?"

The response is followed up with: "What is there about the woman you picked that makes you think that?" Such answers as: "She looks as though she's always in a hurry and can't be bothered with brewing tea," or, "Not that one! She looks rich enough to afford the best; she would have her maid brew tea," are quite revealing of attitudes toward a particular product.

Serial Association

In evaluating the effectiveness of advertising copy, controlled serial association may be used. Prior to exposure of the first ad, the group members are trained in the difficult job of saying words freely one after the other. In this way, they can learn to respond to the test ads with some spontaneity.

For example, to evaluate the impression of the product conveyed to women by a pictorial advertisement in a magazine, group members were shown the advertisement and requested to associate ideas with it. It became readily apparent that this ad suggested licentious intrigue and adventure. While the symbolic meaning of the ad served to attract and hold the attention of the reader admirably well, the dynamic meaning it attached to this particular product apparently was not the most advantageous.

Deprivation Questions

Deprivation questions inquire into the relative value of various products or services. A question such as, "Which of the following canned foods would you miss most if it were no longer available to you?" is somehow more provocative than, "Which canned food is most important to you?"

Deception

A calculated "deception" is often effective in testing the limits of the respondent's convictions. A rich source of information and attitudes is tapped by the group's responses to the blatantly incorrect statement that all of ten very different fabrics are made of the same synthetic fiber.

There are times when none of these methods appears to stimulate any but the most mundane and obvious generalities. This, of course, may be significant in itself if it is not a facade behind which reside motives that are not being expressed. Some other procedures that may be useful in these difficult cases are *false termination* and *playing the devil's advocate*.

It is a rule of thumb in group psychotherapy that the most important material may be produced in the last few minutes of the session. In this way the person who would like to contribute something that may be embarrassing or threatening to him has only a few minutes during which he must endure the discomfort. Also, he may deliberately inhibit ideas that he feels are irrelevant to the discussion proper.

Following this lead, especially in group interviews in which emotionally loaded material is involved, the session is "terminated" early by thanking the group members for being there and inquiring as to whether there are any other comments. Intensive probing into these "final" comments has been rewarding on a number of occasions. For example, a group interview devoted to the motives involved in drinking in taverns as opposed to drinking at home uncovered very little more than mundane and superficial generalities. Following the *false termination*, a group member casually commented laughingly to his neighbor that he is hesitant to drink in a tavern because he holds his liquor poorly and is afraid of making a fool of himself in public. Further probing of this theme with the man who initiated it, as well as others in the group, revealed the specific moral prohibitions against drinking at a bar made by the group member's father. More important, this "casual" comment led to a quite meaningful discussion about the variety and intensity of impulses and emotions that may be expressed in a tavern but are socially unacceptable elsewhere. Anxiety, provoked by the threat of such emotional expression, may be sufficient to limit drinking to the relative "safety" of the home.

Playing the devil's advocate requires that the moderator take a very opinionated role. With the goal of provoking a reaction, the moderator may himself express an extreme viewpoint on the topic under discussion. This is usually sufficient to move the discussion into more productive channels. The same effect can be achieved without involving the moderator, through the use of an accomplice who takes a pre-established and adamantly stated point of view.

Sophisticated Naivete

In most cases, however, the most effective pose is that of sophisticated naïveté. The group members are assigned the role of educating the unknowledgable moderator. He thus forces the group members to explain even the obvious—those unverbalized habits of thought and action that are rarely subject to scrutiny.

Here the moderator may make frequent use of such probes as, "What do you mean?" "I'm afraid I didn't understand that" . . . or, "Remember now, I'm not a buyer; so, would you explain that to me?" Such probing elicited the realization on the part of one dress buyer that in making selections for her extensive clientele she had primarily four of her regular customers in mind.

Parrying Direct Questions

There are occasions in which a *direct question* may put the moderator "on the spot." Often these questions cannot only be diplomatically dodged, but at the same time they may be used to gain additional information. When group members ask, as they frequently do, about identity of the client, this may be used to open a discussion concerning the relative activity in consumer and scientific research of various companies and the interest of these companies in the needs of the consumer. An effective gambit here in response to, "What company is pay-

ing for this anyway?" is something like, "I'm curious about why you ask," or "What's your hunch about who is sponsoring this research?"

Gesture

The use of gestures should not be ignored in conducting the group interview. A raised eyebrow can be an effective probe; leaning forward on the table may encourage more comment by a reluctant or shy person; a shrug of the shoulder can parry many direct questions.

Attention to the gestures of the group members frequently tells more than what is said. Reserve, disgust, disdain, irritation, enthusiasm, and myriad other emotional subtleties are conveyed by gesture. Here is an example. In a discussion of a building material, one woman, while describing her impression of it, continually rubbed her thumb and forefinger together. Here words expressed a mildly favorable opinion, but the gesture revealed a fear of which she was only slightly aware herself. Despite the fact that the material itself was very rigid and hard, probing as to the meaning of her gesture revealed a fear that it would be "crumbly" and soft.

Non-directive Comments

Non-directive comments often help to focus attention on the emotion implicit in a discussion. A non-directive comment such as, "You seem angry about that," or, "That memory seems to give you pleasure," recognizes and accepts emotion, and at the same time encourages the group member to reflect further on his feelings in relation to the topic under discussion. Most people need such encouragement to express strong feelings in a group setting, particularly feelings of tenderness and sentimentality.

Five Requirements of the Group Depth Interview

Five factors are required of the group depth interview in order to serve its research objectives: *objectivity, reliability, validity, intensive analysis,* and *marketing applicability*. While the first four are required of any scientific research, the last is more relevant to marketing studies. Any endeavor that presumes to be marketing research cannot ignore these guideposts of sound inquiry.

1. Objectivity

Avoidance of the bias of the interviewer and client indicates *objectivity*. Respondents are unusually sensitive to the attitudes and opinions of the group moderator; and if these are allowed to manifest themselves without the moderator's awareness, it can grossly affect the nature of the data. To further objectivity, it is usually necessary to disguise the identity of the client, and for the moderator to observe rigorous neutrality (except when being the devil's advocate). Objective summary of attitudes sometimes requires the use of some quantitative technique, such as a scaling device, within the context of the group interview.

2. *Reliability*

The degree to which the information produced is representative of the population to which it is generalized is called *reliability*. The question of reliability of the sample, or generaliation of the results, directs attention to the purpose of the group depth interview. Its basic function is to indicate "why" rather than "how many." That is, it focuses on understanding the motives of behavior rather than cataloging the number of individuals who behave in a particular way.

The group interview is particularly useful in the developmental phases of a research program. It establishes the range of attitudes without, however, asserting the representativeness of these attitudes. Perhaps the major function of the group depth interview is to generate creative and fruitful hypotheses. It does not generally permit broad generalization and thus, in most cases, it should be followed by a probability survey to substantiate these hypotheses.

In certain cases, small-sample group interviews can produce generalizable results. For example, a group panel had represented in its members jobbers who controlled 50% of all automotive parts distributed in a particular city. The opinions they expressed represented a considerable portion of the automotive parts jobber universe in that city.

In special circumstances which limit a study to a small sample for security reasons, the problem of sample representativeness may be academic. A manufacturer may need to limit a study to a small sample, in order to prevent too many people from knowing about a new product prior to its introduction to the market.

Group interviewing does not preclude quantitatively adequate sampling; but in most cases it makes it very expensive.

Another kind of reliability problem is the representativeness of the time sample. Purchasing decisions for higher-priced items begin as vague, general ideas of the product and become progressively more specific as decision-making proceeds. Intersecting this process at any one point in time may not adequately reflect its dynamic nature. The purchasing decision can be viewed as a learning process that may be altered many times from the initiation of the need to the actual purchase of a product.

One way in which this process may be investigated may be illustrated by a problem involving the assessment of consumer reaction to a radical styling innovation of a major appliance. Six groups of eight members each were shown scale models of the appliances at three different sessions held at weekly intervals. At each session, attitudes were intensively probed. A gradual shift in acceptance of the radical change was observed over the three week period. However, when those who had been exposed to the product three times were combined in the same group with people who had never seen the product, the effect was immediate and dramatic: the quality and intensity of their attitudes reverted to what they had been at the very first exposure. Since this kind of interaction duplicates what happens in the market place, it produced a valuable insight into this social-learning process and permitted a more effective marketing decision to be made.

This study suggested that while there may be increasing acceptance of the styling innovation with more exposure to it, this preference was not a stable one and could be reversed by contact with someone who was seeing the radically styled appliance for the first time. Here, it was decided that the style was too radical, and a more moderate style was elected.

3. *Validity*

A source of continual concern to researchers is the *validity* problem, the assumption that a measure really measures what it purports to measure. The group situation attempts to get as close to the actual purchasing decision as possible.

For example, the task given the group member in a problem which concerned purchase of pre-packaged bacon was actual selection from among a number of samples the very bacon that she would serve her family, and not merely enumerating the criteria according to which she usually buys bacon.

Similarly, in a discussion of wine preference, the group members ordered and drank the wine of their choice.

When the topic was that of selecting a garment for themselves, women were asked to act out in detail, using a number of blouse samples, the act of buying one for themselves. Here the moderator took the role of salesman.

A problem involving the factors which are important in home decorating was approached by having groups of married couples go through the actual task of decorating a small-scale model home, using reduced-sized flooring materials, wallpaper prints, drapery fabrics, upholstery fabrics, and a wide variety of miniature furniture of various styles. Each couple decorated in the presence of other couples, and each did so with a conscientiousness that left little doubt that this task had considerable ego-involvement. These various devices tend to decrease the discrepancy between attitude expression and actual purchasing behavior.

4. *Intensive Analysis*

A fourth requirement of the group depth interview is that the often voluminous data be *inten-*

sively analyzed. Discussion material of this kind defies routine analysis. The method of analyses employed here is similar to that by which group psychotherapy sessions are analyzed.

Qualitative analysis of group-interview material focuses on several kinds of data. At the most superficial level are the opinions easily verbalized. They may at times give only some indication of the attitudes that group members are willing to express to others. Subconscious buying motives may be reflected in such data as: what topics are discussed, what kinds of people bring them up and with what degree of intensity, to whom they are said, and, perhaps most important, the temporal sequence in which they are said.

For example, a product that had enjoyed the highest market share in a particular city for fifteen years began to decrease in sales to members of a minority group. The drop in sales did not appear to be attributable to changes in product, package design, or sales policy. In several group sessions, the following sequence of themes was discussed: minority and national groups are becoming more alert and militant all over the world; domination by the more powerful majority must stop; sometimes members of minorities are dealt with unfairly by the police; the company in question makes a good product and is the biggest manufacturer of that product; other companies that also produce a good product are entering the field. These themes, in the context of the total group session, suggested an identification of the minority group member with the smaller producer in opposition to the large "powerful" company. To the extent that their buying behavior was consistent with this psychological identity, the "big" company was being hurt.

5. Marketing Applicability

The group depth interview is designed to *solve marketing problems.* Even if a study satisfies the other four requirements, it is just an "academic exercise" if its findings cannot be put to use in the market place.

A variety of marketing problems in which the group depth interview is applicable have already been indicated. As noted above, the group depth interview is most frequently useful and appropriate in the developmental and exploratory phases of research. Here it is used to make it more likely that the correct questions are asked in large sample surveys to follow.

The group depth interview is also helpful in cases where broad sampling is prohibited by security requirements. For example, when used as a complement to new-product development, group sessions are conducted at several points in the process, to aid management in decisions which are not best left for a point later in the process. In this way, management has available consumer reactions *before* large investments of time and money are committed.

For example, development of a new food product may begin with an exploration of several food concepts in order to expose which of several alternative directions would serve the consumers' needs best. Or, perhaps a manufacturer might wish to know which of several kinds of materials are best suited for a home building item before one of them is committed to intensive laboratory development. When one of these materials is selected by the groups and is developed further, the graphic design of the product also is explored by the group method. In a final research phase the progressively refined and elaborated product may be discussed by various kinds of groups in order to help to guide advertising themes, promotional campaigns, and perhaps distribution systems.

The group depth interview has been used to explore attitudes about corporate images, public relations, personnel-turnover rate, recruiting appeals, health problems, container design, political issues, and many other marketing and social problems. The full potential of the method has yet to be realized.

QUALITATIVE RESEARCH TECHNIQUES:
FOCUS GROUP INTERVIEWS

INTRODUCTION

The focus group interview, or group depth interview, is a technique which grew out of the group therapy method used by psychiatrists. The concept is based on the assumption that individuals who share a problem will be more willing to talk about it amid the security of others sharing the problem. It offers a means of obtaining in-depth information on a specific topic through a discussion group atmosphere which allows an insight into the behavior and thinking of the individual group members. Rather than using a structured question-and-answer methodology, the procedure is to encourage a group to discuss feelings, attitudes, and perceptions about the topic being discussed.

The focus group interview is one of the qualitative marketing research techniques developed in the 1950's in reaction to the large sample polling techniques which provided lots of numbers but little insight into what was really going on, the "why" behind the numbers. One researcher has described the technique as "A chance to 'experience' a 'flesh and blood' consumer . . . to go into her life and relive with her all of the satisfactions, dissatisfactions, rewards, and frustrations she experiences when she takes the product into her home." [44-p.6]

In spite of being one of the most frequently used techniques in marketing research today, there are no prescribed guidelines for focus group interviews, no book of rules, no formulas, and no strategems. [44-p.6] The interviews conducted with researchers and the readings examined in the preparation of this monograph revealed a number of disagreements concerning the use and methods involved in conducting research using focus group interviews. The rest of this chapter will describe the technique, its uses, advantages and disadvantages, noting disagreements among researchers where appropriate.

DESCRIPTION

Merton, Fiske, and Kendall distinguish the focus group as following these criteria:

> Persons interviewed are known to have been involved in a particular situation;... The hypothetically significant elements, patterns, processes, and total structure of the situation have been provisionally analyzed by the social scientist. ... On the basis of this analysis he takes the third step of developing an interview guide, setting forth the major areas of in-

Reprinted from Danny N. Bellenger, Kenneth L. Bernhardt, and Jac L. Goldstucker, *Qualitative Research in Marketing* (Chicago: American Marketing Association, 1976), pp. 7-28.

quiry and the hypotheses which provide criteria of relevance for the data to be obtained in the interview. Fourth and finally, the interview is focused on the subjective experiences of persons exposed to the pre-analyzed situation in an effort to ascertain their definitions of the situation. [54-p.3]

The groups are generally conducted with women, especially house-wives, but can be conducted with any homogeneous group of consumers. For example, Dr. Alfred Goldman has conducted focus group sessions for National Analysts with computer engineers, personnel managers, heads of manufacturing companies, paper-making chemists, retailers, models, doctors, lawyers, and persons whose net worth exceeds a half million dollars.[12]

Focus group interviews typically last one and a half to two hours, which gives the moderator sufficient time to develop a good rapport with respondents and thus get very candid answers. Often the moderator is able to get below the conscious level, and the respondents reveal their personality, emotions, and true feelings. This technique thus allows the researcher to handle sensitive areas more effectively via the group method than with individual interviews.

The technique is particularly suited for new product prototype testing, studying package changes, advertising strategy changes, and advertising copy formulation. It is a very flexible technique, and the interview session can be used to show various products, demonstrations, ads and commercials or even to conduct taste tests or product usage tests as part of the group interview.

The ideal group is 8 to 12 people. Fewer than 8 is likely to burden each individual, while more than 12 tends to reduce each member's participation. With respect to group member selection, Merton, *et. al.* state:

It appears that the more socially and intellectually homogeneous the interview group, the more productive its reports. . . Interviewees of widely differing social status often make comments or refer to experiences which are alien or meaningless to the rest. . . . Some continue to be interested in what is being said, but others become restless and ultimately withdraw their attention.[12]

The number of group sessions conducted depends on the topic being considered, the number of segments to be studied, and expense and time considerations. Covering every possible segment is almost always impossible, so the research must concentrate on the few segments most useful to the specific purposes of the study. For example, if the study requires interviews with broad spectrums of age groups from teenagers to retired people, and heavy users and light users are separated, a large number of group interviews will have to be conducted. The objective, of course, is to try to have as few groups as possible, while at the same time realizing the necessity to replicate the focus group interviews for each segment being studied. If there are two with any one age group and they go in totally different directions, a third session should be conducted.

It is essential to get as much commonality in a group as possible so that the numerous interacting demographic variables do not confuse the issues; to be most productive, all the participants must be on the same wave length. For example, Young and Rubicam, which conducts approximately 600 focus groups per year, almost never puts married, full-time housewives with children at home in the same group as unmarried, working women because their life styles and over-all goals and needs are completely different. They also break teen-age and child groups carefully and rarely interveiw men and women together. [45-p.10]

A number of reseachers think age, then sex are the most important breaks both being better means of separating the group than occupation or income. Great extremes on any of these are bad, however. This is usually not a problem since researchers are typically looking at the middle class only, tending to avoid the extreme of income categories.

Some researchers argue that groups can easily be racially integrated while others feel that separate groups should be conducted with each race. Even those that argue for integration, however, say that one token Black may be worse than no Blacks at all; it is usually better to have two to three Blacks out of ten.

There is much disagreement about the importance of good recruiting to obtain the group members. A minority of researchers feel that because the interview is so subjective and the sample so small and unrepresentative, it does not really matter how you obtain the individuals. A majority of the researchers contacted, however, feel strongly that proper recruiting is essential to the success of the focus group interview. First, it is necessary for the members to have had experience with the product being studied. It is impossible to elicit valuable comments from individuals with no background upon which to draw. Second, people who have participated in group interviews previously (some research firms use a six month limit, some one year, and a very few have no restrictions) should not be allowed to participate. They know what to expect and are too ready to respond, and "show off" for the other participants. As one researcher has put it, "I've heard every excuse and rationalization for repeat respondents, but I will never accept that a repeat respondent can possibly contribute to a session in the same way as a new respondent . . . the only kind of respondent who can make a contribution to my qualitative work is a fresh, spontaneous, involved, honest respondent who has not pre-thought her answers." [45-p.10]

Many researchers believe that an individual should not be allowed to participate in a group containing a friend, neighbor, or relative; they will tend to talk to each other and not to the group as a whole. For that same reason, church groups or organizations should not be asked to send people. The people that arrive in these groups have already established relationships, some being leaders and some being followers.

The physical environment is very important to the success of the focus group interview. The atmosphere should be as relaxed as possible to encourage informal, "off the cuff" discussion. An impressive large table in a big corporate conference room may inhibit many participants and should be avoided. The environment should encourage the individuals to give their opinions and feelings, not their judgments; it is imperative to avoid giving the group members the impression that they are experts and you want their intellectual opinions, and the setup of the room is important in this regard.

Most researchers feel it is important for the client to observe the focus group session. This can be done by having the client actually participate as a group member, or much more commonly, by watching from behind a two-way mirror. It is usually much better to observe from a detached position where there is no danger of disrupting the normal functioning of the group and where the observer can take notes on those findings important to him. A short break may be desirable during the session so the client can specify to the moderator other things which he would like probed in more detail.

DYNAMICS AND THE ROLE OF THE MODERATOR

To give the reader a better feel for the dynamics of the focus group session, an edited transcript (a full transcript from a session usually runs 60 pages or more) from a focus group interview conducted recently with women in Chicago is included in Appendix A. The interview, which originally appeared in *Advertising Age* was one of a series conducted with shoppers throughout the country designed to explore what "typical" consumers think about products and prices in stores today and how they shop.

The one thing on which everyone agrees with respect to focus group interviews is that the moderator's role is of prime importance to the success. This can certainly be demonstrated in the transcript in Appendix A. Rapport, level of verbal ability, relevancy and direction of the discussion are important responsibilities of the moderator. There have been several good articles written telling the moderator how to carry out these reponsibilities effectively. (For example see [47,46])

Proper analysis and interpretation of the data also depend upon the moderator, his experience, insights into group behavior, interviewing techniques, and his knowledge of the subject at hand. Highly skilled moderators are therefore necessary to insure that the information be as free of bias as possible and provide the understanding required concerning the consumers' attitudes, opinions, and buying behavior.

One problem that some moderators have with group interviewing is that they actually conduct separate depth interviews with each of 10 individuals who happen to be sitting at the same table. To avoid this pitfall, a high degree of interpersonal interaction within the group is needed. The degree of interaction can be determined by the focus of the interview. If comments are consistently directed toward the moderator, interaction among the participants is not occurring. If, on the other hand, the discussion centers upon the subject of the research and the moderator has a very minimal role, interaction has been achieved.

Only with interaction can the group interview:

1. provide the desired spontaneity of response by participants.

2. produce the degree of emotional involvement essential to produce "depth" level responses, and

3. produce the kind and degree of rapport which facilitates a "give and take" exchange of attitudinal and behavioral information.

The moderator's skill in achieving interaction among a group of participants who have never met each other before and probably never will meet each other again determines the kinds and the importance of emerging data. Therefore the moderator, often a trained psychologist, must be thoroughly knowledgeable about the category under study and must know when to probe the group members and when to shut up. This special talent can be developed only by specific training and by learning from a great deal of trial and error.

Following are a few key qualifications of moderators adapted from Donald A. Chase, "The Intensive Group Interview"[46]:

1. *Kind but firm* — In order to elicit necessary interaction, the moderator must combine a disciplined detachment with understanding empathy. To achieve this, he must simultaneously display a kindly, permissive attitude toward the participants, encouraging them to feel at ease in the group interview environment, while insisting that the discussion remain germane to the problem at hand. Only with experience can the moderator achieve an appropriate blending of these two apparently antithetical roles.

   It is also the moderator's responsibility to encourage the emergence of leadership from within the group, while at the same time avoiding tendencies of domination of the group by a single member. The kindly but firm moderator must be sensitive to bids for attention and must maintain his leadership without threatening or destroying the interactional process.

2. *Permissiveness* — While an atmosphere of permissiveness is desirable, the moderator must be at all times alert to indications that the group atmosphere of cordiality is disintegrating. Before permissiveness leads to chaos, the moderator must reestablish the group purpose and maintain its orientation to the subject.

   The moderator must be ready and willing to pursue clues to information that may at first appear tangential to the subject for it may open new areas of exploration. He must also be prepared to cope with expressions of unusual opinions and eruptions of personality clashes within the group. The manner in which these are handled may well be the difference between a productive and an unproductive group session.

3. *Involvement* — Since a principal reason for the group interview is to expose feelings and to obtain reactions indicative of deeper feelings, the moderator must encourage and stimulate intensive personal involvement. If the moderator is unable to immerse himself completely in the topic being discussed, the group will sense his detachment, and the depth contribution of the interview will be lost.

4. *Incomplete Understanding* — A most useful skill of the group moderator is his ability to convey lack of complete understanding of the information being presented. Although he may understand what the participant is trying to express, by carefully inserting noncommittal remarks, phrased in questioning tones, the respondent is encouraged to delve more deeply into the sources of his opinion. He is, by this process, able to reveal and elaborate on the kinds of information for which the group interview is designed. The goal is to encourage respondents to be more specific about generalized comments made by group members.

The usefulness of this technique can be endangered if its application is inappropriate. If the "incomplete understanding" is a superficially assumed role, the group will soon detect this artificiality, and will feel that the moderator is playing some sort of cryptic game with the group. The group interview will then deteriorate into a sterile collection of mutual suspicions. Incomplete understanding on the part of the moderator must be a genuine curiosity about the deeper sources of the participant's understanding.

5. *Encouragement* — Although the dynamics of the group situation facilitate the participation of all members in the interaction, there may be individuals who resist contributing. The skillful moderator should be aware of unresponsive members and try to break down their reserve and encourage their involvement.

The unresponsive member offers a real challenge to the group moderator. There are numerous ways in which a resistant or bashful member can be encouraged to participate, such as by assigning him a task to perform, or by providing an opening for his remarks. If this is inappropriately attempted, it may only reinforce a reluctance to participate in a verbal fashion. The ability to interpret nonverbal clues may provide a means of discovering a tactic to broaden the scope of the group's active participation.

6. *Flexibility* — The moderator should be equipped prior to the session with a topic outline of the subject matter to be covered. By committing the topics to memory before the interview, the moderator may use the outline only as a reminder of content areas omitted or covered incompletely.

If a topic outline is followed minutely, the progress of the interview will be uneven and artificial, jumping from topic to topic without careful transitions. This procedure communicates a lack of concern to the participants, for its mechanical nature makes the moderator appear to lack genuine interest in their responses.

At the same time, the interview cannot be allowed to wander aimlessly. Under such conditions, control of the situation soon passes from the moderator to a self-appointed group leader.

The group interview should be conducted the way one walks across a rope bridge. The handrails are gripped firmly and the objective is kept in mind constantly. If the bottom foot rope should break, the walk is continued hand over hand until the destination is reached. This requires an ability to improvise and alter predetermined plans amid the distractions of the group process.

7. *Sensitivity* — The moderator must be able to identify, as the group interview progresses, the informational level on which it is being conducted, and determine if it is appropriate for the subject under discussion. Sensitive areas will frequently produce superficial rather than depth responses. Depth is achieved when there is a substantial amount of emotional responses, as opposed to intellectual information. Indications of depth are provided when participants begin to indicate how they feel about the subject, rather than what they think about it.

There are differing views with regard to the sex of the moderator. Some researchers believe that it is important that the moderator be of the same sex as the group members to insure adequate rapport between the two. Others believe that with a moderator of the opposite sex the participants will not assume the moderator knows what they are talking about (how they wash clothes, for example) and will thus be more specific in their responses.

A problem confronting most moderators is how to control the person who wants to dominate the group and how to stimulate the reticent member. One way to handle the dominant member is to stop the group and poll each person individually on an issue, therefore giving everyone a chance to talk. Also, the moderator may give the person dominating the session a task such as helping the hostess make coffee which takes him out of the room for a few minutes. Reticent persons are often much more of a problem. The moderator must try to determine why they are shy and seek to encourage them to contribute to the session.

The polling technique is often helpful in getting everybody to express his opinion. At the beginning of the focus group interview a question may be asked which requires each member to express something about himself. This tends to reduce the person's reticence and to encourage him to talk. At the end of each session each individual may be asked to sum up what the group resolved. This summary is often very important.

Another helpful device which provides the opportunity to get more input is to call each of the respondents a day or two later to thank him for participating. Often, the respondents have talked to other people after the session, and this may have influenced their opinions. The followup call allows the researcher to find out what they *now* think about the various issues.

It is important to use the same moderator for all the group sessions, even if the sessions are in widely disparate geographical areas. The moderator learns from each session, and becomes more effective in subsequent sessions. He is actually fine tuning his final report with each additional group. Although rarely done, the ideal way to conduct a focus group interview study is to start with several groups and keep going until no new important information is obtained from the session, which may occur after five groups, or after twenty.

ADVANTAGES AND USES

When used properly, the focus group interview technique offers a number of advantages over other techniques. John Hess has described some of the potential advantages of the technique as follows[49] :

Synergism —   combined group effort produces a wider range of information, insight and ideas.

Snowballing —   random comments may set off a chain reaction of responses that further feed new ideas.

Stimulation —   the group experience itself is exciting, stimulating.

Security —   the individual may find comfort in the group and more readily express his ideas.

Spontaneity —   since individuals aren't required to answer

each question, the answers given become
more meaningful.

In addition, the company whose products are being discussed may
benefit by:

Serendipity —   key items or concepts unthought of may
be discovered.

Specialization — the use of highly trained interviewers can
be condensed through group interviewing.

Scientific scrutiny — sessions may be analyzed in detail after the interviews are completed.

Speed —   the use of groups speeds up the interview
process and the data accumulation.

Structure—   group structuring is not so obvious and
leading arrangements can be used that are
unavailable   in   individual   interviewing.

Major benefits accrue from focus group interviews. These interviews provide the researcher with an opportunity to learn directly
from consumers, in their own terms, their reasons for buying a product, their expectations of its performance, and the rewards which
they hope to reap from using it. "No one has done the original
thinking for the women. No one has locked her into little boxes by
'pre-thinking' her reactions and responses. She isn't forced into categorizing her spontaneous and uninhibited reactions so she gives them
to you as they happen."[44-p.6]

Eugene L. Reilly points out an additional advantage of focus
group interviewing. He states that "Our own work in traditional
focus group inquiry had caused us to respect the ability of consumers
(especially in the early stages of ideation),to assess (through reaction)
new product ideas, new concepts, new strategies, etc." [37-108]

Our interviews with researchers yielded a number of different uses
for the technique. Those most often used are:

1. To generate hypotheses that can be further tested
quantitatively;

2. To generate information helpful in structuring consumer questionnaires;

3. To provide overall background information on a
product category;

4. To get impressions on new product concepts for
which there is little information available;

5. To stimulate new ideas about older products;

6. To generate ideas for new creative concepts;

7. To interpret previously obtained quantitative results.

To Generate Hypotheses. An individual whom we interviewed indicated that when a client purchases focus group interviews, he is not buying consumer research. "You are really buying the head of the person who will do the research — the key question is can the person organize information and help you define problems?" With focus groups you are looking for definitions of problems rather than for solutions. What is happening is that you have a loosely defined problem area and want the researcher (moderator) to give you a hand with it. The group sessions give him the guidance to help define the particular problems involved. The researcher and the client draw up a discussion guide together; and when the focus groups are done, what you have is a good operational definition of what the problems are and how they can be stated in the form of hypotheses which can be analyzed via quantitative research.

Because of the qualitative nature of the technique, focus groups are most successful when they allow the researcher to design a better subsequent research study using experimental design or other quantitative techniques. In many major consumer research-oriented companies, any time a major quantitative study is to be conducted, focus groups will be used first to help define the issues and generate appropriate hypotheses for testing.

With sample sizes typically smaller than 100, data which are only directional in nature, and numbers which are not projectable, it is important to recognize that the conclusions generated from focus groups are only hypotheses and that quantitative research must be used to confirm the results before they can be used for decision making.

Several examples can be cited to indicate how focus groups have been used to generate hypotheses. A major gasoline producer, concerned about the future growth of sales of gasoline through service stations, wanted to discover what consumers felt about the gasoline station of the future. It wanted to identify possible opportunities for sales of alternative products and services through its retail network. It used 12 focus group sessions in 5 cities throughout the country to select some possibilities which would be worth investigating in some detail, eventually testing the best ideas with test markets and other quantitative techniques.

Another example of the successful use of focus groups for hypothesis generation concerns research on consumer reactions to bank automated tellers. A series of focus group sessions were conducted with potential users, the results indicating that people found the automatic tellers very impersonal and were afraid of losing their money to the machine. The results of the group meetings indicated that the machines should be personalized, the required secret codes should be easy to remember, and an incentive should be given to the consumer to try out the machine. The hypotheses developed were further tested and confirmed, and a program was created which gave the machine a name and personality all its own. Consumers were allowed to create their own secret code, and free McDonald's hamburgers were given as incentives for using the tellers. The machines now experience the highest usage rate of any automatic tellers in the country with 30 percent of the bank's customers using them, twice the national average.

A third example concerns the use of focus groups to study why women were rejecting vegetable protein products. The quantitative studies found that women said they did not like the taste, but other research showed women could not taste the difference between these products and equivalent meat products. The focus group session found that a possible important reason was that the women did not want to deprive their families of meat.

To Structure Questionnaires. Focus groups are used to help researchers learn and understand the consumer language associated with specific product categories or brands. The language consumers use often may not be at all similar to company technical phrases or buzzwords. One researcher interviewed for this study offered semi-moist dog food, porous-tipped pens, and demand deposits as representative of corporation words not very relevant to consumers. A major use of focus groups is often to find out the key phrases or words used by consumers in talking about the particular product or service.

As an example, a soft drink company, before doing a major study on brand positioning, needed to define the needs people are seeking to satisfy with soft drinks. They know it is not just thirst ("when you see a kid down four cans of cola, you know it can't just be thirst") or a craving for sweets. Such things as social facilitation and escape are also important needs, and 20 focus groups sessions were conducted throughout the country to identify a complete, all encompassing set of needs which were then incorporated into a questionnaire which was used in a quantitative study.

Focus groups are also used to identify new areas to investigate in a quantitative study. For example, a soft drink company used focus groups to examine consumer reaction to several different package changes, including a new wide mouth bottle. The participants indicated that they were concerned with the loss of carbonation in the new package, something that the researchers had not been sensitive to previously. Without the focus groups, the quantitative research would not have investigated this important aspect of the package change.

It is sometimes hard for the researcher to know how to structure a particular question, and focus groups can be helpful in this regard. For example, in studying frequency of use of a laundry product, should the question be put in terms of number of times per month, or in terms of proportion of wash loads?

To Provide Overall Background Information. Focus groups are often used by advertising agencies before making a new business presentation to a potential client. The creative and account personnel are thus able to hear first hand what consumers feel about the product category, the potential client's product, their likes, dislikes, and level of satisfaction with existing products. They are able to hear directly from consumers how they buy and how they use the product, together with their reasons for buying and using it.

In a similar manner, companies considering merger, acquisition, or product line extension into an unknown category may conduct focus group interviews with consumers and/or distributors to determine the attractiveness of the expansion and factors they should consider in their evaluation. In short, what is the product to consumers, how do consumers talk about the category, and how do they judge and evaluate the product?

The wealth of information generated is of great value in introducing someone to a new product category, and as a result, advertising agencies often will conduct focus group interviews when new account teams are assigned to an account.

To Get Impressions On New Product Concepts. One of the most common uses of the focus group technique is the examination of new product concepts to check out ideas at an early stage. As one researcher put it, "So many times the people who work on a project and intellectualize about it almost day and night get so caught up in their reasoning that they no longer can 'see' it clearly. As a result, they can miss the most obvious red flags." [44-p.6]

The following examples show how focus groups can be used to help new product personnel understand how their product fits with consumer needs. First, Texize Chemicals, producers of a wide line of household products including Fantastik®, used a series of focus groups for a new product called Glass*Plus®. Quantitative research had shown that housewives were using Fantastik® to clean glass, a use for which the product was not recommended. The company conducted some focus groups to guide their product development effort and found that there appeared to be a need for a product between Fantastik®, a heavy duty cleaner, and glass cleaners like Windex®. Such a product would be one which could clean glass and also be used as a household cleaner. As a result of the initial concept, they were able to develop Glass*Plus®, which after a great deal more consumer research, both qualitative and quantitative, is being successfully introduced, positioned as an all-purpose light duty spray cleaner. Texize, which has been very aggressive in the new products area, uses focus groups to make preliminary examinations of as many as four to five new product concepts each month, conducting over a hundred group sessions each year.

The focus group technique can also be used effectively by industrial products companies to examine the impressions of dealers toward a new product concept. Owens-Corning Fiberglas is one company which has conducted research of this type.[36] The company's Transportation Marketing Division recently conducted a series of 15 focus group interviews with mass merchandise, oil company and private label tire dealers. The research objective was to see what key benefits and merchandising aids would best help dealers sell glass radials. Previous research had shown that consumers would buy fiber glass radials provided they cost less than steel ones. Owens-Corning marketing personnel watched from behind a one-way mirror as a researcher got groups of 3 to 15 dealers talking about the tire business in general and fiber glass radials in particular. The marketers were very surprised by what they saw as they were convinced that product acceptance would be smooth sailing. But dealers talked about the problems they had when glass bias-belted tires were introduced eight years previously. Even though the bias-belted tires had become big sellers, the dealers were worried that they would have similar initial problems with the glass radials. As a result, the marketing team was able to rework sales themes and promotional copy, with a much higher probability of a successful introduction of the new product.

To Stimulate New Ideas About Older Products. Focus groups can also be used to get consumer impressions of existing products. Such things as consumer satisfaction with what is available now, usage habits, which of several forms or package types are best, possible line extensions, and potential product improvements can all be studied with the focus group technique.

To cite an example, a Texize product, Grease relief®, whose original concept came out of focus groups, was studied using groups to examine some of the above questions. The quantitative research the company had conducted had not indicated any packaging problems, but some focus group participants were found to have a strong underlying distaste for the package. The focus group interviews indicated that the housewives did not like to handle it (pick it up off the shelf). Analysis indicated that the phallic shape of the package was responsible. The company then conducted a series of focus group sessions in Atlanta, a strong Grease relief® market, to determine what type of package might be attractive to the consumers. By the end of each session, respondents had made it clear that a dish detergent-type bottle would be best. In spite of this, participants were sent home with a spray package Texize had developed. Another group session with the individuals was planned for one week later. During these followup sessions the participants said the new spray package was a super package and most thoughts of a dish detergent package were generally downrated. Because members of the group are sometimes so far removed from reality in the sessions that the results are not necessarily indicative of how the product will do in the store, the company decided to do further testing. The final result was the successful introduction of a spray package to attract new users and a large economy sized dish detergent-type package without a spray for heavy users. This example shows how qualitative research can be used most effectively, that is, in conjunction with quantitative research, with each type making important contributions. The qualitative focus groups, for example, were able to identify a problem area which quantitative research was unable to uncover. The groups also identified a possible solution, which was then verified and adjusted via a quantitative followup study.

To Generate Ideas For New Creative Concepts. In addition to helping orient new account teams and gathering information useful for new business presentations, a great number of focus group interviews are conducted by advertising agencies to obtain ideas for new creative strategies for their clients. Myril Axelrod of Young and Rubicam states that:

> Group sessions are, for instance, a most valuable way of letting a copywriter know, hopefully before he has become too emotionally committed to an idea, whether his copy is indeed saying what it is intended to say; whether the consumer is "reading" it in the way he wants her to read it; whether it has meaning to her that is relevant to the way she uses the product and to her needs in the category. [44-p.6]

Most large scale quantitative studies are concerned with the majority, the numbers, and not the single interesting idea that might emerge. For example, during one series of group interviews designed to select a slogan for a new service system, the moderator threw open the discussion for the participants' own ideas. One was particularly succinct and clear, even in perfect rhyme. The phrase was tested further and now is on General Electric trucks all over the country. [12] While this type of experience is admittedly rare, the group sessions often will provide the creative personnel with a wealth of ideas to pursue in their creative process.

Another use of focus groups in advertising is to pretest advertising. The Marketing Workshop in Atlanta, and undoubtedly other research firms as well, conduct short focus group sessions as part of their normal process of testing advertising. They hold a 20 to 30 minute focus group interview after they have administered a quantitative questionnaire to evaluate the effectiveness of the commercials. The purpose of the short group sessions is to provide further insights into why the individuals feel the way they do about ads and to get more detailed information on how respondents interpret the ads.

To Interpret Previously Obtained Quantitative Results. Although not one of the more frequent uses for focus groups, it is one which offers much promise for producing valuable information. This can be demonstrated, using as an example a product of a major soft drink company. The product, a ten percent fruit juice carbonated soft drink, had an acceptable taste, a price which was a little high, and was oriented toward that segment of the soft drink market which was concerned with nutrition.

In the test market, the soft drink started strong, held up for a while, and then dropped off rapidly. Some 30 percent of the market had tried one of the three flavors in a very short time period. The quantitative research which had been conducted had not predicted the falloff in sales and slow death of the product. The company wanted to know why this had happened.

The panel data which had been gathered showed that repeat purchases were slow but did not reveal the reasons why. This was primarily because there was a 6 to 8 week lag between the time that the data were gathered and then disseminated. The research department conducted some focus group interviews and found that the product has a taste that sated very easily but that it was a taste which members of the panel described as " a kind thing that you would have at a wedding. " When asked if that was good or bad, people responded, " It's OK for weddings. " In other words, people liked it but thought of it as being only for special occasions. When asked why they were not buying it, they responded, "Because we've already had it." It seemed that one dose every eight weeks or so was enough. If people wanted to get nutrition in what they drank, it turned out they would buy straight juice or vitamins. If they wanted a soft drink, they did not care about the nutrition at all, and they certainly were not willing to pay extra for it.

DISADVANTAGES AND MISUSES

Some of the advantages of the focus group technique also lead to disadvantages and misuses. For example, focus groups apparently are occasionally used merely as evidence to support a manager's preconceived notions, largely because studies using the techniques are usually cheaper to conduct than quantitative studies using an experimental design.

Focus group interviews are easy to set up, difficult to moderate, and difficult to interpret, and are therefore very easily misused. Often one can find evidence in the interviews to support any position, a reason why many managers use them to support their preconceived ideas. It is obviously very important that extreme care be used in the interpretation, necessitating a highly skilled moderator. This is one of the major disadvantages of the technique, especially since there is an extremely limited number of highly qualified moderators.

In addition, to be most effective, good facilities must be used, as described in the previous section. Unfortunately, there are many cities in the country where adequate facilities are not available.

Another problem with focus groups is that they are used for too many things. Some researchers call this the "quick and dirty" syndrome, again because the groups can be conducted quickly and relatively inexpensively. The problem is the research does not indicate how extensive the attitudes expressed really are, and often the necessary followup using quantitative research is never conducted.

Discussing this problem, one of the researchers interviewed for this monograph offered this advice to future users of focus groups: "Don't use the results as information, and don't believe what comes out of the research. Often, you will make bad decisions using the results, and even worse, you will not know you are making bad decisions. The problem is there is no way to put into perspective what one guy said vs. another guy, or the impact of the group itself on the individual statements." This researcher, who is associated with a consumer products company which conducts several hundred focus groups per year, strongly believes that quantitative research is always required as a followup to the focus group.

Closely related to the problem of the inability to draw firm conclusions from the focus groups is the problem of the nonrepresentative sample used. It is so tempting to leave respondents with a questionnaire. Unfortunately, as one research manager indicated, "The product managers will then project these results to a larger population. For example, with 30 people in the focus groups, if 80 percent said X, the product manager would translate this into so many million people.''

The data are not at all projectable because (a) the sample is so poor with respect to the way in which the individuals are recruited (seldom are they recruited randomly), and (b) because everyone does not have an equal say. The mouse-type person in the corner may be the heaviest user of your product, yet may not say much during the focus group session.

In the words of one researcher, ''All you are really looking for are the few mavericks who will give you good operational definitions for your future study.'' At the same time, care must be taken not to place the respondents in the role of marketing experts. The purpose of the focus groups is not to get the consumers to make intellectual judgments, but to determine their feelings and emotions about the subject being studied, and to get help in designing a quantitative study to measure the pervasiveness of these feelings. Many firms, however, want to use focus groups instead of quantitative research, and then ask, ''How many?'' instead of ''Why, how, what concepts were presented?'' Clients have a tendency to ask, ''How many people does that apply to?'' This of course, cannot be answered with focus group interviews, one of the major limitations of the technique.

Another danger with group interviews is that so much depends on the experience and the perceptions of the moderator. He has his own biases, and the things that impress a moderator may or may not be typical. Is the moderator reading things into the interview that were not there, or is he overstating or understating the findings? The moderator is usually involved in the study right from the beginning and thus has certain biases. For example, he knows what kinds of things a client is looking for and often has seen much past research which may influence his observations.

The environment in which focus groups are conducted leads to other limitations. For example, it is difficult to test pricing in focus groups. People are overly sensitive to pricing questions and the participants are only able to respond to relative type questions such as, ''Is this worth more or less than this?'' Because of this, store tests must be used for pricing studies. A related disadvantage is that the participants are not in their kitchens or homes during the focus groups, and they are therefore outside the environment in which they would normally use the product. This may cause some difficulty in responding to some of the discussion topics.

Another disadvantage is the difficulty in recruiting participants for focus group sessions. This, of course, depends on how many groups are actually conducted and the difficulty in recruiting participants; for specialized sessions this may run as high as $1500. Focus groups are thus not a cheap method, although the total investment is smaller than quantitative research projects, which often cost at least $8,000 to $12,000.

A final disadvantage of focus groups is that there are many charlatans in the business of conducting focus groups, and the marketer must exercise great care in selecting a research firm to conduct the interviews. Some factors to consider in this regard are presented in Chapter Four.

Turning focus groups inside out

by **William A. Cook**
General Foods Corporation

Abstract

A comparison of two group-interaction methodologies was used to suggest some opportunities for improvement of focus groups to be explored in methological research. The Synectics® group problem solving methodology was chosen for the comparison because it had been developed from an extensive research program.

Introduction

Research on ways to improve the focus group interview has been quite limited. Somehow, our emphasis on developing moderator expertise has produced an art form more than a scientific tool. Consequently, there are many skilled moderators, but little canonized knowledge on record. Lists of "do's and don'ts" have proliferated, but testable hypotheses have been infrequently postulated and less frequently put to test.

We have expressed strong reservations about the use of focus groups for a variety of purposes, but we have been less clear about those applications for which they are suited. Even though many of us decry the use of focus groups for decision making, their output looms larger than life and, indeed, often does influence our decisions.

The intent of this paper is to highlight some lines along which we might develop research programs to improve our use of the focus group interview. The vehicle for this is a comparison of focus group methodology with that developed by Synectics® Inc. for group problem-solving meetings. My choice of Synectics was motivated by their heavy reliance on research as the basis for development of their methods. In fact, they continue to modify their process as further experimentation indicates ways of improving such meetings.

Both the focus group and the Synectics group share the same mixed blessing. The group interaction which is integral to them both is at once a blessing and a curse. To achieve the desired synergy, the group leader must relinquish some control to the group and that introduces certain risks and complexities.

Definition of Terms

Let me clarify what I mean by these two terms. By focus group interview, I refer to an interview between a trained moderator and a group of 6-12 willingly recruited participants. The composition of the group varies according to the needs of the client, but generally they do not know each other or, at least, lack any working relationship. By a synectics group I refer to one using the group problem solving procedures developed by Synectics® Inc. in Cambridge, Massachusetts. Most often these groups are composed of fellow workers who bring with them certain pre-established roles and relationships. Their participation may be in response to managerial fiat instead of their own choice. A smaller group is likely with six considered optimal in most cases. Like focus groups, synectic groups generally have a pre-established agenda, but there is wide latitude in following it.

Objectives

The objectives for the focus group interview are generally stated in such nebulous language as:

■ **To provide a source** of ideas or hypotheses to be tested in subsequent research.

■ **To improve our understanding** of how a given segment talks about or thinks about this topic.

■ **To provide the creative team** with input for creating an ad or a campaign.

The objective for a synectics problem solving group is to develop oné or more possible solutions to the problem before the group. An acceptable solution must be novel, feasible and sufficiently well-developed to have identifiable next steps from the point of view of the person whose problem it is. The group approach is usually dictated by the failure of the person whose problem it is to come up with a satisfactory solution alone and/or the need for group participation in the implementation of any solution.

Roles

In the focus group there are two designated roles: moderator and participant. The moderator is responsible for both the content, or **what** gets discussed, and the process, or **how** it gets discussed. Typically, the content focus shifts within a session from the general to the specific. The procedure can vary from a "serial interview" where the moderator poses the same question to each participant in turn to the moderator sitting as a silent observer of a free discussion among participants. The moderator usually is fairly active in the discussion as he tries to balance participation among group members, direct the content toward some focal area, and to get participants to be more self-disclosing than they typically are in a statement of opinion. The participant's role is to "be herself", to tell what she does or doesn't like or want to understand or whatever. Sometimes participants choose other roles for themselves rather than the implicity assigned one. Under such circumstances, the moderator may find that there is suddenly:

Reprinted from *Advances In Consumer Research* 9 (October 1981), 62-64. Used with permission.

■ **A Co-moderator,** who interjects her own questions into the proceedings, and often her own opinions, too.

■ **The Interpreter,** who explains to the moderator what everyone else just said.

■ **The Expert,** who speaks for the group on every topic and takes issue with any who disagree.

■ **Or any of a number** of other disruptive, counterproductive roles.

In synectics groups, the roles are explicitly identified. They may change during the meeting with the consent of the group, but a training session is used to convey what is permissable behavior for each role and what is not. At the end of the training an attempt is made to secure an informal verbal contract with each participant so that they understand the importance of each one filling their role. Leadership of the meeting is divided between two people: one taking process leadership and one content leadership. The Process Leader, or Facilitator, serves as: scribe, recording the meeting activity on a large easel pad; traffic cop, insuring the free expression of ideas and that the rules are followed; time keeper, seeing to it that breaks and session endings occur on time, etc; and catalyst, by changing pace or focus when needed to stimulate activity. The client is the person who owns the problem and has chief responsiblity for implementing the solution. He tries to stay out of the process and to listen receptively to the ideas offered by the group. The rest of the group are designated as participants. Their job is to aid the client principally by offering evocative ideas. Criticism of ideas is primarily restricted to the client and at specified points in the meeting. Both clients and participants are urged instead to try to build on existing ideas overcoming any negative aspects they see.

Communications Networks

It is not surprising that a communications network analysis of these two types of groups reveal substantially different patterns of interaction. The presence of the client in the latter case is quite a significant difference in composition.

Ideally, the focus group would have balance and abundant interaction among participants with minimal involvement by the moderator (See Figure 1). Frequently, the moderator or another member of the group will evolve into a "node" with communications primarily channeling through that person as shown here. Where this occurs, group participation is reduced.

With the synectics group, the client ideally is a node in the communications network (See Figure 2). The participants want him to understand and consider their ideas. At times the communications will be formally restricted to interaction between the Content and Process Leaders for brief periods while the Content leader or Client indicates his desire for the group to redirect its attention. Typically, the group is privy to this diologue but their input is limited. Since ideas are recorded by the Facilitator, there is a tendacy to speak to the chart pad or to the group at large. Too much of this may weaken group cohesion and the willingness of participants to listen to each other and build on one another's ideas. Consequently, the Moderator must exercise some effort toward pushing communication back down so that participants interact more. A light, friendly atmosphere is very valuable here just as it is in a focus group session.

Figure 1

FOCUS GROUP COMMUNICATIONS NETWORK

A.

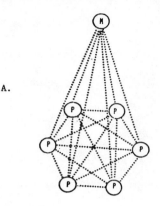

B.

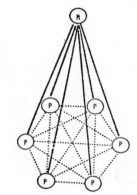

C.

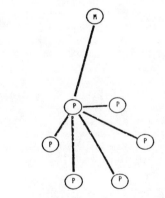

Barriers to Effective Interaction

There are numerous barriers to effective group interaction in these two types of meetings. In the focus group, a common inhibitor to participation is one's perceived lack of expertise on a topic. Similarly, if a person views her opinions as uniquely different from the rest of the group, she is less likely to expose herself as an oddball. Other sources of group heterogeniety (race, sex, SES, product usage, etc.) may also restrict interaction and self-disclosure. Where both spouses are pre-

Figure 2

SYNECTICS® COMMUNICATIONS NETWORK

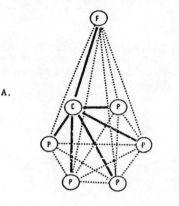

A.

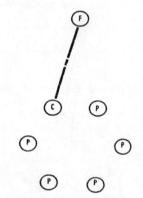

B.

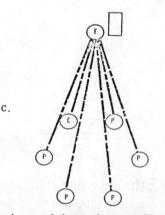

C.

previous working relationships with each other and with the problem being addressed. Issues of turf and lack of trust are common in large organizations and bear heavily on how a group interacts. Similarly, there are various pre-conceived notions regarding what the "real" problem is and how it should be attacked. Getting all the hidden agenda out on the table is not always possible, but deserves some time. The practice of gathering a list of alternative problem statements from which the client is to choose is a good means of accomplishing this.

Implications

There are several means used by Synectics practitioners to restructure group interaction. These may have applicability to improving focus group methodology. For mnemonic purposes I have identified four R's of Restructuring as:
1. Relegating new roles
2. Rechanneling criticism
3. Recognizing contributions
4. Relating to reality

In the *relegation* of a specific person to the role of client, the ability to focus the meeting is substantially enhanced. At the same time, by removing process control from the client, the participants are assured that whatever the clients views, their ideas will receive a fair hearing. Freeing the participant to serve as an uncritical resource permits them to consider riskier, more fanciful ideas than they might otherwise.

The *rechanneling* of critical thinking is brought about through various means. The use of more open-ended language such as "I wish..."or "How to..." is part of that. Allocating separate periods to expand or alter the groups perception of the problem (to blue-sky it) and to narrow the focus and introduce practical considerations insures that blue-sky thinking can occur without the risk that it will stop there. Encouragement to seize on that which is of value in an idea and to build on that doesn't lead to an immediate elimination of our knee-jerk critical response, but it does reduce the frequency of such behaviors.

The formal recognition of contributions does more than just get an idea recorded for future reference, it bolsters the participant's sense of security and rewards her for actively participating. In addition to summarizing an idea up on the chart pad, the facilitator may request elaboration or clarification of the idea from its contributor. The facilitator may turn to the group and specifically ask for a build on that idea to provide additional reinforcement for it, or comment that a new idea is a nice build on someone's previous idea.

Relating the synectic's problem solving activites *to reality* does more than provide a concrete, practical outcome, it serves as a milestone, a tangible reference point for the group, representing how far they have moved toward solving the problem. Of course, a reality-oriented solution is more likely to be translated into action than a blue-sky one. The need for both kinds of thinking derives from the difficulty we have with our practical approaches in escaping our old ways of thinking about the problem with all their inherent limitations.

This notion of closing the loop is one I have found very helpful. It provides a chance for the group to see just what they have accomplished. To determine that they have brought something new to bear on the problem and that it is implementable is very rewarding. The articulation of the next steps to be pursued provides a bridge between the meeting and the future where the ideas will be realized.

sent there is a good change that one will speak for the couple while the other sits silently. In the case of various professional groups, such as doctors, the participants are inclined to state the "party line" instead of disclosing their own views or feelings when they are surrounded by their peers.

Additional barriers to effective group interaction are found in the typical synectics group. They center around the groups

Speaking of closing the loop, I would like to ask you to join me in considering some ways of translating the elements of synectics into researchable hypotheses for studying focus group methodological development. Perhaps you have experimented some in a less formal fashion and have an idea you would like to share. I would like to study the impact of recording the ideas in a focus group up on a pad. I would expect that it would reward the participants for contributing and would serve to focus attention. A simple experiment might involve the note taking in the presence of the group for one set of groups and behind the mirror for another.

I have experimented with presence and absence of client in a focus group session, but not to the point that I would generalize my experience. I would hypothesize that group participation would be increased if the client was present but restrained in her level of activity. I would further hypothesize that group participation would decline if the client took a more acitive role. I doubt that the bias toward expressing only positive views is a serious issue if the client expresses sincere interest. I hope that you will join me in seeking answers to these and other relevant issues.

CONDUCTING FOCUS GROUPS — A GUIDE FOR FIRST-TIME USERS

by A. Caroline Tynan and Jennifer L. Drayton
University of Edinburgh and University of Strathclyde

Introduction

Many authors have drawn attention to the increased use of qualitative techniques by commercial marketing researchers over the last decade (Greenberg *et al.*, 1977; Cooper and Branthwaite, 1977; Goodyear, 1978; de Groot, 1986). These methods have been recommended for use in both consumer (Goodyear and Vineall, 1976) and more recently in industrial settings (Welch, 1985). Despite their importance, qualitative research methods are frequently misunderstood and even ignored by students of marketing. Fahad (1986) stressed this omission and advocated the use of one kind of qualitative research; namely, the focus group interview, at least by the postgraduate researcher. This, however, seems over-cautious. The benefits obtained from qualitative research methods render them worthy of consideration by all students engaged in research projects. These techniques can be used to conduct a preliminary exploration of an under-researched area, to sort and screen ideas as the project progresses, to explore complex behaviour or to experience a consumer's eye view of the world. The accepted advantages of speed, flexibility and economy, together with the rich data generated, make qualitative methods eminently suitable for student research at both undergraduate and postgraduate level.

Of all the techniques available, the focus group is probably the most familiar, having provoked a wealth of comment from both commercial and academic researchers; as such, it offers a realistic starting-point for the study of qualitative research.

Focus group interviews are a qualitative method in which a small sample of respondents discuss elected topics as a group for approximately one to two hours. A moderator focuses the discussion onto relevant subjects in a non-directive manner. The method is a development of the group discussion. This article presents a practical guide to the procedures for conducting focus groups. A full discussion of the theory, role, uses, advantages and disadvantages of qualitative research in general, and focus groups in particular, can be found in Drayton and Tynan (1986).

There is a dearth of useful, practical information on how to run group discussions. The Market Research Society Research and Development Sub-committee on Qualitative Research (1979, p. 116) reported that "there are no widely agreed rules on how discussions should be conducted". Axelrod (1975a, p. 52) concurs: "There are no prescribed guidelines for qualitative research, no books of rules, no formulas, and no strategems". An added complication is that the process of running a group discussion seems simple to the onlooker, ". . . to the uninitiated, the amateur, or the outsider, group interviewing appears to be a simple casual process. . ." (Payne, 1976, p. 69), yet to organise a group discussion yielding useful and usable data requires a thorough understanding of the process and very careful planning.

Preparation

The first step in conducting qualitative research is to discover "what information is being sought, and how insights derived will be used" (Axelrod, 1975b, p. 55). The researcher, or moderator, as they are usually known, should then prepare a discussion or interview guide which is essentially an outline of the key issues, areas and questions to be covered (Payne, 1976). Merton and Kendall (1946, p. 541) see the interview guide as "setting forth the major areas of inquiry and the hypotheses which locate the pertinence of data to be obtained in the interview". It is important that the questions are open and non-committal, leaving the respondents to discuss the issue without being biased by the wording or presentation of the topic. It is at this point that the moderator must consider all the avenues the group might discuss on a given subject, and how he/she might present them in such a way that will not influence the results (Axelrod, 1975b). Hannah (1978, p. 77) suggests that the moderator and the client, i.e. the student and supervisor, should review and discuss the proposed guide thoroughly to ensure that they are both "comfortable with the outline" before proceeding.

Group Size

The most widely recommended size for a group discussion is between eight and 12 respondents (MacFarlane Smith, 1972; Bellenger *et al.*, 1976; Cox *et al.*, 1976; Qualitative Research, 1977; Prince, 1978;

Reprinted from *Marketing Intelligence & Planning*, 6 (1988), 5-9. Used with permission of MCB University Press.

Fern, 1982). For more difficult projects, or more sensitive subject matter, using fewer respondents is advised (Falconer, 1976; Mendes de Almeida, 1980). However, it should be noted that for normal topics, too small a group may result in the loss of useful data. An experiment by Fern (1982, p. 12) proved "focus groups of eight members generated significantly more ideas than focus groups of four members". At the other extreme, 12 respondents are viewed as "a maximum for decent moderation" (Mendes de Almeida, 1980, p. 119). With more than 12 members, the group becomes difficult to manage and may disintegrate into two or even three small groups, each having their own independent discussion.

Sample Selection

The relatively small number of respondents used in a focus group study makes it important that the sample is properly selected (Market Research Society R&D Sub-committee, 1979), but it should not be assumed that the limited numbers in any one group preclude the use of scientifically drawn samples. Normal practice is to use brand or product usage characteristics and demographic controls as a basis for selecting respondents (Prince, 1978).

The issue of inadequate sample size is one of the criticisms most frequently levelled at focus group research. The most convincing case to refute this criticism comes from Lipstein (1975, p.34). He used data from the US Census of 1970 to prove that "increasing sample size is not a guarantee of increasing accuracy. On the contrary, the sheer size makes many kinds of errors highly likely". Errors that increase with sample size are called non-sampling errors. They include errors due to factors such as interviewer bias, mistakes in coding, respondent and interviewer fatigue. Sampling theory states that sampling error decreases as a function of $1/n$. Therefore, increasing the size of a sample decreases the sampling error; but it also increases the non-sampling error. So, for any given sample size, there is a trade-off between sampling and non-sampling errors.

Composition

The composition of the group is related to the research problem. Usually, the group chosen will be fairly homogeneous, with a little diversity to ensure different points of view and to stimulate discussion (Kelman and Lerner, 1952; Smith, 1954; Bessel, 1971; Peterson, 1975). For a group to develop a relaxed, comfortable, natural discussion, its members must have a "community of interests", according to Goldman (1962, p. 61). The respondents must have some common interest they can establish, be it in background, product use, attitudes, etc, to help them form themselves into a group.

Levy (1979) draws attention to the hazards of using a heterogeneous group:

> Perhaps the results are potentially intriguing — but they are more likely to be a fiasco as the participants struggle to find some common ground, or fight the battles of age, sex and class differences (p. 35).

Recruitment

The recruitment of respondents is an issue which is currently the subject of much debate between marketing research practitioners (Market Research Society Qualitative Research Study Group, 1985; Firth and Goffey, 1986; Willis, 1986). Many of the instances of bad practice quoted, stem from the use of inadequately supervised recruitment agencies, a situation which is unlikely to be paralleled in an educational setting.

However, the recruitment of group members can be difficult and expensive. To locate respondents who meet the sample criteria quickly, efficiently and accurately, the Market Research Society R&D Sub-committee (1979) and, more recently, Welch (1985) advise the use of a recruitment questionnaire, whereas Wells (1974) suggests recruiting by telephone or door to door, but only as a last (expensive) resort. All recruiting methods should mask the precise subject matter of the discussion, and provide demographic and "usership" data which can be used in interpreting the research findings. Researchers should take steps to "minimise exclusion of busy, impatient . . . hard to get people" (Falconer, 1976, p. 21), and be aware of the "volunteer bias" indicated by Belson's research (1960, 1963).

One issue of the debate which "has not been adequately resolved", according to Fern (1982, p. 12), is the effect of acquaintanceship on the results of group discussions. Mendes de Almeida (1980) indicated that group discussions are vulnerable to any "group cultures" that existed prior to the discussion because they may enable members to bring prevalidated ideas to the debate. On this basis, he excludes the possibilities of recruiting from churches, clubs or associations, but is not unduly worried about the possibility that a couple of the participants of a group may be acquainted. Kaden (1977) is not perturbed about acquaintanceship among his group members, as he advises the use and re-use of the same respondents, claiming they become more useful as they learn their art. This use of trained respondents has, more recently, been advocated in a British context by Schlackman (1984). The widely held middle view is expressed by Wells (1974, p. 137). He reports that "the assets and liabilities of allowing friends to participate almost balance out".

An allied problem to those of acquaintanceships is the issue of repeaters. Ideally, most writers expressed their preference for "virgin participants" (Axelrod, 1975b; Payne, 1976; Mendes de Almeida, 1980). Their preference is best summed up by Axelrod (1975b):

> Once the respondent thinks, censors, intellectualizes, it no longer is a qualitative insight. Therefore, the only kind of respondent who can make a contribution to my qualitative work is a fresh, spontaneous, involved, honest respondent who has not prethought her answers (p. 10).

It appears that there may be difficulties in locating "virgin respondents" in some areas because of the rate at which they are being used due to the sheer volume of research.

The Moderator

A good moderator is normally described in terms of the traits he/she must have rather than in terms of academic qualifications and professional experience. Langer

(1978, p. 10) lists the characteristics of a good moderator as being:

(1) Genuinely interested in hearing other people's thoughts and feelings;

(2) Expressive of their own feelings;

(3) Animated and spontaneous;

(4) A sense of humour;

(5) Empathic;

(6) Able to admit their own biases;

(7) Insightful about people;

(8) Expressing thoughts clearly, and

(9) Being flexible.

To do their job well, moderators must have "personality, sensitivity and ability" (Drossler, in Caruso, 1976, p. 14). These characteristics and attributes are not impossible for the motivated students to assume. Practising by means of "dummy sessions" will accelerate the learning process.

The Moderator's Role

"The moderator's objective is to focus the discussion on the relevant subject areas in a non-directive manner" (Cox et al., 1976, p. 77). To facilitate this, he/she must establish rapport with the participants, make them relax and promote free discussion. It is important that he/she does not bias the result by imposing his/her ideas or language on the group. The moderator is actively working throughout the whole discussion, thinking about "what is happening now, where the discussion goes next, what it will all mean afterwards" (Langer, 1978, p. 86).

One of the most difficult tasks facing the moderator is that of suppressing the dominating respondent(s) while encouraging any passive group members to participate. This must be achieved as far as possible without alienating or embarrassing respondents, which would destroy the group cohesiveness. The use of body language, gesture and non-directive questioning are the usual techniques moderators employ to achieve this end.

Occasionally, a respondent will refer a question to the moderator in order to resolve some group difficulty. This attempt at reversing roles is best dealt with by countering a question with a question. The implied content of the group member's question then becomes a cue for further discussion (Merton and Kendall, 1946).

In an experiment published in 1982, Fern examined the assumption that moderators are crucial to the focus group process. He concluded that "groups led by focus group moderators did not produce significantly more ideas, or ideas of better quality, than unmoderated discussion groups". However, it is interesting that the respondents who participated in a moderated group felt more enthusiastic in doing the task, as they found it more exciting and enjoyable than those in unmoderated groups. Perhaps the use of a moderator is the price the market research industry will have to bear to keep up a supply of unpaid and co-operative respondents. It should be noted that Fern stands isolated on this issue; other authors see the moderator's role as crucial.

Location

The venue for the focus group must be one in which the respondents feel comfortable and at ease (Macfarlane Smith, 1972). It must also be one they can find and reach easily. Payne (1976) claims that groups can be held "literally anywhere". However, a normal and familiar setting, where there is sufficient space to examine samples or copy if necessary and where the group will not be disturbed are minimum requirements. "Given the accommodation available, people should be seated as comfortably as possible in full view of each other and the leader" (Sampson, 1978, p. 29). An adjacent power socket for the tape recorder is another essential, which, if once missed, is never subsequently forgotten.

The Discussion

The moderator's opening remarks will set the style and tone of the discussion. He/she must indicate the scope of the interview and the topics to be covered. The use of a tape recorder should be explained at this point as an aide-memoire for the moderator, and respondents encouraged to talk one at a time so the play-back will be comprehensible (Wells, 1974).

Wells suggests opening the interview by asking the members of the group to introduce themselves and say a little about their family, occupation, etc. This should break the ice and start the process of the respondents relating to each other.

There is some debate concerning the overall structure of the interview. Both Payne (1976) and Axelrod (1975a) advise moving from the general to the specific when the objective is to obtain a basic orientation into the product category. To obtain a reaction to a specific concept or advertisement, a reverse movement, from the specific to the general, is more appropriate. Axelrod (1976, p. 440) justifies this on the grounds that "when consumers see an ad on television or in a magazine, they have not been thinking about the category for an hour or three quarters of an hour before". She recommends presenting the concept, product or advertisement as the original stimulus for the discussion to get the respondents' fresh and spontaneous responses, then moving to a discussion of the general category.

Payne (1976) considers two hours is approximately the outside limit for a productive group session. The moderator must pace the discussion so that all the topics in his/her guide are covered, and an interesting subject is not allowed to crowd out a topic which should have been discussed towards the end (Wells, 1974).

The use of a tape recorder at group discussions of any kind is well covered by Murphy's Law, "if it can go wrong, it will", with most mistakes being human rather than mechanical in origin. Establishing the routine of always using a new tape for each discussion will alleviate the problems caused by recording a second discussion over the first. Always using new batteries will save having to attempt to interpret "gobbledegook" when playing back a tape recorded on a machine with failing batteries. Using a battery-powered recorder saves

MIP 6,1
1988

having to rely on the existence of a convenient mains supply at the venue, and is also considerably lighter than carrying an extension lead to each discussion. The major disadvantage of using tape recorders is that they inhibit the respondent (Berent, 1962), but a skilful moderator will minimise this effect by treating the recorder routinely (Wells, 1974).

Analysis and Interpretation

Prior to analysing and interpreting the data, it is appropriate to remind the reader that focus groups share the "behavioral science foundation of group depth interviews, but differ from them in that they entail greater moderator involvement and less reliance on psychological theories for interpretative analyses" (Szybillo and Berger, 1979, p. 29). Katz (1946, p. 33) warns that "if research findings are to have any scientific meaning, they must be interpreted in terms of the conditions and assumptions of the investigation of which they are the outcome". When applied to focus groups, Katz's proviso is endorsed by Kennedy (1976), Templeton (1976) and Hannah (1978).

At the beginning of the study it is important that sufficient thought and consideration is given to the method by which the data will be analysed. The data generated by focus groups do not lend themselves to literal interpretation (Templeton, 1976). A good analysis "includes not only what was said, but more importantly includes the implications to the client of what was said or left unsaid" (Hannah, 1978, p. 8). Templeton (1976, p. 445) gives a clear description of the process of analysis and interpretation

> . . . the act of interpreting our group interview data consists in the bringing together of disparate materials (private, written records, interactive discussion, observed behavior, drawings and stories), weighing and sifting of all inputs, and organization of these multiple clues into an articulated set of premises and speculations.

This is done by playing back the tapes, preparing edited typescripts, systematically relating and classifying the information according to problems, objectives and respondent source (identifying and listing factors, dimensions, language, etc.), the seeking of patterns, relationships and ideas by relating new-found with existing data, seeking to construct, support or explode hypotheses (Market Research Society R&D sub-committee, 1979). It is tempting to illustrate and spice the report with examples and quotations from "typical" respondents. Katz (1946) warns against using this kind of case material "when no rigorous procedures have been employed to establish the typicality of the quoted material", but if rigorous selection procedures are utilised, the quotations add life to the final report.

There has been a move among academics to develop a more scientific method of analysing qualitative data to replace the currently pre-dominating methods of the "gut feel and instinct" school. Sue Jones (1981) has described a technique and technology for facilitating the analysis of exploratory qualitative marketing research data. This innovative and complex technique is fully described in her paper. Kassarjin (1977, p. 11) has promulgated the application of "content analysis" (Berelson, 1952) to various methods of consumer research in general and focus groups in particular. Claxton et al. (1980, p. 308) have suggested the use of Delbecq et al's (1975) Nominal Group Technique as an attractive alternative to many existing research

methods. They compared the Technique with focus groups and claimed the following advantages for the former over the latter:

> The structured nature of the session output makes the analysis of individual perceptions possible. Second, using the data analysis extensions developed in the current research, it is possible to do both intra- and intergroup comparisons.

This move by academics has not been mirrored by a similar response among practitioners.

Perhaps the last word on analysis and interpretation should go to Leslie Collins as quoted by May (1981, p. 205), "It is worth bearing in mind that any educated fool can carry out complicated analyses but the ability to be simple is rare."

Conclusion

The focus group interview is a method of qualitative research which is much misunderstood and frequently maligned. As detailed in this article, it is as user-friendly as the ubiquitous survey, and, in many situations, offers substantial benefits, in terms of the quality and nature of data collected, over more familiar techniques. Their attributes of cheapness, speed and flexibility are particularly appropriate for student research with its attendant limitations on time and money. The technique is not without flaws and has been questioned on the grounds of reliability and validity. However, rigorous sampling, honest recruiting and careful moderation will mitigate these errors. This technique should be in every creative researcher's repertoire.

Our contention is that the theory and practice of qualitative research is an integral part of a comprehensive marketing course. Students of marketing, at both postgraduate and undergraduate level, may be expected to be familiar with, and to have experience of, qualitative techniques. Wells and Lunn (1986) highlighted the demand for trained qualitative researchers, the growth in the number of practitioners having failed to keep up with the growth in the quantity of commissioned research. Amongst their suggestions to overcome the problem, the possibility of recruiting graduates with existing skills and experience apparently did not occur to these authors. We may permit ourselves to ask the question why? ∎

References

Axelrod, M.E. (1975a), "Marketeers Get an Eyeful when Focus Groups Expose Products, Ideas, Images, Ad Copy etc, to Consumers", *Marketing News*, Vol. 8, 28 February, pp. 6-7.

Axelrod, M.E. (1975b), "Ten Essentials for Good Qualitative Research", *Marketing News*, Vol. 8, 14 March, pp. 10-11.

Axelrod, M.E. (1976), "The Dynamics of the Group Interview", in Anderson, B.B. (Ed.), *Advances in Consumer Research*, Vol. IV, Association for Consumer Research, Ann Arbor, Michigan, pp. 437-41.

Bellenger, D.N., Bernhardt, K.L. and Goldstucker, J.L. (1976), *Qualitative Research in Marketing*, American Marketing Association, Chicago, pp. 7-28.

Belson, W.A. (1960), "Volunteer Bias in Test Room Groups", *Public Opinion Quarterly*, Vol. 24 No. 1, pp. 115-26.

Belson, W.A. (1963), "Group Testing in Marketing Research", *Journal of Advertising Research*, Vol. 3 No. 2, pp. 39-43.

Berent, R.H. (1962), "The Depth Interview", *Journal of Advertising Research*, Vol. 6 No. 2, pp. 32-9.

Berelson, B. (1952), *Content Analysis in Communications Research*, Free Press, Glencoe, Illinois.

Bessell, R. (1971), *Interviewing and Counselling*, Batsford, London.

Caruso, T.E. (1976), "Moderators Focus on Groups: Session 7 Yields Hypotheses Covering Technology Trend, Professionalism, Training Techniques, Reports, etc.", *Marketing News*, Vol. 10, 10 September, pp. 12-6.

Claxton, J.D., Brent-Ritchie, J.R. and Zaichkowsky, J. (1980), "The Nominal Group Technique: Its Potential for Consumer Research", *Journal of Consumer Research*, Vol. 7 No. 3, pp. 308-13.

Cooper, P. and Branthwaite, A. (1977), "Qualitative Technology: New Perspectives on Measurement and Meaning through Qualitative Research", 20th Market Research Society Annual Conference, March, pp. 79-92.

Cox, K.K., Higginbotham, J.B. and Burton, J. (1976), "Applications of Focus Group Interviews in Marketing", *Journal of Marketing*, Vol. 40 No. 1, pp. 77-80.

de Groot, G. (1986), "Qualitative Research. Some Reflections on Current Approaches", *Admap*, February, pp. 72-6.

Delbecq, A.L., Van de Ven, A.H. and Gustafson, D.H. (1975), *Group Techniques for Program Planning*, Scott, Foresman and Co, Glenview, Illinois.

Drayton, J.L. and Tynan, A.C. (1986), "The Focus Group Interview: A Controversial Technique", Strathclyde University Working Paper No. MWP 86/6, November.

Fahad, G.A. (1986), "The Use of Focus Group Discussions by First Time Users", Marketing Education Group Conference, July, pp. 454-71.

Falconer, R. (1976), "Group Discussion in Research", *Marketing*, November, pp. 20-3.

Fern, E.F. (1982), "The Use of Focus Groups for Idea Generation: The Effects of Group Size, Acquaintanceship and Moderation on Response Quantity and Quality", *Journal of Marketing Research*, Vol. 19 No. 1, pp. 1-13.

Firth, D. and Goffey, L. (1986), "Recruitment Comes out of the Closet", *Market Research Society Newsletter*, No. 239, February, pp. 20, 28.

Goldman, A.E. (1962), "The Group Depth Interview", *Journal of Marketing*, Vol. 26 No. 3, pp. 61-8 (reprinted in Seibert, J. and Wills, G. (Eds.), (1970), *Marketing Research: Selected Readings*, Penguin, Harmondsworth, Middlesex, pp. 266-71.

Goodyear, J.R. (1978), "The Impact of Economic Growth and Recession on Qualitative Research Agencies and on the Use of Qualitative Research", 21st Market Research Society Annual Conference, April, pp. 53-65.

Goodyear, J.R. and Vineall, M.G. (1976), "From Hats, Rabbits and Magicians to the Present Day: An Up-to-date Appraisal of the Role and Value of Qualitative Research as an Aid to Marketing Decision Making", ESOMAR Congress, Venice, pp. 263-92.

Greenberg, B.A., Goldstucker, J.L. and Bellenger, D.N. (1977), "What Techniques are Used by Marketing Researchers in Business?", *Journal of Marketing*, Vol. 41 No. 2, pp. 62-8.

Hannah, M. (1978), "A Perspective in Focus Groups", *Viewpoints*, July, Market Research Association, pp. 4-8.

Jones, S. (1981), "Listening to Complexity-analysing Qualitative Marketing Research Data", *Journal of the Market Research Society*, Vol. 23 No. 1, pp. 26-39.

Kaden, R.J. (1977), "Incomplete Use Keeps Focus Group from Producing Optimum Results", *Marketing News*, Vol. 11, 9 September, p. 4.

Kassarjian, H.H. (1977), "Content Analysis in Consumer Research", *Journal of Consumer Research*, Vol. 4, No. 1, pp. 8-18.

Katz, D. (1946), "The Interpretation of Survey Findings", *Journal of Social Issues*, Vol. 2, May, pp. 33-44.

Kelman, H.C. and Lerner, H.H. (1952), "Group Therapy, Group Work and Adult Education: The Need for Clarification", *Journal of Social Issues*, Vol. 7 No. 2, pp. 3-10; Vol. 8 No. 2, pp. 1-88.

Kennedy, F. (1976), "The Focused Group Interview and Moderator Bias", *Marketing Review*, Vol. 31, February/March, pp. 19-21.

Langer, J. (1978), "Clients: Check Qualitative Researcher's Personal Traits to Get More; Qualitative Researchers: Enter Entire Marketing Process to Give More", *Marketing News*, Vol. 12, 8 September, pp. 10-11.

Levy, S.J. (1979), "Focus Group Interviewing", in Higginbotham, J.B. and Cox, K.K. (Eds.), *Focus Group Interviews: A Reader*,

American Marketing Association, Chicago, pp. 34-42.

Lipstein, B. (1975), "In Defense of Small Samples", *Journal of Advertising Research*, Vol. 15 No. 1, pp. 33-40.

Macfarlane Smith, J. (1972), *Interviewing in Market and Social Research*, Routledge and Kegan Paul, London, pp. 103-11.

May, J.P. (1978), "Qualitative Advertising Research — A Review of the Role of the Researcher", *Journal of the Market Research Society*, Vol. 20 No. 4, pp. 203-18.

Mendes de Almeida, P.F. (1980), "A Review of Group Discussion Methodology", *European Research*, Vol. 8 No. 3, pp. 114-20.

Merton, R.L. and Kendall, P.L. (1946), "The Focused Interview", *American Journal of Sociology*, Vol. 51 No. 6, pp. 541-57.

Market Research Society Qualitative Research Study Group (1985), "Qualitative Research Study Group", *Market Research Society Newsletter*, No. 237, December, p. 14.

Market Research Society R & D Sub-committee on Qualitative Research (1979), "Qualitative Research — A Summary of the Concepts Involved", *Journal of the Market Research Society*, Vol. 21 No. 2, pp. 107-24.

Payne, M.S. (1976), "Preparing for Group Interviews", in Anderson, B.B. (Ed.), *Advances in Consumer Research*, Vol. IV, Association for Consumer Research, Ann Arbor, Michigan, pp. 434-6.

Peterson, K.I. (1975), "The Influence of the Researcher and his Procedure on the Validity of Group Sessions", in Mazze, E.M., *Combined Proceedings*, American Marketing Association, Chicago, pp. 146-8.

Prince, M. (1978), "Focus Groups Can Give Marketers Early Clues on Marketability of New Product", *Marketing News*, Vol. 12, 8 September, p. 12.

Qualitative Research (1977), "Supplement", *Market Research Society Newsletter*, No. 132, March, pp. i-xv.

Sampson, P.M.J. (1978), "Qualitative Research and Motivation Research", in Worcester, R.M. and Downham, J. (Eds.), *Consumer Market Research Handbook* (2nd ed.), Van Nostrand Reinhold Co (UK), London, pp. 25-48.

Schlackman, W. (1984), "A Discussion of the Use of Sensitivity Panels in Market Research", 27th Market Research Society Annual Conference, March, pp. 279-94.

Smith, G.H. (1954), *Motivation Research in Advertising and Marketing*, Greenwood Press, Westport, Conn., pp. 58-72.

Szybillo, G.J. and Berger, R. (1979), "What Advertising Agencies Think of Focus Groups", *Journal of Advertising Research*, Vol. 19 No. 3, pp. 29-33.

Templeton, J. (1976), "Research as a Giraffe: An Identity Crisis", in Anderson, B.B. (Ed.), *Advances in Consumer Research*, Vol. IV, Association for Consumer Research, Ann Arbor, Michigan, pp. 442-6.

Welch, J.L. (1985), "Marketing Research with Focus Groups", *Industrial Marketing Management*, Vol. 14, November, pp. 245-53.

Wells, S. and Lunn, A. (1986), "Sample of Two", *Market Research Society Newsletter*, No. 242, May, p. 8.

Wells, W.D. (1974), "Group Interviewing", in Ferber, R. (Ed.), *Handbook of Marketing Research*, McGraw-Hill, New York, pp. 133-46.

Willis, K. (1986), "A Two Way Process", *Market Research Society Newsletter*, No. 241, April, p. 34.

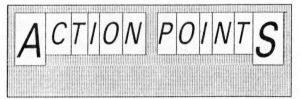

(1) What use do your market researchers make of focus group interviews?

(2) Have you discussed the contribution that focus groups could make to new product development in your company?

(3) Have you thought about the use to which focus group interviews could be put in problem solving in your company?

MIP 6,1
1988

Focus groups are divided into 4 distinctive categories

by Raymond Rowe Johnson

Raymond Rowe Johnson is a consultant in Washington, D.C.

Focus groups can never fully satisfy the demands of orthodox researchers for order and consistency.

Groups are too spontaneous and improvisational. But a close look at how they are used routinely in marketing research reveals that the method is surprisingly methodical, despite its reputation for laxity. There is a strong underlying pattern that links form and function, procedure and purpose.

A survey of more than 100 tapes from the project files of several qualitative research vendors revealed the range of questions focus groups answered and the main variations in interviewing methods observed among experienced moderators.

This survey led to the identification of four basic types of focus groups, each defined by a significant adaptation of interviewing technique to answer one of four basic research questions.

Focus group moderators adjust their interviewing techniques to meet the requirements of a particular study. They vary the way a topic is "framed" as it is presented to the group, and they influence the way the topic is discussed, eliciting either descriptions or interpretations.

Weak framing allows the members of the group to decide for themselves what aspects of the topic are most important or interesting to talk about; strong framing provides a more explicit agenda and limits what is appropriate discussion.

Moderators also vary interviewing procedure by eliciting discourse in which either interpretation or description predominates.

Descriptions, to be readily understood, require an act of selection. The speaker must emphasize what is most important and minimize irrelevant and distracting detail.

Interpretation, likewise, requires the speaker to single out those aspects of a topic which indicate its "real point" and to ignore those elements which are inconsistent with this understanding.

To illustrate the four basic types of focus groups, relatively pure examples have been chosen. Each "ideal" type poses its own key question for analysis. In practice, moderators often mix procedures, but not without some risk of degrading the quality of an interview.

■ **Type 1:** In this category are all of the exploratory studies of consumer lifestyles and the probing to "just find out what's on consumers' minds these days."

The goal usually is to identify possible holes in the market where no existing product or service satisfies consumer needs. Participants describe their generic experiences as consumers, with little framing by the moderator.

At the beginning, these interviews wander aimlessly. But a productive session eventually will achieve some cohesion as participants settle on what to talk about. The key question for analysis is the extent to which this initially desultory conversation finally coalesces around one or two main themes that everyone considers the most relevant aspects of the topic.

■ **Type 2:** Here we are interested in how a group, without undue prompting, interprets a deliberately sketchy idea for a new product or service.

The interview provides an opportunity to float a trial balloon, giving potential users a chance to react to a concept still in its formative or experimental stage.

The key question for analysis is the extent to which the participants highlight those aspects of the idea that were uppermost in the thinking of the product development people.

A company envisions a new product or service as providing specific benefits to the consumer. But does the consumer see the product the same way? Are the benefits clearly understood? Are they valued as highly as the product designers believed they would be? The ease with which the participants use a common vocabulary to talk about the idea may also indicate the ease with which it can be later explained to potential purchasers.

■ **Type 3:** Studies in this category deal with the real world of actual consumers. The topic is framed by the moderator's instructions to describe, usually in the form of situation-specific narratives, the details of personal experiences in using a particular product or service.

Participants are typically recruited from past or current customers.

The key question is the extent to which participants are able to agree on what makes up a prototype narrative: those story elements essential in describing the most typical experience. This class of interview can also give the client an inkling of the word-of-mouth that is circulating about a product or service.

■ **Type 4:** In this version, bane of the creative staffs at ad agencies, participants are asked to interpret the message conveyed in TV or radio spots, print ads, and other media products, usually seen in rough form.

The ensuing discussion is strongly framed by the content of the presentation. Group members talk about their understanding of the message and evaluate the extent to which they find it credible, interesting, and emotionally involving.

Because many in a mass audience can misconstrue the most carefully crafted ad, the key question posed in the analysis of these interviews is whether participants interpret the message in the way intended by its creator.

A Type 4 focus group constitutes a micro-audience for evaluating whether a message is pitch-perfect in exciting the desired resonances in the minds of the participants.

Reprinted from *Marketing News*, **22** (October 24, 1988), 21, published by the American Marketing Association.

BOBBY J. CALDER*

Use of the focus group technique is widespread in qualitative marketing research. The technique is considered here from a philosophy of science perspective which points to a confusion of three distinct approaches to focus groups in current commercial practice. An understanding of the differences among these approaches, and of the complex nature of qualitative research, is shown to have important implications for the use of focus groups.

Focus Groups and the Nature of Qualitative Marketing Research

INTRODUCTION

There have come to be two kinds of commercial marketing research. One is commonly called qualitative, the other quantitative. For most marketers, qualitative research is defined by the absence of numerical measurement and statistical analysis. Qualitative research provides an in-depth, if necessarily subjective, understanding of the consumer. In practice, qualitative research has become almost synonymous with the focus group interview. This technique involves convening a group of respondents, usually eight to 10, for a more or less open-ended discussion about a product. The discussion "moderator" makes sure that topics of marketing significance are brought up. The research report summarizes what was said, and perhaps draws inferences from what was said and left unsaid, in the discussion.

One can detect in several quarters conflicting feelings about focus groups. The results do seem useful to management. But there is concern about the subjectivity of the technique, and a feeling that any given result might have been different with different respondents, a different moderator, or even a different setting. Most commercial reports contain a cryptic statement acknowledging this conflict. The statement cautions that focus group research should be regarded as preliminary. Results should not be generalized without further quantitative research. Most users

probably have a vague sense of uneasiness with the technique. As aptly put by Wells [18, p. 2-145], "How can anything so bad be good?"

In addition to the general uneasiness, numerous procedural questions surround the use of focus groups. The following are typical questions.

Should focus group research ideally be generalized through additional quantitative research?
When should focus group research be used?
How many focus groups constitute a project?
What is the role of interaction among the group members?
Should focus groups be composed of homogeneous or heterogeneous people?
What expertise and credentials should a moderator have?
How important is the moderator's interviewing technique?
Should management observe focus group sessions?
What should a focus group report look like?

These questions currently are debated by marketing researchers on the basis of their professional experiences.

Neither the conflict between the apparent utility of focus groups and the reservations expressed about them, nor the typical procedural questions have been the subject of systematic argument. The marketing literature has been of little help to qualitative marketing researchers. There have been occasional descriptions of applications [e.g., 7] and expositions of techniques [e.g., 2, 10, 17], but this work has not established a general framework for thinking about focus group

* Bobby J. Calder is Associate Professor of Behavioral Science in Management and of Psychology, Northwestern University.

Reprinted from *Journal of Marketing Research*, 14 (August 1977), 353-364, published by the **American Marketing Association.**

research. The purpose of this article is to provide such a framework through a critical inquiry into the fundamental nature of qualitative marketing research.

Qualitative marketing research is considered first from a philosophy of science perspective. This perspective is not used simply to hold up the focus group technique to a list of ideal criteria for scientific methods. The author fully realizes that many practitioners are not interested in being "scientists." They are, however, interested in developing knowledge from research. The philosophy of science provides a valuable perspective on knowledge—not just scientific knowledge, but the entire realm of knowledge. The point of the philosophy of science perspective developed here is to analyze the type of knowledge sought by qualitative research, be it scientific knowledge or otherwise, to determine what this implies about the use of the focus group technique. The implications of seeking either nonscientific or scientific knowledge through focus group research are not well understood.

Though many practitioners might avoid the "scientist" label, the distinction is not as simple as it may seem. There are actually three different approaches to focus group research in current practice. Drawing upon the philosophy of science perspective developed, this article shows that each of these approaches reflects a different kind of knowledge being sought. Though none of the three approaches seeks scientific knowledge in its strictest form, two are meant to yield knowledge which is in some sense scientific.

A PHILOSOPHY OF SCIENCE PERSPECTIVE

What comes to mind when most people think of research is the image of "scientific" research. This image is somewhat fuzzy, and it is not easy to articulate. Thus it may help to begin with a consensus view of what science is. Science is a particular way of trying to understand the real world. For social scientists the real world is the full physical complexity of objects and behaviors. But the real world is much too complex to be understood in and of itself. At the heart of science is the process of conceptualization, which seeks to *represent* the real world in a simple enough way to allow understanding. Scientific constructs are abstracted forms and represent only limited aspects of real-world objects and behaviors. If scientific constructs mirrored the full complexity of the real world, one could no more understand science than one can directly understand the real world.

Constructs are simplifications and idealizations of reality. They are, in short, abstractions of the real world. Some may seem more "real" than others—say, "taste buds" as opposed to "attitudes"—but they are all abstractions; they "exist" only within the realm of scientific discourse. Scientific theory consists of constructs and the interrelationships among them [5]. The value of this theory depends on the fact that abstract conceptualization is not a one-way process.

As depicted in Figure 1, scientific conceptualization must work in reverse, too. One must be able to use constructs to interpret the real world, to determine whether real objects and behaviors possess the properties and relationships embodied in scientific theory [cf. 19]. This is the business of theory testing. It is the most visible part of science, for it entails all of the methods and procedures associated with "being scientific." Basically, these methods are simply systematic procedures for determining whether a theory is consistent with the workings of the real world. If consistency is detected, the theory is retained, though it is not considered proved; otherwise the theory is modified. The uniqueness of science is in the logical rigor and documentation employed in testing scientific constructs and relationships against the real world.

Let us return to the nature of scientific constructs. An important question is, how do we develop scientific constructs? Where do they come from? In all of science, the origin of constructs is somewhat problematic [cf. 11]. Part of the answer seems to be that good theory spawns its own constructs (the best example being particle physics). There is also the process of modifying constructs on the basis of empirical evidence. Still, there must be an external origin at some point in theory development, and this origin is the world of everyday thought and experience. As shown in Figure 1, the world of everyday thought is separate from scientific discourse. It is composed of the terms and ordinary language that people use to give meaning to the world in their everyday lives. As such, its function is analogous to that of science. It allows one to interpret the real world by use of simplified ideas. The only difference is that scientific constructs are supposed to be more powerful and to be subject to more rigorous and critical verification than are everyday ideas. Although everyday thought may initially supply ideas for scientific constructs,

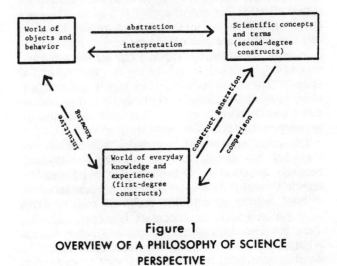

Figure 1
OVERVIEW OF A PHILOSOPHY OF SCIENCE PERSPECTIVE

the two types of knowledge are independent. Scientific knowledge is subject to its own rules of evidence. But this independence is not absolute. Modern philosophers of science agree that all knowledge is highly presumptive [8, 13, 16]. No single hypothesis can be examined without at the same time assuming the truth of the bulk of all other knowledge, both scientific and everyday.

Neither scientific explanations of consumer behavior nor explanations based on everyday knowledge can be proved. All knowledge reduces to the choice between alternative explanations. It is thus entirely reasonable to compare scientific and everyday explanations. The truly scientific explanation may be expected to have advantages, but it is not automatically superior. In the case of social science, these advantages are seen by many as more assumed than real. Such considerations have led Campbell [6] to argue for the cross-validation of social science by qualitative common-sense explanation. This step rarely is taken, and is probably generally considered to be "unscientific." Nonetheless, some form of comparison between scientific and everyday explanation should be part of a sophisticated view of science, and this relationship accordingly appears in Figure 1.

An example may clarify the nature of this comparison. Suppose that a researcher postulates an attitude process (scientific) explanation for a brand choice which to most consumers is so low in involvement as to be, say, strictly a function of shelf-facings. The foregoing discussion suggests that the researcher should reconsider his attitude process explanation. The everyday explanation certainly does not prove that the scientific explanation is wrong, but it does indicate the need for increased skepticism.

The overall conclusion emerging from this discussion is that the philosophy of science clearly implies a separation, though not an impenetrable boundary, between everyday and scientific discourse. Explanatory concepts of the everyday kind are sometimes called "first-degree constructs" (cf. Fig. 1). They are based on the social construction of reality by a set of actors; they are imparted to a person as a consequence of socialization within a culture. In contrast, second-degree constructs belong to the realm of science. They are supposed to be highly abstract and to be subject to scientific methods, but they are no less a construction of reality. It is not "unscientific" to compare the everyday and the scientific.

The categorization of knowledge as scientific or everyday has strong implications for the division between quantitative and qualitative marketing research. Quantitative research commonly is associated, at least implicitly, with the realm of science. This connotation is not always accurate, however. Actually, there are two approaches to quantitative research. What can be referred to as the descriptive approach supplies numerical information relevant to everyday,

first-degree constructs. Demographic analyses, such as breakdowns of consumption figures by age, are a prime example. This research, in itself, bears more upon everyday than scientific explanation. Age, used purely descriptively, is not a scientific construct. Quantitative research which does seek scientific explanation can be referred to simply as the scientific approach. Here, quantitative means much more than merely working with numerical amounts or rating scales. It implies the use of second-degree constructs and causal hypotheses which are subjected to scientific methods. The methods in common use are the experiment, some types of cross-sectional and panel surveys, and time series analysis. Scientific quantitative marketing research, in sum, aspires to the scientific knowledge depicted in the philosophy of science perspective.

Qualitative marketing research similarly cannot be restricted to a literal definition of "doing research without numbers." *Unlike the case of quantitative research, the relationship of qualitative research to the scientific and everyday knowledge dichotomy is very ambiguous.* An underlying confusion about this relationship has led to three approaches being lumped under the label of "qualitative marketing research." The three approaches should be kept distinct. Each

Table 1
SUMMARY OF RESEARCH APPROACHES DISCUSSED

Approach	Type of knowledge desired	Rationale
Quantitative		
Descriptive	Everyday	To find numerical patterns related to everyday concepts (e.g., consumption breakdowns by age)
Scientific	Scientific	To use numerical measurement to test scientific constructs and causal hypotheses
Qualitative		
Exploratory	Prescientific	To generate scientific constructs and to validate them against everyday experience
Clinical	Quasiscientific	To use second-degree scientific constructs without numerical measurement (i.e., clinical judgments)
Phenomenological	Everyday	To understand the everyday experience of the consumer

represents a different version of the relationship between qualitative research and the partition of scientific and everyday knowledge.

The first two approaches seek knowledge that is on the boundary between scientific and everyday, whereas the third clearly seeks everyday knowledge. The following sections describe the approaches in turn. A lack of understanding of the differences among them is responsible not only for much of the uneasiness surrounding qualitative marketing research, but also for misuses of this research.

THE EXPLORATORY APPROACH

Qualitative marketing research frequently is undertaken with the belief that it is provisional in nature. Focus groups often are conducted before the fielding of a large sample survey. This exploratory approach can take one of two somewhat different forms. Researchers may be interested in simply "pilot testing" certain operational aspects of anticipated quantitative research. Their objective might be to check the wording of questions or the instructions accompanying product placements. Alternatively, researchers may have the much more ambitious goal of using qualitative research to generate or select theoretical ideas and hypotheses which they plan to verify with future quantitative research. For this purpose, focus groups are usually less structured; respondents are allowed to talk more freely with each other.

When focus groups are conducted in anticipation of scientific quantitative research, their purpose is really to stimulate the thinking of the researchers. They represent an explicit attempt to use everyday thought to generate or operationalize second-degree constructs and scientific hypotheses (cf. Fig. 1). Though the subject of exploratory qualitative research is everyday knowledge, the knowledge desired is best described as prescientific. The rationale of exploratory focus groups is that considering a problem in terms of everyday explanation will somehow facilitate a subsequent scientific approach. Focus groups are a way of accomplishing the construct-generation process shown in Figure 1.

As was noted, however, the process of generating second-degree constructs from first-degree ones, of moving from the everyday to the scientific, is very poorly understood. The philosophy of science supplies no precise guidelines. Nor has any thought been given to this process in the marketing research literature. This is not to say that the exploratory approach is not worthwhile, only that it is being attempted without benefit of any well-developed ideas of how to do it. The most relevant sources to which qualitative marketing researchers might turn are sociologists concerned with the notion of "grounded theory." This term refers to theory systematically generated from qualitative as well as quantitative research as opposed to theory generated by its own internal logic. The

idea is that "grounded theory is a way of arriving at theory suited to its supposed uses" [9, p. 3]. In other words, such theory is developed within the context of its application. The aim of the exploratory approach might well be described as grounded theory.

Much qualitative research follows the exploratory approach even though it never leads to quantitative research. The putative second-degree constructs and hypotheses developed from focus groups frequently are not subjected later to scientific methods. Most often this omission is due to the high costs of a second quantitative stage. In such cases, concern commonly is expressed about the risk of generalizing from the small samples of qualitative research. But there is much more at risk than sample generalizability. What happens with this truncated exploratory approach is that what is still essentially everyday knowledge (that of the researchers and focus group participants) is cast in ostensibly scientific terms and treated as if it were a scientific finding, instead of being at best a prescientific starting point. The problem is that this knowledge has not been subjected to scientific methods for any sample; to assume that it is scientific is risky indeed.

Exploratory qualitative research which is not followed by a quantitative stage is not necessarily useless. Taken as everyday knowledge (as will be shown in discussion of the third approach), it may well be very useful. The mistake is to represent prescientific everyday explanation as fully scientific but merely lacking sample generalizability.

One final point with regard to the exploratory approach is almost never recognized in marketing research practice. The approach concentrates solely on the construct-generation relationship from the everyday to the scientific (cf. Fig. 1). Of equal importance in terms of the philosophy of science is the comparison relationship from the scientific to the everyday. It is useful to think of this relationship as cross-validating scientific explanations against everyday ones. If the two explanations are not consistent, a choice must be made. Given the current development of social science, this choice sometimes will favor the everyday explanation. That is, consumers' explanations will sometimes be favored over theoretical hypotheses.

Thus, it is potentially misleading to assume that qualitative research must always be provisional. It is also desirable to conduct independent exploratory qualitative research. In this way, scientific explanations can be compared with everyday ones. Contrary to current practice, it is just as appropriate to conduct focus groups *after* a quantitative project as before it. Scientific explanations should be treated as provisional also.

The exploratory approach to qualitative research seeks prescientific knowledge. This knowledge is not meant to have scientific status. It is meant to be a precursor to scientific knowledge. Its status is ultimately rooted in the creativity of the individual. The exploratory approach could be adopted to compare scientific with everyday explanations. In this case, the objective would be not prescientific, but everyday knowledge.

THE CLINICAL APPROACH

Whereas the exploratory approach seeks to generate scientific constructs from everyday thought and to compare scientific and everyday explanations, a second approach expressly attempts to conduct qualitative research as a scientific endeavor. With this approach qualitative methods are viewed as an alternative to scientific quantitative ones. In marketing this approach most clearly reflects the perspective of clinical psychology. A "clinical" heritage has deeply influenced qualitative marketing research practitioners, both those with and without actual clinical experience.

Two premises underlie the clinical approach. One is that the constructs of everyday thought are often misleading as explanations of behavior. The explanations people can verbalize, by which they can describe themselves, commonly conceal the real underlying causes of behavior. Self-reports, the grist of many quantitative techniques, cannot be taken at face value. Indeed, the actual causes of behavior may be at least partly unconscious. Self-reports are filtered through a variety of defense mechanisms such as rationalization and thus do not directly reflect these unconscious determinants.

The second premise follows directly on the first. It is that the real causes of behavior must be detected through the sensitivity and "clinical judgment" of a specially trained analyst. The usual *tools* of quantitative research are not adequate for this purpose. Clinical judgment is an analytical skill of somewhat nebulous dimensions, though much faith is placed in it. It is an ability developed largely from practical experience for diagnosing the major causes of behavior from the complex overdetermination of both unconscious and conscious causes. Although it is basically an art, as is the medical model in general, it is widely held to be scientific because clinical judgment is supposed to take scientifically valid theory as a starting point and as a problem-solving framework. The clinical approach thus attempts to make use of scientific knowledge without being bound by quantitative methods of analysis.

The clinical approach was most obviously in vogue in marketing during the ascendancy of "motivation research." The wide variety of qualitative techniques (e.g., projective tests and free association) employed by motivation researchers were intended to provide informational input for clinical judgment. The popularity of many of these techniques has now receded. Though perhaps not as visible, the clinical approach is definitely alive, having largely assumed such names as "depth research." The statement perhaps most indicative of the present clinical approach is Goldman's [10] description of the "depth" focus group interview. The term "depth" expressly "implies seeking information that is more profound than is usually accessible at the level of interpersonal relationships" [10, p. 63]. Moreover, the depth focus group "defies routine analysis" and an approach similar to the way "psychotherapy sessions are analyzed" [10, p. 68] should be used. In other words, focus groups provide a qualitative source for clinical judgment.

The clinical approach has led to some excesses in marketing. The nature of clinical judgment is such that faulty or even far-fetched explanations may be accepted too easily by uncritical lay clients. This problem apparently has led some marketers to conclude that the clinical approach is inherently unscientific. On the contrary, put in proper perspective, it is the most scientific of the three approaches to qualitative marketing research. One must be very careful, however, about the relationship between the clinical approach and the partition of scientific and everyday knowledge. The clinical approach is not scientific in precisely the same sense as scientific quantitative research. Clinical judgment does not conform to the rules of scientific evidence. But, ideally, such judgments are based on second-degree constructs and scientific explanations.

The depth focus group interview is not meant to be (or at least ought not to be represented as) a scientific method. It is merely a device for obtaining the kind of information useful for clinical judgment. The group discussion is intended to stimulate the participants to produce relatively unguarded comments. This is why Goldman stresses the creation of rapport among participants by the moderator. The claim of the clinical approach to being scientific rests not on this method, but on the presumed scientific knowledge of the analyst. This knowledge underlies his clinical judgment and presumably renders it more scientific. Explanations developed in this way might best be described as quasiscientific.

Because the clinical approach assumes the existence of scientific knowledge as a basis for clinical judgment, it is crucial to appreciate the nature of the scientific theories favored by clinicians. Though any scientific theory could logically be treated clinically, the concern of clinicians is with the underlying causes of behavior which are not directly available from self-reports. This concern is what leads them to the need for clinical judgment as a means of scientific interpretation. The theories they employ are thus psychodynamic ones which postulate constructs that are personal to the individual and develop over the course of his life history. These theories are at root *intrasubjective*. They explain in terms of individual, subjective experience. Given this theoretical basis, it is reasonable that the depth focus group interview should concentrate on causing participants to reveal their inner experience in a way that is susceptible to clinical judgment and therefore clinical scientific interpretation.

Contrary to what one might expect, the most troublesome aspect of the clinical approach is not the use of the depth focus group, or even more exotic devices such as TAT pictures. The major cause for concern is the scientific knowledge on which clinicians rely. It is fairly well known that psychodynamic theories can be classified only questionably as scientific knowledge. They have not been subject to extensive scientific verification, nor are they even thought to be in testable form. The clinical approach is thus at best a calculated risk, but a risk that could pay off. More disturbing, and this is less well known, clinicians frequently draw more from everyday knowledge in making judgments than from psychodynamic theory. London [14, p. 22] describes this as a confusion of morality and science, "the imposition of value and fact upon each other." He contends that if the clinician "knew a little more of astrology or charlatanism or faith healing or the development of priestly castes, he might see some ironic and perhaps worrisome parallels between his own and some less-honored crafts" [14, p. 22].

Such a breakdown in the ideal of clinical interpretation very likely carries over to marketing research. Many qualitative researchers may believe that they clinically interpret behavior in terms of scientific causation, while in practice they explain why people do things, even involuntarily, in terms of everyday motive and meaning.

The clinical approach to qualitative research seeks quasiscientific knowledge. This knowledge is meant to have scientific status. It is not fully scientific, however, because it has not itself been subject to scientific methods, only to clinical judgment. To the extent that the process of clinical judgment fails, the clinical approach results in everyday knowledge which masquerades as scientific. Therefore, at its best, the clinical approach yields quasiscientific knowledge; at its worst, it yields phony scientific knowledge.

THE PHENOMENOLOGICAL APPROACH

A third approach to qualitative research in marketing is summed up succinctly by Axelrod's description of the focus group [2, p. 6] as:

> A chance to "experience" a "flesh and blood" consumer." It is the opportunity for the client to put himself in the position of the consumer and to be able to look at his product and his category from her vantage point.

This statement may not seem much different from the exploratory or the clinical approach. However, the difference is profound, it has the strongest implications for appreciating the nature of qualitative marketing research, and it is to be understood only in terms of the partition of scientific and everyday knowledge.

Certainly many practitioners would recognize Axelrod's statement as descriptive of their own use of qualitative research. It is common in agency circles, for instance, for creative people simply to say that they would "like to hear consumers talk" in requesting focus groups. The experiential utility of focus groups is accepted even by persons who implicitly think of their own research as mainly exploratory or clinical. This acceptance does not seem in any way at odds with an exploratory or a clinical approach. Unfortunately, the notion of experiential utility has received little reflection beyond its practical acknowledgment, despite the fact that this notion is the primary concern of the richest literature on qualitative research. Sociologists are the most active contributors to this literature.

Their work is by no means unified; in fact, it has several current streams. Perhaps the best general name for it is "sociological phenomenology," and thus the label "phenomenological" is chosen here to refer to the approach in marketing. The core ideas of sociological phenomenology derive from writings of the philosopher-sociologist Alfred Schutz [cf. 15, 17]. In philosophy, the study of phenomenology is concerned with the representation of knowledge as conscious experience. Schutz approached this experience as *intersubjectivity*. Essentially, intersubjectivity refers to the common-sense conceptions and ordinary explanations shared by a set of social actors. It corresponds to the everyday knowledge depicted in Figure 1. The term "constructs of the first degree" is Schutz's. Toward the world of everyday knowledge one assumes "the natural attitude." This is the philosopher Husserl's term and can be defined as [17, p. 320]:

> The mental stance a person takes in the spontaneous and routine pursuits of his daily affairs, and the basis of his interpretation of the life world as a whole and in its various aspects. The life world is the *world of the natural attitude*. In it, things are taken for granted.

The individual adopts the natural attitude from birth, accepts everyday knowledge, and functions in terms of this knowledge.

The seeming objectivity of everyday knowledge depends on the natural attitude. In turn, the natural attitude, Schutz argues, depends on the actor's assumption that others see the world in the same way. The natural attitude is based on the assumption of a reciprocity of perspectives. Intersubjectivity is thus defined socially, not individually.

Schutz contends that every actor is born with a unique "biographical situation." No two people experience the world in precisely the same way. But for everyday knowledge to be usable, and to seem objectively reliable, it must for the most part be shared by other actors. Not only must it be shared to some extent by all actors, but it must be shared increasingly with the closeness of interpersonal contact among actors. For any given actor, intersubjectivity arises from his contact with other actors (including common patterns of general socialization). Thus intersubjectivity is relative; different sets of actors will differ in their particular intersubjectivity to the extent that they have less contact and have had dissimilar socialization. Intersubjectivity will be greatest within primary groups and will be less within larger, more encompassing groups.

The key variable is the degree of personal contact and similarity of socialization, which is basic to all social groupings, such as those based on social class, geographic location, race, or whatever. For example, intersubjectivity is less between social classes in the United States than within them. Although major aspects of everyday knowledge are shared by different social classes, many features are not. The unshared features of everyday knowledge conform to different intersubjectivities. Each class adopts the natural attitude toward its own intersubjectivity but is ethnocentric toward that which is not shared by other classes.

This capsule version of Schutz's ideas captures much of the spirit of recent work on phenomenological sociology within the areas of ethnomethodology and symbolic interactionism. Note especially the dependency of intersubjectivity on the reciprocity of perspectives arising from the contact of a set of actors. The conclusion emerging from this work is that qualitative research requires actual contact between the researcher and his subjects. For the researcher to describe the intersubjectivity of a set of subjects, he must interact with them to the extent that he acquires the ability to take their perspective so that their intersubjectivity seems natural to him. A recent sociological qualitative research text [4, p. 8] puts this very simply: *"In qualitative methods, the researcher is necessarily involved in the lives of the subjects"* (original italics). As Blumer [3, p. 86] argues:

> . . . the student must take the role of the acting unit whose behavior he is studying. Since the *interpretation* is being made by the acting unit in terms of objects designated and appraised, meanings acquired, and decisions made, the process has to be seen from the standpoint of the acting unit. . . . To try to catch the *interpretative* process by remaining aloof as a so-called "objective" observer and refusing to take the role of the acting unit is to risk the worst kind of subjectivism—the objective observer is likely to fill in the process of interpretation with his own surmises in place of catching the process as it occurs in the experience of the acting unit which uses it [italics added].

The necessity of contact for truly grasping the intersubjectivity of a set of actors has led phenomenological sociologists to favor the method of participant observation. The text [4, p. 5] referred to previously broadly defines this as *"research characterized by a period of intense social interaction between the researcher and the subjects, in the milieu of the latter"* (original italics). Also favored is unstructured interviewing in which, according to the same text [4, p. 6], *"people reveal in their own words their view of their entire life, or a part of it, or some other aspect about themselves"* (original italics). Both participant observation and unstructured interviewing seek the description of the intersubjectivity of a set of actors through the researcher's own experience of that intersubjectivity. The focus of any interview technique becomes vicarious experience.

The goal of the phenomenological approach to qualitative marketing research is identical to that of phenomenological sociology. Both attempt to experience a set of actors and to describe that experience. Though sociologists historically have been more interested in deviant groups (e.g., gangs), marketing researchers are concerned with the intersubjectivity of different groups of consumers. Although deviant groupings vary more in intersubjectivity than most consumption-related groupings, the exercise of qualitative research should be the same in principle. Marketers for the most part belong to social groupings whose intersubjectivity is not the same as that of many of their target segments. Reality in the executive suite differs drastically from that of most kitchens. Qualitative research is an excellent way of bridging social distance.

There is more to be seen in phenomenological sociology, however than a confluence of purposes. The ideas of phenomenological sociology provide greater methodological direction than is currently available in marketing research practice. Focus groups following the phenomenological approach amount to an effort to get consumers to talk to each other about product-related issues. But the role of the moderator in this interaction is very poorly prescribed. The moderator's behavior most often is left to the idiosyncracies of the person moderating. To the extent that the moderator's technique is not idiosyncratic, it most likely is drawn implicitly from the exploratory or clinical approaches. These two approaches are not compatible with the phenomenological approach. Exploratory focus groups entail creative prescientific intellectualization. Clinical focus groups concentrate on *intra*subjectivity, on quasiscientific interpretations based on second-degree constructs which are personal to the individual. Neither allows the active involvement, the highly interactive personal contact, called for by the phenomenological approach.

A bias toward the seeming objectivity of the exploratory and clinical approaches forces an unduly detached moderator style in many applications of the phenomenological approach. Similarly, too much reliance sometimes is placed on the professional qualifications of moderators. It is more important in the phenomenological approach to employ moderators whose own backgrounds make it easier for them to take the role of a particular consumer segment.

These considerations lead to the question of the relationship between the phenomenological approach and the partition of everyday and scientific knowledge. Clearly, the intersubjectivity that is the *object* of inquiry constitutes everyday knowledge. But does the treatment of this everyday knowledge itself belong to the world of everyday knowledge or to that of scientific knowledge? Most researchers would contend that, as ordinary description derived from experiencing the role of the other, the phenomenological approach results in everyday knowledge.[1] This description, however systematic and thorough, still relies by its nature on first-degree constructs. For most phenomenological sociologists, this status does not preclude the development of a social science of second-degree constructs. It does raise a difficult problem, though. Some sociologists, mainly the ethnomethodologists, lodge a powerful criticism against conventional social science. They claim that all too often researchers confuse first-degree constructs with second-degree ones. The explanatory constructs of everyday life are assumed implicitly to have some scientific status.

The concern of the ethnomethodologists is that the validity of most of the supposed second-degree social science constructs rests more on their utility in everyday knowledge than on scientific evidence. Consider an example. In everyday life it is natural to explain the behavior of people in terms of personality traits. Nearly 5% of the English language is given over to trait names [1]. The first-degree constructs of traits have been carried over into the realm of social science. Traits have certainly received considerable attention in consumer behavior research. Nor is this an improper way of generating a second-degree construct. It is possible, however, trait explanations are not scientifically valid. Empirical evidence indicates that trait theory needs considerable elaboration [e.g., 12]. That simple trait theory persists in social science may be attributable to its entrenchment in everyday explanation rather than to its scientific merits.

The point is that much of what is considered to be scientific may belong more to everyday explanation. Phenomenological qualitative research therefore may have a stronger claim to the use of conventional social science constructs than does scientific research. In any event, this criticism should give pause to marketers who would condemn the nonscientific status of the phenomenological approach to qualitative marketing research. Not only does this work have practical utility, but it is also entirely defensible as the approach of

choice, given the current development of social science.

To summarize, the phenomenological approach provides a systematic description in terms of first-degree constructs of the consumption-relevant intersubjectivity of a target segment. The description is of how consumers interpret reality in their own terms. In contrast, the clinical approach gives what is hoped to be a scientific interpretation of reality. This interpretation employs second-degree constructs representing the intrasubjectivity of individual consumers. The logic of the phenomenological approach dictates that the researcher have close personal involvement with consumers. He or she must share, participatively or vicariously, the experience of consumers. It is misleading, on reflection, to say that the value of phenomenological focus groups is in the experiencing of consumers. What they should yield is the experiencing of the experience of consumers.

The phenomenological approach to qualitative research seeks everyday knowledge. This knowledge is not meant to have scientific status. It is the everyday knowledge, the experience, of the consumer.

IMPLICATIONS FOR MARKETING RESEARCH PRACTICE

Qualitative marketing research is more complex than any simple notion that quantitative research permits objective numerical analysis which qualitative research sacrifices for intensive analysis and fast turnaround. That there is more involved than a trade-off between precision and flexibility is especially evident in light of the three distinct approaches to qualitative research in current practice. These approaches must be viewed in terms of the partition of everyday and scientific knowledge. The exploratory approach seeks prescientific explanations stimulated by everyday thought. The clinical approach seeks quasiscientific explanations based on clinical judgment. The phenomenological approach seeks everyday explanations derived from personal contact. The three approaches are summarized in Table 1.

These three approaches are not well understood by those who use them. Frequent confusion of the approaches testifies to this lack of understanding. Marketing researchers often subscribe to the exploratory and clinical approaches (as evidenced by the usual statements included in the introductions of commercial reports) but commonly pursue something more akin to the phenomenological approach. It is hoped that discussion of each approach provides a deeper understanding of them. The discussion also has several specific implications for questions typically raised about the use of focus groups.

Perhaps the most common question is about generalizability, which usually is considered by analogy with the quantitative survey—how can one project to a larger universe results which are not stated as numeri-

---

[1] It should be noted that social psychologists have sought specifically to investigate the constructs and hypotheses of everyday knowledge scientifically. This was the goal of Heider's original work on "näive psychology." It continues to be ill-acknowledged rationale for current attribution theory studies in social psychology.

cal scores and are based on poor sampling? The conventional answer is that such results can be generalized only by a followup quantitative stage. But analogy to quantitative techniques is the wrong point of reference. One must consider the nature of qualitative research in thinking about generalizability.

For the exploratory approach, sample generalizability is not even particularly meaningful. The goal is either to generate ideas for scientific constructs or, as urged here, to compare scientific with everyday explanations. It is difficult to specify what projection to a larger universe means in this context. The likelihood of generating an idea or confidence in a comparison should depend to some extent on the number of focus groups, but this is not the same as sample generalizability. What researchers presumably have in mind is generalizability *when* the scientific construct or explanation is employed in quantitative research. However, this is a problem for the quantitative research procedure, not a concern of the qualitative research. The error is to assume that focus groups are provisional in the sense of yielding preliminary versions of quantitative findings. On the contrary, exploratory focus groups only suggest a construct or provide a comparison with everyday knowledge. They do not constitute a scientific test. Sample generalizability is a property only of subsequent quantitative research. It is misleading even to speak about the generalizability of exploratory focus groups.

Generalizability is more meaningful for the clinical approach. Here a scientific interpretation is being made, and one would like to know whether it holds beyond the focus group sample. Recall, however, that the basis of this interpretation is clinical judgment. Clinical judgment is not itself sufficiently specifiable to permit systematic extrapolation. Generalizations of clinical judgment can be accomplished only through intuition, and this has no claim to being scientific. Poor generalizability is inherent in clinical focus groups. It might be thought that generalizability can be assessed through subsequent research designed to test the clinical interpretation with a quantitative technique. This notion is somewhat paradoxical, however. The justification for the clinical approach is that it allows the use of scientific constructs (unconscious thoughts, etc.) which are difficult to investigate quantitatively. Attempting then to base the generalizability of a clinical interpretation on quantitative results, and not on clinical judgment, makes no sense. If it did make sense, there would have been no rationale for the original use of clinical judgment. A quantitative technique would have been more appropriate from the first. Generalizability is thus a critical issue with clinical focus groups; unfortunately, no one really knows how to determine it, aside from conducting more and more groups.

Generalizability is also important for the phenomenological approach, though it has a different meaning.

The problem is to determine the extent to which a particular intersubjectivity manifested in focus groups is shared. That is, how large is the social grouping which has a particular perspective in common? Here it does make sense to address generalizability through a descriptive quantitative survey. Both opinion polling and psychographic/life-style surveys can be seen as attempts to do just this. These are not attempts at scientific explanation so much as checks on the extent of everyday perspectives. The present popularity of using pictures of consumers to illustrate different psychographic profiles is indicative of the phenomenological character of this work. Surveys do seem effective in establishing the generality of different patterns of intersubjectivity. But recall that the phenomenological approach is predicated on experiencing the experience of consumers. This is best done through personal contact. Quantitative surveys, though they permit estimates of generality, are a poor substitute for even vicarious experience. The best way to generalize from phenomenological focus groups is to conduct additional groups in an attempt to cover as many different social groupings as possible. The widespread faith in the superiority of quantitative over qualitative research is clearly reversed for the phenomenological approach.

How then does one answer the typical question, *"Should qualitative research ideally be generalized through additional quantitative research?"* Conventional wisdom says yes. The foregoing discussion says no. This strategy makes sense only for the phenomenological approach. And even then it is neither an effort to attain scientific legitimacy nor the preferable method of generalizing. Focus group research basically must stand alone!

The ideas discussed here bear upon other typical questions as well. *When should qualitative research be used?* The phenomenological approach should be used when management is out of touch with the consumer, or when target segments consist of minority or rapidly changing social groupings. The exploratory approach should be used when scientific explanation is desired but researchers are uncertain about second-degree constructs, or when a scientific explanation is at hand and researchers wish to compare it with the consumer's interpretation. Finally, the clinical approach should be used when researchers invoke scientific constructs which are not amenable to self-report or direct inference.

How many focus groups constitute a project? It is usually said that focus groups should be continued until the moderator can anticipate what is going to be said in the groups. This typically happens with the third or fourth group of a particular kind. This rule of thumb seems adequate for the phenomenological approach: anticipation probably reflects vicarious experience. But one can anticipate without having yet made a clinical judgment or having formed an idea for a second-degree construct. The number of groups for the other two approaches should vary according to when the desired results are actually achieved.

What is the role of interaction among the group members? One of the few real dictums of focus group research is to avoid serial questioning where a number of people are simply being interviewed at once. Interaction among the participants is thought to be a major virtue of the technique. Group dynamics, members stimulating other members, is held up as the basic rationale for the technique. In contrast to this consensus about the importance of interaction, there seems to be little agreement about the role of interaction. What does it accomplish? Interaction is clearly important for the phenomenological and clinical approaches. But to understand the role of this interaction, one must specify the relation of the moderator to it. This relation is different for the two approaches. With the phenomenological approach, the moderator must be part of the interaction. He or she must participate in the group dynamics as a member. It is necessary to feel a part of the group in order to experience the group's shared perspective. With the clinical approach, the moderator is not a part of the interaction. He or she must be detached from it so that the group dynamics can be used as a tool to probe and manipulate the defenses of the members. Interaction has a different purpose for each approach. For the exploratory approach, however, interaction is not nearly so important. The group functions as a convenient device for interviewing a number of people, one or more of whom might stimulate the moderator's scientific thinking. The exploratory approach implies more participation from key members and more one-to-one interaction with the moderator than do the other approaches.

Should focus groups be composed of homogeneous or heterogeneous people? Heterogeneous groups might yield rich information for the exploratory or clinical approaches. Clinical groups, however, should most often be homogeneous to facilitate rapport. Phenomenological groups require homogeneity. A shared perspective cannot be expected to emerge if the people are not similar.

How important is the moderator's interviewing technique? Many focus group moderators affect stylized interviewing techniques which encompass everything from how respondents are seated, and whether or not they are addressed by name, to how nondirective the moderator is. From the present perspective, these techniques do not seem crucial for the exploratory or the phenomenological approach. Anything which is comfortable for the participants is probably consistent with these two approaches. One technique or the other is not likely, in itself, to help much in obtaining ideas for scientific explanations or in understanding the consumer's experience. The phenome-

nological approach even seems to call for the absence of any style that would be apparent to the group. Such a style might make it difficult for the moderator to take part in the group as a member. Interviewing technique may be much more crucial, however, for the clinical approach. The process of clinical judgment is related intimately to interviewing technique. Clinicians believe that some techniques facilitate clinical judgment and others do not. There may well be effective and ineffective styles for the clinical approach, though it would be no simple task to identify which are effective and which are ineffective.

What expertise should a moderator have? The clinical and exploratory approaches demand a high degree of sophistication with scientific theory. In contrast, most important for the phenomenological approach are previous experiences which are maximally compatible with those of the focus group participants. There may also be dispositional characteristics which allow some people to take the role of others more readily.

Should management observe focus group sessions? Opinions differ sharply on this question. From the present perspective, observation is of no use with the clinical and exploratory approaches. What is being revealed cannot be seen by the lay observer. Observation makes sense for the phenomenological approach if it helps the manager to experience the consumer's experience.

What should a focus group report look like? Obviously the approaches identified call for different

Table 2
PROFILES OF THE THREE APPROACHES TO FOCUS GROUP RESEARCH

	Exploratory	Clinical	Phenomenological
The approach can be generalized with a followup quantitative stage	No	No	Yes
The approach should be used when the goal is to experience the consumer	No	No	Yes
The anticipation rule-of-thumb is appropriate for determining the number of groups conducted	No	No	Yes
Obtaining a high level of interaction among the group members is essential	No	Yes	Yes
A homogeneous group of people is necessary	No	No	Yes
The moderator's interviewing technique is crucial	No	Yes	No
The moderator must have scientific credentials	Yes	Yes	No
Observation by management is appropriate	No	No	Yes
Verbatim quotes should be emphasized in the report	No	No	Yes

styles of reporting. The phenomenological report should include extensive quotes ("verbatims") from consumer comments. It might be supplemented by edited tapes of the sessions. Oral presentations also should be helpful. Anything which better conveys the reality of the consumer's perspective is appropriate. Reports of clinical or exploratory groups should concentrate much more on the analyst's own reasoning in reaching conclusions.

To sharpen the distinction among the three approaches to focus group research, the implications discussed are summarized in checklist form in Table 2. The columns of this table provide a convenient profile of each approach. Remember that the only claim being made is that these approaches are discernible, though often blurred, in current practice; qualitative marketing research would profit greatly by fuller appreciation of the differences among them. These differences stem directly from the types of knowledge sought (see Table 1). Important questions about focus groups should not be resolved by convention, predilection, or happenstance. Different approaches, reflecting the need for different types of knowledge, require different answers.

THE FUTURE OF QUALITATIVE MARKETING RESEARCH

As previously stated, the three approaches detected and elaborated on are not sharply distinguished in the minds of marketing researchers. It is hoped that the foregoing discussion, if nothing else, shows that qualitative marketing research is a diverse activity. Otherwise the confusion of approaches may worsen. Most troubling is an increasing fuzziness of the clinical approach. Recall that the rationale for this approach is that it allows scientific interpretation where constructs cannot be investigated quantitatively; hence the need for clinical judgment. Increasingly, however, all kinds of theories are being applied with "clinical" judgment. Focus groups are interpreted in terms of any available social science construct (e.g., attitudes, values, traits, roles, norms, etc.). This is not an application of the exploratory approach. It is an attempt to extend the clinical approach to all constructs, without regard to their amenability to existing scientific methods. This is a misuse of qualitative research. It is an attempt to shortcut the scientific process, without the attendant justification of the traditional clinical approach. The result is often explanations which have no claim to being even quasi-scientific. Social science constructs are used merely as convenient (and probably overly intellectualized) ways of describing the phenomenology of consumers.

This trend leads to purportedly scientific interpretations which either (1) are needlessly based on clinical judgment or (2) are in fact phenomenological descriptions couched in social science jargon. Perhaps these are useful to marketing management. But they may be more a license to "qualitative clairvoyance" than good research.

Scientific integrity might best be maintained by having two largely separate realms of marketing research. Most routine qualitative research would follow the phenomenological approach. The exploratory and clinical approaches would be used with caution, and only when clearly dictated. Present misconceptions about the desirability of linking qualitative and quantitative research would be abandoned. Marketers would recognize the need for *both* qualitative phenomenological research and scientific quantitative research.

Whatever trends emerge in qualitative research, one thing is certain. Focus groups should not be the exclusive technique. The nature of qualitative research does not limit it to any one best technique. Other techniques are just as legitimate as the focus group, and should be explored. The greatest threat to qualitative research findings is not lack of generalizability but lack of validity. Validity can best be assessed with multiple methods. The commitment to focus groups, like the conventions surrounding their use, is based on opinion conformity rather than the nature of qualitative marketing research.

REFERENCES

1. Allport, G. W. and H. S. Odbert. "Trait-Names: A Psycholexical Study," *Psychological Monographs*, 47 (1, Whole No. 211).
2. Axelrod, M. D. "Marketers Get an Eyeful When Focus Groups Expose Products, Ideas, Images, Ad Copy, Etc. to Consumers," *Marketing News* (February 28, 1975), 6-7.
3. Blumer, H. *Symbolic Interactionism: Perspective and Method.* Englewood Cliffs, New Jersey: Prentice-Hall, Inc., 1969.
4. Bogdan, R. and S. J. Taylor. *Introduction to Qualitative Research Methods.* New York: John Wiley & Sons, Inc., 1975.
5. Bunge, M. *Scientific Research I: The Search for System.* Berlin: Springer, 1967.
6. Campbell, D. "Qualitative Knowing in Action Research," *The Journal of Social Issues*, in press, 1974.
7. Cox, K. K., J. B. Higginbotham, and J. Burton. "Applications of Focus Group Interviews in Marketing," *Journal of Marketing*, 40 (January 1976), 77-80.
8. Feyerabend, P. K. "Against Method: Outline of an Anarchistic Theory of Knowledge," *in* M. Radner and S. Winokur, eds., *Analysis of Theories and Methods of Physics and Psychology. Vol IV. Minnesota Studies in the Philosophy of Science.* Minneapolis: University of Minnesota Press, 1970.
9. Glaser, B. G. and A. L. Strauss. *The Discovery of Grounded Theory: Strategies for Qualitative Research.* Chicago: Aldine, 1967.
10. Goldman, A. E. "The Group Depth Interview," *Journal of Marketing*, 26 (July 1962), 61-8.
11. Kaplan, A. *The Conduct of Inquiry: Methodology for Behavioral Science.* New York: Intext Educational Publishers, 1964.

12. Kassarjian, H. H. "Personality and Consumer Behavior: A Review," *Journal of Marketing Research*, 8 (November 1971), 409–18.
13. Lakatos, I. "Falsification and the Methodology of Scientific Research Programmes," *in* I. Lakatos and A. Musgrave, eds. *Criticism and the Growth of Knowledge*. Cambridge: Cambridge University Press, 1970.
14. London, P. *The Modes and Morals of Psychotherapy*. New York: Holt, Rinehart & Winston, 1964.
15. Schutz, A. *The Phenomenology of the Social World*. Evanston, Illinois: Northwestern University Press, 1967.
16. Toulmin, S. E. *Human Understanding. Vol. 1. The Evolution of Collective Understanding*. Princeton, New Jersey: Princeton University Press, 1972.
17. Wagner, H. R. *Alfred Schutz on Phenomenology and Social Relations: Selected Writings*. Chicago: The University of Chicago Press, 1970.
18. Wells, W. D. "Group Interviewing," *in* R. Ferber, ed., *Handbook of Marketing Research*. New York: McGraw-Hill Book Co., Inc., 1974.
19. Zaltman, G., C. R. Pinson, and R. Angelmar. *Metatheory and Consumer Research*. New York: Holt, Rinehart & Winston, 1973.

SECTION II

Planning And Preparing Focus Groups

This section contains six articles dedicated to helping the researcher plan and prepare for focus groups. Two articles are again "classics" from the first edition of this text. Three of the six articles emphasize the role of the moderator in planning successful focus group efforts.

"Preparing for Focus Groups" by Melanie Payne is a "classic" article that emphasizes the need for the researcher to understand the objectives of the proposed research. She goes on to illustrate how these objectives must be translated into a sound research design and the importance of supervising recruitment of participants and the writing of a report that is useful.

"Dimensions that make Focus Groups Work" by Kimbal and Flexner describe twelve dimensions that the researcher might consider in finding a research style that fits the individual and allows for better research.

"Focus Groups Don't Have to be Expensive" by Daume provides twelve excellent suggestions on how to save money when planning focus group research. These recommendations are practical in their approach without sacrificing the research objectives.

The second "classic" in this section is by Frank Kennedy and also represents the first of three articles concentrating on the role of the moderator in executing successful research efforts. This article is dedicated to illustrating how the moderator can bias research results and provides tips on how to minimize such occurrences.

"Beyond 'Moderator Chemistry': Guidelines for Judging Qualitative Research" is a short, yet solid article. It describes the important characteristics one might look for in distinguishing among all the moderators available for one's research efforts.

The last article in this section by Mariampolski presents twenty-one different techniques available to a moderator to increase the effectiveness of focus group interviews. This article is very well written and concise.

Preparing for group interviews

Melanie S. Payne
Elrick and Lavidge Inc.

Abstract

Proper preparation for group interviews is essential to achieve meaningful study results. Responsibility for conducting the groups should be given to a well-trained qualitative researcher whose job it is to understand the research objectives and how the results will be used. Other aspects of preparation include writing the discussion guide and supervising recruitment of respondents. Prior to the groups, decisions must also be made concerning where the sessions will be held and the type of audio or video recording that will be done.

Preparing for Group Interviews

Once you have decided that groups are the proper research tool to use and before you actually run the sessions, considerable attention should be devoted to preparing for them. Because group interviewing appears to be such an easy thing to do and the process itself seems so casual, the important step of preparation is often neglected and left to chance.

One of the most crucial elements of preparing a group study is to place the responsibility for it in the hands of a well-trained moderator/analyst. This may seem obvious, but because the technique has gained such popularity and because it seems so simple, more people are getting into the act, and they are often the wrong people. I have seen too many instances where, to save money, a company will turn the job of conducting groups over to a secretary. They give the assignment to her because she is a pleasant individual who gets along well with people and she is a good conversationalist. That is not enough, however, because what is required is someone thoroughly grounded in the theory and technique of what group interviewing is all about.

Once the assignment has been placed in the hands of the right person, the first order of business in preparing for a group interview is to gain a thorough understanding of the problem. Occasionally this means helping the client understand the problem, too. Many clients, of course, know precisely what their needs are and how they will use the results, but all too often the person requesting the focus group research does not really know what he wants to find out or what he will do with the information once the study is completed. In this latter instance, he may know simply that he has a problem, and because the group approach is simplistic, he decides that is what he will do, without really thinking through the issues involved.

In either case, it becomes the researcher's job to clearly spell out the reasons the research is being done, the specific areas to be covered in the groups, and how the results are going to be used once the research is completed. Let me give you an example. Assume you have been asked to do some work for a company that has, (1), done virtually no consumer research and, (2), does not have an understanding of what its customer's attitudes about the company's products are. In this instance, your first job will be to educate the client about what the group interview technique can and cannot do. Secondly, when you actually conduct the group discussions you will probably have to devote some of your efforts to gathering basic attitudinal informaton about the product category in general and your client's product in particular.

The approach just outlined will be very difficult from one you would use with a client who has a long history of researching his products and now wants some group sessions to help him develop the concept for a line extension of an existing brand. In these sessions, you would shorten the background gathering and move quickly to the heart of the matter—the new product. My point here is that all groups do not follow the same format and the correct approach to use is a function of the nature of the problem to be tackled.

As you gain an understanding of the problem, you should begin making a list of specific questions to be explored in the research. Some of these questions will be raised by the client, others will occur to you, and the combined list will become the skeleton for your discussion outline. The easiest and most useful way to handle the questions is to organize them by areas or topics so they become clustered in logical groupings. For example, if you are doing some research on a new hot breakfast cereal, you might want to begin with a general discussion of what is served at breakfast and then refine that by having respondents describe weekday versus weekend breakfasts. From there you might move on to focus on cereals, both hot and cold, then narrow down to hot cereals only. At this point, you would probably introduce the concept for the new product, and you might even have some actual product prepared for respondents to taste. Just like a good story, a group discussion should have a beginning, a middle, and an end. Typically, as in this example, the movement is from the general to the specific.

The discussion guide itself should be fairly simple—two or three typed pages, double spaced. It is an outline of the key areas and questions to be covered and not an exhaustive dissertation of every conceivable issue that might be probed for. If you understand what you want to do in a group and have the questions pretty well fixed in your mind, you should hardly have to refer to your outline once you are in the group setting itself. I suppose we all have our own little tricks for achieving this goal. My own personal quirk is that I must sit down at the typewriter and personally bat out the discussion guide I am going to use. Even if someone has prepared a perfectly adequate guide for me, I cannot seem to internalize it unless I type it myself.

Another essential element in the preparation of a guide, whether you have my kind of hang-up or not, is an adequate amount of time to think about the topic of your discussion. I feel that a minimum of a couple days is necessary to allow the topic area to sufficiently sink in. I don't mean to say that one should spend two or three days working on an outline, but you do need time to mull over in your mind what you are going to cover in a session. I find that I do this when I am preparing dinner, or riding the train to work, putting on my

Reprinted from *Advances In Consumer Research*, IV (1976), 434-36. Used with permission.

makeup, or whatever. No moderator, no matter how experienced he or she is, can be handed a group discussion guide half an hour before a group and be expected to conduct a first-rate interview.

At the same time you are involved in the process of understanding the problem and preparing the discussion guide, recruiting for the group should be getting under way. This will generally be taken care of by someone other than yourself. Just as the moderating should not be handled by an amateur, recruiting too should be supervised by a specialist. It may seem simple enough to gather together several "warm bodies" for a group discussion, but once again I have seen the amateurs who thought this was such a snap fall flat on their faces. So the moral of the story is pay a little more and find someone who knows what they are about to recruit your groups.

Your responsibility in working with the recruiters is to tell them exactly who you want and who you don't want in your groups. Let's look at the exclusions first. You do not want people who work for marketing research companies or advertising agencies or those employed by your client or any of his competitors. This is fairly obvious. You will also want to screen out certain groups who, for some reason, might bias your results. One of the worst examples I ever heard along those lines happened to a researcher who was doing some conceptual work on baby food and wanted to interview mothers of infants concerning feeding practices. The project director did not learn until the group had assembled that all the respondents belonged to the Leche League. These are women who breast-feed their babies and, not only do they breast-feed, they belong to a league of breast feeders. Needless to say, their responses were hardly typical of all young mothers.

The recruiter should have known better than to have pulled a stunt like that, but that little episode which happened more than 10 years ago taught me to never leave anything to chance. You should always stipulate that you want respondents recruited from a wide area, and that you do not want them to come from the same neighborhood or church or club or ethnic group. My own feeling is that it's okay if two people, but no more than two, know each other in a group, that is they may come in pairs if necessary. This is simply being realistic because often a woman will not agree to participate in a session unless she can come with a friend.

The question of professional respondents always arises— these are the people who make a habit or perhaps even a living of participating in groups. The opposite of the professional respondent is the so-called virgin respondent—the person who has never taken part in a group session. What you should ask for and can realistically expect lies somewhere between these two extremes. If a recruiter is providing you with the same faces again and again, you had better take your business elsewhere. Keep in mind that if you have seen those people repeatedly you can be pretty sure that they have recently been respondents in someone else's groups, too.

On the other hand, be fair with your recruiter and do not demand that they provide you with virgin respondents. There is simply too much group interviewing being done these days for that to be a reasonable request. I once calculated that with the number of groups being done each week in Chicago, if everyone demanded virgin respondents we would have exhausted the entire population of the city in a period of eight years. I generally ask that respondents in my sessions have not participated in a group within the preceding six months or perhaps within the preceding year. You will find, however, that even with this sort of screening, people enjoy participating in groups so much that they will lie about not having been interviewed so that they can come back soon again.

After you have stipulated whom you don't want attending, you must be very specific about whom you do want. For example, if you are conducting a study on a new brand of frozen french fries, you do not simply ask for people who eat french fries. Rather, you ask for women who have bought, and prepared for their families, at least two pounds of frozen french fries within the past month. Set your qualifications specifically and precisely and you won't be disappointed by coming face to face with a gourp of women who have little interest in your product category and who, therefore, connot be the least bit of help to you.

How many respondents to include in a group is another key issue and one that I find myself getting into arguments about all the time. I am going to be very dogmatic on this point and say that no group discussion should ever have any more than eight respondents. If you, as a moderator, are performing your job correctly, six or seven people is perfectly adequate. I am appalled at the trend which seems to be in vogue now to demand ten or twelve respondents per group. What we want to accomplish with these people we have recruited is to carry out a discussion in which everyone participates as a group. With more than eight people, this process simply cannot occur naturally. The group breaks down and you, as moderator, are faced with the chaos of two or more splinter conversations going on simultaneously. To maintain control you then have the choice of policing the group conversation, thereby destroying the dynamic process you wanted to set up in the first place, or you retreat to the position of having to conduct a series of individual interviews in a group setting. Either solution is unsatisfactory.

At the time respondents are recruited for a group they should be told how long it will last. I generally ask people to be prepared to stay two hours even if I don't expect the session to last that long. What you want to avoid is underestimating the time involved. Men and women who come expecting to spend an hour get very fidgety when that hour is up. At that point they will say anything just to get the group over with and get out, leaving you with a lot of results that you can't have very much faith in. Two hours is about the outside limit for a productive group session. Occasionally some respondents get so wound up with a topic they will, of their own choosing, stay on and on. But normally a group will have said all that it's going to say by the end of the second hour.

It is possible to conduct a group interview literally anywhere there is enough room to seat the respondents and yourself. I have done them in church basements and in posh boardrooms and just about anywhere else you can imagine in between. I personally do not feel that the setting is nearly as important as the tone you set and the rapport you establish with the respondents. If they feel you are on the same wave length with them, you'll get a good interview no matter where you are.

The most desirable facility these days, especially from a client's point of view, is an interviewing room equipped with a one-way mirror and a comfortable room from which to view the group in progress. That viewing room should be as sound-proof as possible so that the conversations of the observers cannot be heard by the respondents. Some research companies seem to be especially proud of the fact that they have well-stocked open bars in their viewing rooms. I find this not only unnecessary but offensive because it tends to turn the group session into some sort of charade rather than the serious business that it should be.

The furnishings in the interviewing room, per se, should be comfortable, but they need not be elaborate. There are some who prefer a living room atmosphere with coffee tables and easy chairs. My own preference is for a large conference room table that will seat eight or nine people without crowding. I prefer the table because I think it gives respondents something to hang on to—both literally and figuratively. Many men and women are very nervous when they come to a group discussion because they don't know what to expect. If they can sit down at a table, set down their coffee cups and fill out a short questionnaire covering product usage and demographics, it seems to put them at ease. Theoretically, people can accomplish the same end sitting in easy chairs clustered around coffee tables. But I find that in such a setting there is a lot of fumbling with clipboards, pencils, coffee cups and ashtrays. Also, women feel compelled to pull their skirts down to cover their knees, especially in a room with a very obvious one-way mirror. I prefer to avoid this altogether by conducting sessions around a conference table.

The presence of such a table also sets a somewhat businesslike tone to the session, and I don't think that's at all undesirable. While you want the respondents to be comfortable, this is a research session and not a neighborhood coffee klatch, and they surely know that ahead of time. They are not there just to shoot the breeze; they are being paid for their participation, and their conversations are being tape recorded. So it seems to me that to force all of this into a simulated home setting doesn't really accomplish very much.

I mentioned tape recording, and the extent to which you will record the proceedings is another decision you will have to make. The less gadgetry you have to worry about, the easier your life will be. If the facility you are using is equipped with an overhead microphone and sound system, this can be an advantage. But if you don't have this, it's no cause for alarm. Any reel-to-reel tape recorder that can pick up the conversation will do. Also, I routinely take along a small cassette

tape recorder to use as a back up. These recorders generally run on batteries, which can be a lifesaver if the electricity fails—something that has happened to me more than once.

In at least 99 percent of the group interviews you do, audio taping is all you should need. But I have found as this group interviewing business becomes more elaborate, clients are requesting video taping more frequently. My guess is that in many of these cases the video tapes end up being stored on a shelf and are never looked at again. Few people have the interest or stamina to sit and stare at eight to ten hours of film after the fact, so if the tape is going to be used at all it should be edited. This is an extremely time-consuming process, and no one can have an appreciation of how much time it takes until he has been through it once. And believe me, once is enough. Both the filming and the editing are expensive, and my feeling is that much of the time and money spent on video tape might have been better invested elsewhere. But it is the client's money, and he can spend it in any way he chooses.

Just remember that if you are planning to videotape you must meet some special conditions, including lots of ceiling light and no windows or back lighting behind the respondents (or you will end up with shadows instead of faces). Also, to obtain a tape that has any visual interest at all, you should hire a professional cameraman whose job it is to follow the discussion with the camera and zoom in and out to pick up the person speaking. The alternative to this is a fixed camera with a wide-angle lens that is visually no better than an audio tape.

In the past 15 minutes I have taken you through approximately two weeks worth of preparation for a group interview. Some of the issues I covered may have seemed obvious, others trivial, but from where I sit, all are essential. Going back to the point I made at the outset, to the uninitiated, the amateur, or the outsider, group interviewing appears to be a simple, casual process that one just waltzes through. But as the case with everything from raising children to making a soufle, if it ends up being done well, it didn't just happen; it was planned for.

Dimensions that make focus groups work

BY KIMBAL L. WHEATLEY
and WILLIAM A. FLEXNER

TWO ISSUES about focus groups need to be challenged.

The first is that one technique, usually the author's, is better than another. One's success in leading focus groups is much like one's success as a psychotherapist: most any paradigm, theory, technique, or construct is good as long as the psychotherapist is comfortable in working with it and feels confident in what he or she is doing.

The second issue is the notion that you must, above all, keep the group focused on a set of preconceived questions. We have witnessed the loss of valuable and pertinent data as a group leader stopped discussion because the topic was not on the agenda. If you know generally what you are after and you have done your homework before the session, you can be assured of extracting the information you need from the group even if it takes the discussion fairly far afield.

Here is a general set of dimensions to pay attention to as you find the methods that work best for you.

1. Purpose. Before a focus group is conducted, its purpose should be clearly understood. You can arrive at the hierarchy of purpose by continually asking "Why?" until the question has been exhausted.

"To find out about what our customers value in our services" is a purpose, but asking "Why?" takes you up a level in the hierarchy to "We need to find out what our customers value, because we want to meet their needs."

Again, "Why?" generates "Because we want to invest our resources where our customers see value." "Why?" "Because we want the customers to find more value in our services than in our competitor's." "Why?" "So they will choose us."

To satisfy the purpose of the focus group, look for input relevant to the whole continuum. For example, determining "what our customers value in

Kimbal L. Wheatley is general manager of Option Technologies Inc., Mountain Green, Utah. William A. Flexner is president of Flexner & Associates Inc., Mendota Heights, Minn.

our services" does not answer the higher-level questions of whether they will choose us if our services manifest such values.

2. Quality of data. Before the group is conducted, develop several key hypotheses relevant to the purpose. Then ask yourself: "What would the evidence from the group have to look like to force me to accept or reject each hypothesis."

This technique can create two important perspectives: you will have rehearsed the possible outcomes relevant to your purpose, and you will know when the discussion is generating input that will be useful in reaching conclusions.

3. Expectations (yours). Before the group sessions, but after the development of your hypotheses, consider what input you expect from the group, in terms of length, quality, and tenor of discussion, and the overall opinion you expect the group to give.

Remember that your expectations will bias the way you do things and perceive things. If you expect a great discussion on a topic and do not get one, you will likely feel frustrated and behave differently. You will also pay more attention to results that differ from your expectations.

4. Expectations (theirs). No matter what, group members will develop expectations about what they are participating in and what their role is in it.

Consider the management of these expectations to be a very important before-group activity and carefully craft your initial phone call and follow-up letters and calls. Every word spoken or written should be carefully selected to create the expectations you want them to have.

If your group members think they are coming for one thing, and you surprise them with something else, you will end up using precious time to align the group.

5. Framing the group dynamic. What you do and say and what you have the group do and say in the first 10 minutes will set the group dynamics throughout the session. This is where you set the "rules" for the group and participants set them for each other. Depending on how you want the group to go, you can frame the group along several dimensions. For example:

● A friendly chat or scientific research.

● Unstructured, structured.

● Go where they take you, agenda to follow.

● Discussion among group, group only talks to you.

● People talk when they wish, call on people to talk.

● Fast pace, slow pace.

● Humorous, serious .

● Idea session, griping session.

Although you can modify the dynamic as you go, it is easier and more productive to remain fairly consistent in approach throughout a session.

6. Legitimizing opinions. Most participants in a focus group will assume that their opinion cannot be all that important and that others in the group are more qualified to give opinions.

You can help to make all participants feel their opinions are legitimate by having each describe his or her experience with the service, product, institution, etc., to which you respond with a statement of how that perspective will be valuable to the discussion.

7. The questions. Remember that the participants will respond to the question they perceive you are asking, which includes their guess as to why you are asking it.

As the group discusses an issue, it is building a context that will influence how subsequent questions are per-

---

Reprinted from *Marketing News,* **22** (May 9, 1988), 16-17, published by the American Marketing Association.

ceived and answered. There are several types of questions, all serving a different purpose in handling the group:

● The main research questions focus discussion on issues directly at the purpose of the session. Exactly how you are going to ask these questions should be thought out beforehand.

● Leading questions are useful for carrying a discussion toward deeper meaning and are especially useful if the group seems hesitant to pursue it. Formulate the questions using the group's words and ideas and asking "Why?"

● Testing questions can be used to test the limits of a concept. Use the group's words and ideas to formulate the question, this time feeding the concepts back to participants in a more extreme, yet tentative form, as though you may have misunderstood.

● Steering questions are used to nudge the group back onto the main research questions, following its frequent excursions into what it wants to talk about.

● Obtuse questions. Often the discussion will go into territory uncomfortable to the group. To further pursue topics into such areas, you need to back the questions off one level of abstraction, allowing the group to discuss other people's reactions or opinions, not necessarily their own: "Why do you suppose somebody else would feel this way?"

● Factual questions are questions that have a factual answer and permit the group to answer without personal risk. These questions can be useful for neutralizing emotionally charged groups or discussions.

● "Feel" questions ask for opinions surrounded by personal feelings. Feel questions ask participants to take risks and expose their personal feel-ings. They are the most dangerous and most fertile of question types.

The rule to remember here is that every person is entitled to his or her feelings, and no one else can disagree with or discount them, though many will try.

● Anonymous questions are used to get a group talking, comfortable with each other, or refocused on a key question. They generally take the form "Please take the index card in front of you and write down the single idea that comes to mind regarding this issue."

● Silence. Often the best question is no question. Many group leaders tend to fill in every void in the discussion. Simply waiting for a response allows those who are a little slower or uncertain to formulate their ideas.

8. Feedback. Intently listening to a discussion or statement, then rephrasing it for participants in a succinct but complete form using their words and ideas accomplishes several objectives: it makes participants aware that you are hearing what they are saying, it provides structure and reduces ambiguity for postsession analysis of the tapes, and most importantly, it makes the group feel you are part of it.

9. Divergent/convergent processing. The whole session should be a stream of converging on specifics and diverging back to generalities. It does not matter which way you go, starting with detail and moving out to a general concept or vice versa.

Writing a single topic on the board or asking "Can you give me some specific example of..." creates convergence. Writing a bunch of blank lines (clearly meant for filling in) or asking "Think of all the reasons that..." creates divergence.

10. Disengagement. Clinical psychotherapists develop the ability to display a certain "clinical facade" to their patients or group while intellectually removing their being to a "metacritical" viewpoint.

As the persons responsible for controlling the outcome, they can't afford to get caught up emotionally in what is going on. Neither can you. Pay attention to your own feelings and emotions, developing the ability to sense when you are becoming "engaged."

11. Pace, scope, and rhythm. Every group has a unique rhythm, where going any faster or slower, more or less structured, will reduce the value of the results. Always be prepared to accomplish more or less of your agenda once you get a feel for the group.

12. Electronic assistance. Two types of electronic tools are available to the leader: tapes (video or audio) and computerized voting systems that capture the group opinions and feed them back to the group for interpretation.

The primary advantages of taping are that the group leader can pay attention to the group (instead of taking notes), and the tapes can be studied later for otherwise missed information.

Computerized voting allows all participants to have a voice, provides quantitative descriptive information, and, most important, creates a "feedback loop" in which the participants interpret their own feelings when the results of the vote are displayed back to them (see *Marketing News*, Feb. 27, 1987, for a description of Option-Finder, one example of this technology.)

If you elect to use either of these electronic aids, take care that they remain useful; that they do not end up being so intrusive as to make the participants uncomfortable or end up dominating the process.

Focus groups don't have to be expensive

by Harold C. Daume Jr.

Harold C. Daume Jr. is president and cofounder of Daume/Swenson Inc., a marketing research firm in South Pasadena, Calif.

Not too many years ago, consumer focus groups cost about $2,000 ($3,000 for business groups), but today costs have shot up by a third or more for a variety of related reasons.

Back in the mid-1960s, focus groups often cost less than $1,000. We would convene a panel of people and pay them $5 or $10 to come to, say, a church meeting room, where we'd use a portable recorder and sit behind a room divider to listen and take notes.

By the 1980s, focus groups were a major business venture and, like other research methodologies, had developed their own infrastructure: the moderator, the facility, and in some areas of the country, the panelist recruiter.

Facilities became more luxurious and electronically sophisticated. Sound systems were installed for recording and monitoring. Then came one-way mirrors for on-the-spot observing. All of this, of course, cost money.

Next came videocassettes and the ability to record focus groups. Then panelist qualifications changed. No longer could one be satisfied with people who used mouthwash. Now they had to use a particular brand or use mouthwash at least twice a day. The more refined the requirements, the more it cost to find the right people.

Coupled with tighter screening requirements came increased honorariums, caused by inflation as well as the desire to recruit the best panelists.

Finally, there are the observers' amenities. We have graduated from sandwiches and soft drinks to much more exotic menus: chicken cordon bleu, sushi and sashimi, veal picatta, and more, usually accompanied by bottled mineral water or, occasionally, Corona and a dry chardonnay.

During this same period, costs for moderating and analysis also have gone up. At my company, moderating has increased by 10% in the past five years, and analytical costs have risen by nearly 20%.

Of course, there are always "loopholes." Take the focus group facility that five years ago hired a videotape operator and equipment for $125 per group, and charged $250. Today, the outside operator and equipment have been replaced by a $10-an-hour employee and a facility-owned camera, changing the gross profit per group for videotaping from $125 to over $300.

The bottom line is this: We have seen an across-the-board budget increase of some 33% in just the past five years. A corporation that commissions 100 focus groups a year is likely to spend at least $100,000 more today than five years ago.

The big issue, of course, is how to keep focus group costs from increasing while maintaining their value. Here are 12 suggestions:

1. Consider smaller rather than larger groups, six to eight panelists instead of the historic 10 to 12.

With 12 panelists, after removing the time it takes to warm up (usually about three minutes) and the moderator's questions and probes, the average panelist in a 90-minute focus group has some three minutes of actual talking time.

Cut the number of panelists and you'll increase their ability to speak. Instead of conducting a group survey, the moderator can begin to get "inside" the panelists. Cutting the number of panelists recruited can save up to $400 a group.

2. Never conduct an odd number of groups unless they can somehow be bundled into three groups in one day.

The "odd" group on a subsequent evening will cost you at least 10% more than if it were one of a pair. When focus groups cost $3,000 and more, this can add up very quickly.

3. Consider contracting for a volume of work, not just by project or brand.

One focus group facility we work with offers a 10% discount for a commitment of five or more focus groups in a 12-month period. Of course, this has to be paid for in advance, so the time-value of money needs to be taken into account. But this does serve to demonstrate that "buys" are still available.

4. Think about restricting the discussion topics to the issues actually at hand.

This will save in discussion guide development costs, reward you with more germane discussions, and hold down analysis costs.

Many focus groups (so moderators frequently observe) often become "the community Christmas tree"—everyone wants to hang his or her own ornament on them. Holding the line on the variety of topics covered can save incremental development, moderating, and analytical costs.

5. When you need purely background information from panelists, use a prediscussion questionnaire.

This can cover occupation, buying habits, household income, etc., all the information needed for analysis without

Reprinted from *Marketing News,* **22** (October 24, 1988), 20, 26, published by the American Marketing Association.

using up valuable discussion time.

6. Get the facility to have the 6 p.m. panelists arrive between 5:30 and 5:45 instead of the usual 5:45 to 6, and don't let the facility feed the 6 p.m. panelists in the discussion room.

This may seem like a minor point, but here's what happens:

The panelists arrive closer to 6 than 5:45. They're checked in. They wait a few minutes, then go into the discussion room and begin to make their sandwiches. By the time they've eaten, and the moderator can actually begin, it's now close to 6:10 or 6:15. Effectively, you've just lost up to 15% of your total discussion time or you back yourself into the second group, with no time in between to debrief your people or the moderator.

In the same regard, don't waste time with a deli platter for the panelists. Deli platters may look nice, but they use up the precious time you're paying for. Get premade sandwiches.

7. Don't use a videotape as merely a record. If that's all you'll use it for, skip it.

If you do videotape, don't bring an army of observers; let them watch the tape the next day, when you can fast-forward to the parts that are critical, and offer running commentary.

8. When you're traveling out-of-town, buy a package of airline tickets and hotel rooms.

Often, you can get discounts that would not be available if everyone traveling, including the moderator, booked reservations individually.

Take care of the moderator's travel arrangements along with your own. This will keep the moderator or research company from having to add a charge for the administrative costs of making arrangements. It also ensures that you'll all travel together.

9. Realize that most companies and independent moderators have to include in their project budget a factor for "selling time."

Instead of seeking competitive bids—inappropriate for something as subjective as focus groups—select those you wish to work with and tell them they've got your business. You'll be rewarded with leaner budgets, even if you still "buy by the project."

10. Plan ahead, geographically, when running out-of-town groups.

If your company is on the West Coast, don't start out in New York; it takes a full day's travel to just get there. This means you and your mod-erator have to budget for an extra day.

Instead, where possible, go to the Midwest on the first day (you can get to, say, Chicago and run groups on the same day), reserving East Coast groups for the second day. If you are based on the East Coast, with groups to be scheduled across the country, consider doing your West Coast groups first, then picking up the remaining groups as you travel back east.

11. If using a full, formal report is more archival in nature than actionable, don't use it.

Instead, have your moderator prepare a one- or two-page summary of each discussion, highlighting aspects critical to you and dispensing with a recitation of everything that was discussed, whether germane or not.

12. Make your focus groups evolutionary, not confirmatory.

Don't repeat, word-for-word, the same discussion guide each time. Use each prior group as a springboard for new learning.

This, while not saving money in a budgetary sense, will vastly increase the value of what you set out to accomplish in the first place.

The Focused Group Interview and Moderator Bias

by Frank Kennedy, President
Frank Kennedy Inc.

The nature of the problem

One of the unique features of the group interview and an important source of its strength as a research tool, is the enormous flexibility, scope, and freedom of action permitted the moderator. Not bound by the rigid constraints of a formal questionnaire, the adept moderator constructively uses this freedom to take full advantage of the spontaneous, dynamic give-and-take of the group experience, and to make countless on-the-spot judgments as to what course of action will be most responsive to his research objectives.

Yet, this very freedom——so essential to good moderating——implicitly carries with it a risk and a challenge which is the subject of this paper: the introduction of bias, and the loss of objectivity.

We must recognize at the outset that no moderator can be fully objective; it is inevitable that to some extent subtle biases, pre-conceptions and pressures toward "consistent" findings will unconsciously call for expression during the course of a group interview. Biases and pre-conceptions, once recognized as such, can actually be helpful to the moderator. Yet, unrecognized, these pressures can erode the potential value of the group interview technique.

What must be examined, then, are (a) those factors and needs which provoke these pressures, (b) how they are actually reflected in practice, and (c) what can be done constructively to bring them under control.

Sources of moderator bias

Essentially, there are three quite different pressures at work which threaten to distort moderator objectivity:

—The all-too-human predisposition to welcome and reinforce the expression of points of view which are *consonant with our own.*

—The predisposition to welcome and reinforce the expression of points of view which are *consonant with those of our clients.*

—The predisposition to welcome and reinforce the expression of points of view which are *internally consistent.*

Let us examine each of these potential sources of bias in turn.

(a) Personal bias

What good and bad moderators share in common, of course, are those personal and professional experiences, beliefs, prejudices and emotionally-grounded needs which define our individuality and "humanness." We interface with and interpret new experiences within the context of our past. Our perceptions of reality, and how we manipulate that reality, are inevitably conditioned by needs which transcend the intrinsic properties of "raw" experience.

We are all driven by powerful needs to find reality compatible with our pre-established beliefs, and we all tend to greet dissonant perceptions with selective inattention, if not with anxiety or hostility.

What differentiates the good from the poor moderator is not the absence of needs which predispose us all to bias, but (a) a recognition that these forces exist, (b) an awareness of their power and of how they can subtly influence the course of a group discussion, and (c) mastery of skills designed to minimize their expression.

This is not to say, of course, that the ideal moderator is an unfeeling robot free from hunches, hypotheses, expectations or prejudices. Indeed, every phase of his work, from guide development to moderation and analysis, requires the *constructive* use of hunch, speculation, past experience and provisional hypotheses. Yet the moderator role also requires an effort to make conscious all preconceptions, assumptions and prejudices, and to assure that these potential sources of bias are under continual scrutiny.

Perhaps in the end, the best antidote to moderator bias is the old maxim, "Know Thyself." And perhaps because this goal is so critical during the on-going, dynamic give-and-take of the group experience, moderators with psychological training have a major advantage over those who do not.

In this regard, it should be stressed that it is not the flagrant, obvious introduction of personal bias that must concern us most, since these distortions are usually quite apparent to group participants, observers, and clients alike. It is the subtle, unconscious introduction of bias which is most dangerous, since it typically escapes the attention of even experi-

Reprinted from *Marketing Review*, 31 (Feb./March 1976), 19-21, published by the **New York Chapter/American Marketing Association.**

enced moderators, and of most psychologically untrained clients. And it is for this reason that no moderator can remain complacent about the issue of bias, or sidestep the need for continual self-scrutiny.

(b) Unconscious needs to "please the client"

A second challenge to objective moderating is the unconscious need to "please the client," and to manipulate group discussions in such a way as to support *client* prejudices and preconceptions. (One prerequisite in this regard is some knowledge of what *will* make the client happy——an issue we'll turn to shortly.)

Bias in favor of client prejudices, preconceptions and hopes is not an easy thing to acknowledge, and for that very reason, it can become a significant roadblock to effective moderating. There is probably no other area of market research in which there is a greater working intimacy between client and "supplier" than in group interview research, with clients frequently going "on the road" with moderators, and sharing with them their observations, reflections, interpretations, and emotional reactions to what is taking place.

A close working relationship between client and moderator during the course of a group interview study can, of course, have considerable value. It encourages a deeper understanding by the moderator of the underlying marketing objectives, and permits him to be fully responsive to these needs. Moreover, by working together, client and moderator may jointly decide to "shift signals," and take full advantage of the flexibility of the technique.

Yet one consequence of such an intimate working relationship is that the hopes, fears, aspirations and preconceptions of the client often become all too apparent. What moderator would not honestly prefer to prepare a report in which he could assert with conviction that a new product concept has merit, that a new advertising theme is responsive to consumer need, or that exciting opportunities exist to capture a critically important market segment? And what moderator could candidly deny that he shares with his client a sense of disappointment when

the advertising or marketing implications of his work are frankly "unfavorable" in character?

It is, of course, true that for most moderators, there are meaningful and gratifying rewards in pulling a client back from the brink of a disaster, or in making a very real——if temporarily painful——contribution to his assessment of reality. Yet it is nonetheless true that as human beings in a very human art, moderators can be caught up in the enthusiasms and the fears of their clients, and as a consequence become unconsciously motivated to "make them happy."

It must be said in passing that knowledge of client hopes and expectations can provoke a very different kind of bias. There can be perverse pleasures in "enlightening" clients, and in dramatically reporting findings which fly in the face of pre-established assumptions. Quite aside from the heady delights of "ego trips," moderators occasionally feel the need to prove the value of the group procedure, and to demonstrate that the technique (and the supplier in question) is essential to client survival. One way to do so, of course, is to "rock the boat," or "find something new," and inevitably, some moderators succumb to the temptation.

For the psychologically trained moderator, these temptations are obvious and are generally held in check. Yet the client-related sources of bias represent a major hazard for the untutored moderator.

(c) The need for consistency

Still another potential source of bias is the need for consistency, both within and across group sessions. Unconscious pressures to bias a group discussion are most powerful during the later stages of a study, particularly when the initial sessions have been highly consistent in their implications. When a group threatens to react in a way which is at variance with research-based expectations, and promises to present us with unexpected and unwelcome analytic and interpretive headaches, our unconscious impulse is to nip this insurrection in the bud ——or, as a last resort, to tune out, or reject such a group as "odd-ball."

Good moderators know, of course, that apparent inconsistencies often have a way of serving up unanticipated insights upon careful analytic scrutiny, and that they can be blessings in disguise. Moreover, inconsistencies and paradoxes can usefully instruct us that an issue is perhaps more complex than we had imagined, or that additional work is legitimately required. Yet in spite of our intellectual willingness to accept occasional inconsistencies, there remains some unconscious pressure to coercively wring conformity out of our group discussions.

It should be said that unconscious efforts to bias a group so that its message is consistent with other groups can backfire, occasionally provoking the "maverick" response that one so wishes to avoid. Respondents tend to be very alert to any covert "signals" which suggest that the moderator is less than objective and has some axe to grind. Once a group recognizes unconscious efforts to bias, the value of that group is often destroyed.

Knowing "what the moderator wants to hear," respondents tend to react in a very different way to this kind of psychological arm-twisting. Some will simply surrender, or withdraw into silence. Yet many will balk and bristle at signs of psychological dishonesty, and will often take vengeful delight in scuttling the moderator ——and his favorite position——in spite of how they might genuinely feel about the issue at hand.

We have seen, then, that there are three major sources of unconscious bias which threaten to challenge moderator objectivity: personal assumptions, client expectations, and the need for consistency. How is moderator bias typically manifested in actual practice? What are its tell-tale signs?

How bias is reflected in practice

It is, of course, true that bias can be introduced at any stage of a group interview study——from guide design to interpretation and presentation. Yet opportunities for unconscious distortion are most accessible in the dynamic, spontaneous give-and-take of the group session itself, where we do not have the time to reflect, evaluate or assess the "objectivity" of each question, comment, nuance of language or gesture.

From the point of view of moderator bias, three different kinds of respondent reactions exist: (a) comments the moderator *wants* to hear, (b) comments the moderator *does not want* to hear, and (c) comments to which he is indifferent. Biasing techniques focus almost wholly on efforts to reinforce "favorable" comments (defined as those which concord with moderator expectation or hope), and on efforts to punish or inhibit the expression of "unfavorable" comments (defined as those which are dissonant with moderator expectation or hope).

How, specifically, are these biasing efforts expressed in practice?

—Most often, by greeting favorable comments with appreciative nods, smiles or reinforcing comments, and by responding to unfavorable comments with indifference, perplexed stares, or body movements which reflect discomfort.

—By being patient, permissive and encouraging when someone finds it difficult to articulate a favorable thought, but by providing no such assistance to one who finds it difficult to express an unfavorable position.

—By more actively directing questions to those who seem most likely to hold favorable views, and by ignoring those who seem most likely to hold unfavorable views.

—By initiating a round of questioning with a favorably-inclined respondent, so that a favorable view will set a precedent and context for subsequent inquiries.

—By failing to probe for contrary sentiments when favorable comments are expressed, but by probing actively when unfavorable comments are articulated.

—By permitting "out of context" favorable comments, while telling those who offer an unfavorable view out of context that "we'll talk about that later."

—In periodic summaries of group positions, understating or omitting "minority" points of view.

—By "turning on the charm" so that respondents will tend to go along with the position you have unconsciously conveyed you want to hear.

—Conversely, by failing to develop any rapport at all with a group asked to assess a competitive product or advertisement, so that not only you, but the product or ad will be rejected.

These examples are meant simply to illustrate rather than to catalogue the many ways in which bias can be introduced. We should note, however, that these devices, when well executed, are often successful in accomplishing their purpose because they are subtle and often escape conscious self-scrutiny.

How moderator bias can be minimized

The group interview technique is a very human art. While one of its unique strengths rests in the character of moderator-respondent interaction, and in the flexibility and scope accorded the moderator, that very freedom poses challenges which must be recognized by client and moderator alike. Absolute objectivity can perhaps never be achieved, yet there are concrete steps which clients and moderators can take to reduce the problem of moderator bias to inconsequential proportions. What, then, can specifically be done to maximize moderator objectivity?

As clients:

—Use moderators with clinical or psychological training, particularly moderators who have had therapeutic experience.

—Understand the unconscious pressures on moderators to "make you happy," and make a conscious effort to keep them in the dark as to your *personal* expectations and hopes.

—Refrain from holding detailed "post-mortems" with moderators after each session, particularly any discussions which attempt to formulate "tentative findings."

—Stay away from "do it yourself" moderation, particularly if in all honesty, you feel you are emotionally invested in the outcome of the research.

—Do not require "top line" findings of the moderator, or even ask him for his "impressions" during the course of a study. Once he commits himself, there are additional pressures to prove himself right.

—Increasingly make "objectivity" one of your criteria for moderator eval-

uation. When in the role of an observer, reward objectivity in your conversations with the moderator, and call him to task when you feel there is evidence of unconscious bias.

As moderators:

—Recognizing the potential hazards of unconscious bias is half the battle. Before a study begins, learn to ask yourself what you expect will happen, what you would like to happen, and why. By doing a little soul-searching and by bringing potential sources of bias to the surface, you will find yourself operating on a much more objective level.

—Learn to be increasingly sensitive to your own feelings during the course of a session. When—and why—are you feeling angry, uncomfortable, anxious, bored, disappointed, frustrated, relieved or happy? How—and why—are you unconsciously expressing these feelings to the group?

—When auditing tapes, learn to be sensitive not only to content, but to interaction patterns and to evidence of unconscious bias on your part. Take the time and trouble to analyze your own performance from time to time by way of videotape.

—After completing a given session in a series, try not to discuss your impressions with your client, or to attempt any formulation of tentative conclusions. Do not write interim memos or take notes in lieu of tape recordings.

—Avoid the temptation to prematurely demonstrate your interpretive skills and marketing know-how to observer-clients. The time for synthesis and closure is after the last session has been completed, and not before.

—Recall to mind the times when apparent inconsistencies "made sense" on another level of abstraction, and when they triggered fresh inquiries in unanticipated yet useful directions.

—Though requiring courage, it is sometimes useful at the close of a group session to hold a brief post-mortem with respondents, quite candidly asking them if there had been a full opportunity for all opinions to be expressed, or whether in their view, you have in any way communicated a personal bias.

—Recognize the fact that if your personal expectation or hypothesis is valid, it will withstand the most vigorous scrutiny. By providing full opportunities for contrary positions to be expressed and explored (and in taking the courage to do so), you will be on far more secure grounds in asserting and documenting its validity.

In summary, while the potential hazards of moderator bias are very real, we should not overstate the degree to which these pressures can distort group interview findings, particularly when both client and moderator are aware of the problem and take sensible steps to forestall its expression. Truth is obstinate and persistent, and will generally make itself heard. What is at issue is not the likelihood of massive distortion, but the failure to fully exploit a technique which offers so many unique and valuable rewards to those who use it well.

Beyond 'moderator chemistry': Guidelines for judging qualitative research

**BY ROBERT J. KADEN
and GAYLE D. MOBERG**

ALTHOUGH THE RANGE of quality among quantitative market research sources varies widely, criteria for evaluating them seem fairly definable and objective.

Clients assess performance in such areas as cost estimates, questionnaire development, field validation, data collection, tabulating, ethics, and communications.

The importance assigned to those and other areas may vary in importance among clients and research sources, but at least the criteria exist and provide some measurable means for distinguishing one source from another.

Judging qualitative sources, however, often seems much more subjective, as in "Well, I just have good chemistry with that moderator."

Although that chemistry is an important part of a successful qualitative relationship, there are many other specific, measurable, and meaningful criteria by which to judge qualitative expertise.

This makes recognizing good qualitative research all the more important.

We have assigned ratings of very important, occasionally important, and rarely important to various items. Following is how clients should judge qualitative sources:

Very important
● Marketing acumen.
● Upfront involvement in defining the problem.
● Creativity in qualitative design.
● Developing new qualitative techniques for better understanding the problem at hand.
● Proper screening of respondents.
● Ability to recruit articulate and

Robert J. Kaden is president of Goldring & Company Inc., Chicago, and Gayle D. Moberg is a group account manager for the firm.

creative respondents when necessary.
● Ability to shift gears quickly and follow lines of respondent thinking that were not anticipated.
● A wealth of moderating techniques to handle any group situation.
● Reporting the findings clearly and succinctly.
● Generally creative analysis.
● Ability to make insightful, action-oriented recommendations.
● Issuing the report on time.
● Being able to translate qualitative planning, thinking, and acquired knowledge to next-step quantitative studies.

Occasionally important
● Organized, comprehensive, and flexible discussion guide.
● Moderating style.
● Ability to uncover issues the client hasn't thought of.
● Analyzing group reactions or debriefing immediately after the group.

Rarely important
● Whether the focus group seems animated and excited.
● Thick reports.

QUALITATIVE researchers can be tougher on themselves than clients are. Often, there seem to be more areas that we consider very important than they do.

The focus of the client tends to remain on areas traditionally expected to fall under the qualitative domain: screening, writing discussion guides, moderating, and issuing reports.

It is vital that the client demand excellence in these areas, but there are areas we deem important, for which many clients don't think to ask or demand involvement, much less expertise. These include marketing acumen, preresearch involvement in problem definition, design, development of new research techniques, action-oriented analysis, and recommendations.

Even fewer clients think to choose a qualitative source on the basis of their or their companies' ability to be continually involved once the qualitative portion of a study is technically finished.

Yet the value of the qualitative work and the researcher's expertise should continue to play a role in subsequent quantitative research and can further be evaluated on such criteria as the following:
● Assessment of whether the right qualitative information is available to properly define the direction of a quantitative study.
● Ability to look for the most effective quantitative design based on the qualitative data.
● Effective interpretation and translation of qualitative findings to questionnaire development.
● Understanding the qualitative nuances of the quantitative data.
● Recognition of whether further qualitative work is needed after the quantitative portion.
● Ability to effectively design further qualitative work, if deemed necessary, based on the quantitative learnings and on understanding the overall marketing implications and decisions to be made as a result of the study.

WE LOVE the chemistry we have with our clients, but we strongly believe they should, when judging a qualitative source, move beyond that to broader areas that affect the entire process of solving research problems.

Reprinted from *Marketing News,* **21 (August 28, 1987), 2, published by the American Marketing Association.**

Probing correctly uncovers truth behind answers in focus group

by Hy Mariampolski

Hy Mariampolski is president of QualiData Research Inc., Brooklyn.

Probing is the primary way to validate focus group responses and establish the truth behind glib answers, but many moderators are unable to do this.

Questioning and probing strategy that lacks variety can result in a monotonous and tedious session, with resulting threats to respondent interest and involvement. Furthermore, predictable probes can raise respondents' defenses and promote hostility toward the interviewer.

The following techniques should prove useful to moderators as well as market researchers who pursue open-ended responses and those who conduct one-on-ones:

1. The silent probe.

Often the best way to probe is simply to say nothing after a respondent has made a statement, and to suggest through your eye contact and body language that you expect to hear more. Experienced interviewers know that silence is a powerful weapon.

2. Request elaboration.

In this, the simplest form of probing, the operative word is "more." For example, "Can you tell me more about why you chose ExBank for your checking account?"

3. Request definition.

The respondent is asked to provide the meaning of an adverb or adjective that is used to describe a product. "When you say you like healthful breakfast cereal, what do you mean?"

4. Request word association.

This method is particularly helpful when the goal is to develop copy or advertising, because it can provide breakthrough alternatives to overused and hackneyed product descriptions.

The success of this probing technique depends on rapidity and a machine-gun style of asking for additional associations. For example, "You said you want to buy condoms that are sensitive. Quick, give me another word for that...Another... Another."

5. Request context or situation.

This technique requires respondents to establish the domain for an expressed product preference. For example, "Do you drink bourbon every time you're at a bar? With a date? With coworkers?"

6. Shift context or situation.

Like the previous method, this technique requires the interviewer to shift situations to bring unexpressed motivations to the surface. For example, "You said you prefer ABC Airlines for your business travel. How about when you're going on vacation? What if you had to go to another city for a family emergency?"

7. Request clarification.

The operative word here is "explain." The interviewer says he or she would better understand a participant's response if it were explained differently or more thoroughly.

8. Request comparison.

After respondents have described a particular product or service, have them provide a list of additional products for which they would use the same description.

Alternatively, this can be turned into a game in which the moderator names a category and respondents are asked to provide comparable products. For example, "You said Ivory soap was a 'classic.' What would be the Ivory soap of cars...of airlines... of packaged meats...of credit cards?"

It should be obvious that this is an effective strategy for generating commodity images for consumer or business services.

9. Request classification or typology.

This involves sequencing questions so that the first response opens up the possibility of creating a typology for additional responses.

Several of the probing techniques listed above can be used as the first stage. For example, "What is your favorite type of candy?" "Truffles." "Can you tell me about some types of candy that you enjoy?" "Licorice, jelly beans, and gumdrops." "Do you buy them all for the same occasions or for different ones—what are those occasions?"

10. Compare and contrast to a previous statement.

An effective way to get respondents to enlarge on an answer is to ask them

Reprinted from *Marketing News,* **22** (October 24, 1988), 22, 26, published by the American Marketing Association.

to relate it to real or imagined inconsistencies with things they previously stated.

For example, "Before you said you use coffee in the morning to 'get you going.' Now you tell me you don't like that 'caffeine buzz.' Is there a contradiction between those answers or not?"

11. Compare and contrast to remarks by other group members.

Group debate and challenge are among the most effective aspects of focus group sessions. The moderator can use group dynamics to probe a respondent by asking him or her to compare a definition, classification, etc., to one stated by another participant.

For example, "You said you read a daily newspaper to keep up with your favorite sports. He said he reads a weekly magazine to keep up. Do you both mean the same thing when you say 'keep up?'"

This group of probing techniques works by raising the discomfort level of participants. Interviewers should use them only when high levels of cooperation and openness have been established in a discussion session.

Refrain from using them during most interviews on sensitive subjects (such as those involving sexual behavior, body functions, deviant behavior, etc.). Most of all, make certain that respondents know that it is only a style of questioning and not an attack on their dignity and integrity.

12. Challenge veracity.

This can go from mild to hot—spoken with a wink or a curled eyebrow. For example, "You can't be telling me the truth," or "OK, now that you've told me what's socially acceptable, can you tell us how you really felt when you called your insurance agent to say your car was wrecked?"

13. Challenge completeness.

In this technique, the subject is pressed for more information with the subtly expressed implication that something is being held back. A well-targeted statement of empathy can be a useful adjunct here.

14. Confrontational probes.

This is an extreme version of the provocative probe in which the researcher adopts a very testy tone. Few individuals have the personality to pull this off without alienating at least some to the other focus group participants.

It is, however, sometimes an effective technique for breaking beyond "acceptable" responses. For example, "OK, I've heard enough of the same stupid, safe answers. Let's hear something original for a change."

Most of the preceding techniques directly follow a given response. The next group usually depends on some lapse of time before the interviewer takes up the issue again.

These techniques are effective as a validity check for previously expressed attitudes. They also can indicate whether information introduced during the session helped to change subjects' minds.

15. Echo probe.

This requires the interviewer to play back an earlier response using the same words that the subject voiced.

16. Interpretive probe.

The interviewer's goal is to expand the meaning of implications of an attitude expressed earlier. For example, "Before you said that you chose your overnight delivery service because it provides you with written verification of delivery. Can I assume that if your fax machine provided you with delivery verification, it would serve your purposes just as well?"

17. Summary probe.

After following the drift of a discussion, the moderator can outline briefly the thrust or range of opinion. For example, "Am I getting this right; some of you care most about the reputation of your accounting firm, while for others, what's foremost in your mind is the specific person handling your account?"

This group of techniques requires going beyond mere questions and answers into the realm of fantasy and play. The basic purpose here is to

break down defenses and the tendency to provide acceptable responses. These are particularly effective in studies involving idea generation, product development, positioning, and copy development.

18. Purposive misunderstanding.

The interviewer can misunderstand and answer in a way that's either straight-faced or in obvious jest. In both cases, conveying an incorrect interpretation of a response, puts a subject on the spot to clarify and enlarge upon the meaning of what was said.

19. Playing naive.

The naive style of questioning was developed in the 1970s by a school of qualitative sociology known as "ethnomethodology." The objective here is to get the subject to respond as though the researcher knew absolutely nothing about a behavioral pattern.

This technique can be used in conjunction with other probing methods, and depends on a rapid-fire style of questioning. For example, "OK, you said you picked XYZ cola because it's 'refreshing.' That sounds fine, but it assumes I know what that means. I want you to assume that I don't have the slightest idea of what it takes for something to be 'refreshing.' Tell me about it from the very first principle. Should it be hot or cold? Wet or dry? Flavored or unflavored? Sweet, spicy, salty...?

20. Wrong answers.

Turn around and ask the subject to give you an incorrect or dishonest answer, rather than the acceptable one. Focus further discussion on why it is wrong.

21. Projective probe.

It is effective to probe projectively by getting subjects to shift their psychological frame of reference. For example, ask the respondent to imagine he or she is someone else: "How would you answer that if you were over 65?" Alternatively, ask subjects to answer on behalf of "most people" so that the sources of their own motivations can be explored.

SECTION III

Case Studies And Applications

The six articles in this section give the reader some insights on using focus groups in particular situations or industries. One of the articles is a "classic" from the first edition and one article presents six case studies which exemplify proper and improper applications of the focus group methodology. The remaining articles offer insights on particular problems or situations in which the focus group techniques may assist marketers or managers in their information gathering activities.

Keown's article, "Focus Group Research: Tool for the Retailer" suggests a step by step approach to using focus groups as part of a strategic planning process in retailing. In addition to some basic guidelines for using focus groups, Keown offers some practical advice for the retail strategist on managing the research process and a brief case history on how a food retailer effectively used focus groups to frame future research and planning efforts.

As the title suggests, "Six Focus Group Cases: 3 correct, 3 incorrect" presents very clear examples of how focus groups are used and misused. With this article, Buncher makes the point that one can expect too much from the focus group technique.

The "classic" for this section, "Applications of Focus Group interviews in Marketing", illustrates the usefulness of the focus group approach for marketing mix problems.

In "Focus Groups: An Innovative Marketing Research Technique", Hisrich and Peters give useful guidance in using focus groups in the health care industry. While they advocate the use of focus groups they also offer good cautions about misusing focus groups.

J. Mitchell Elrod, Jr., in his article "Applying Business Methods and Techniques: Improving Employee Relations with Focus Groups" gives an example of how this technique can be applied to non-marketing problems.

"Are Focus Groups a Viable Tool for PR Practitioners to Help Their Companies Establish Corporate Responsibility" presents another problem area where focus groups can be used as an effective data development approach for strategic planning.

FOCUS GROUP RESEARCH: TOOL FOR THE RETAILER

by Charles Keown

ABSTRACT: LA RECHERCHE DES GROUPES DITS "FOCUS": UN INSTRUMENT A L'USAGE DU DETAILLANT

Dans cet article, dans le but d'aider le petit ou moyen détaillant qui désirerait évaluer ou changer sa stratégie, nous nous proposons de donner quelques indications sur l'usage de l'interview "focus group" pour le recueillement de données chez les consommateurs. En premier lieu, nous recommandons un procédé en cinq étapes, où la direction: (1) déciderait sur quelle matière doivent porter les recherches; (2) déciderait également quels seraient les consommateurs-cibles; (3) organiserait, dirigerait, et soumettrait à un contrôle, les discussions du "focus group"; (4) formulerait une méthodologie permettant d'analyser les données; et (5) dresserait plusieurs plans parmi lesquels l'on pourrait choisir, selon les circonstances. Ensuite, et pour terminer, nous présentons un cas concret afin de faire voir la valeur du procédé recommandé.

One of the most popular of recent management developments in large corporations has been the emphasis on strategic planning, the process of developing long-term programs for survival and growth. Strategic management has been defined as "the managerial process of developing and maintaining a viable relationship between the organization and its environment through the development of corporate purpose, objectives and goals, growth strategies, and business portfolio plans for company-wide operations."[1]

The prospects (as well as the problems) for adapting strategic planning to the field of retailing have been addressed recently in the *Journal of Retailing.*[2] One of the major problems facing the small- to medium-sized retailer is assessing the environment and target market in order to effectively develop and evaluate strategic programs.

Berman and Evans state that: "Retailers are often tempted to rely upon *nonsystematic measures* in evaluation of strategies because of time constraints, cost constraints, or lack of research capabilities."[3] These authors strongly recommend the use of marketing research as a systematic method for the collection and analysis of data so that the retail organization can develop or modify its strategies.

Marketing research data may be obtained from secondary or published sources, and primary sources such as surveys. Most often, however, published

---

[1] Philip Kotler, *Marketing Management: Analysis, Planning and Control.* 4th ed. (Englewood Cliffs, N.J.: Prentice-Hall, 1979).

Dr. Keown is an assistant professor of marketing at the University of Hawaii's College of Business Administration. He teaches marketing and retail management and has consulted with retailers in the Honolulu area. Dr. Keown had twenty years of experience in industry prior to obtaining his Ph.D. from the University of Oregon in 1980.

[2] Bert Rosenbloom, "Strategic Planning in Retailing: Prospects and Problems," *Journal of Retailing,* 56 (Spring 1980), pp. 107-120.

[3] Barry Berman and Joe R. Evans, *Retail Management: A Strategic Approach* (New York: MacMillan Publishing Co., Inc., 1979).

Reprinted from *Journal of Small Business Management,* **21 (April 1983), 59-65. Used with permission.**

data sources do not pertain to the specific retailing strategy under consideration, and collecting primary data by survey is time-consuming, costly, and usually requires outside help. A relatively new technique for collecting primary data from consumers is the focus group interview. The technique was first applied to a retail store in the early 1960s.[4] More recently, *Advertising Age*[5] conducted a series of focus groups with shoppers in various parts of the country in order to assist planners in their national advertising campaigns. It appears that the focus group technique may be an under-used research tool, particularly for small business retailers who want to evaluate and/or redirect their strategies.

What Is a Focus Group?

For the reader unfamiliar with focus group research, an excellent compendium of various articles describing its application, dangers, and advantages is available from the American Marketing Association.[6] In brief, focus group research involves a moderator conducting several small-group discussions about a particular topic of interest. Under the guidance of this trained moderator or "facilitator," the groups, ranging from eight to twelve people, "focus" their discussions on a selected topic. The principal advantage of focus groups is synergism; that is, group interaction generally provides more and better data than would individual indepth interviews. The prime disadvantage, however, is the lack of generalizability due to the small sample size. Focus group research is considered a qualitative tool, as compared to the quantitative technique of large, statistically controlled surveys.

The arranging and conducting of the focus groups is best performed by a market research firm or a consultant. Normally, the moderator should not be connected with the retail business under discussion, since this could inhibit participants' comments. The firm or consultant should have experience with focus group research and the ability to know when to "probe" a particular topic and/or participant, as well as when to "shut off" or redirect discussion of a non-pertinent subject.

The discussion can take place in any quiet room (to allow for tape recording) with comfortable seating, generally around a table. A restaurant or hotel meeting room is often ideal, since it permits ease in parking and the opportunity to serve refreshments. In some instances, however, a special room with a one-way mirror is used so that the retail strategist can monitor the discussion unobserved. Such rooms are available in the facilities of the larger research firms.

Scheduling of the discussions depends upon the availability of participants; for example, late mornings or luncheons for non-working housewives, or early evenings for day workers. Recruiting of participants can be done in several ways. Some consulting firms have lists of people who have participated in other studies; generally, these people have been identified as outgoing and able to express themselves. Another way to recruit is simply to ask shoppers (assuming they compose the target market of interest to the study) if they would be willing to participate in a group discussion, and follow up with telephone calls. Other recruiting methods include ads in the newspaper, telephone solicitation, and requests to social clubs or civic associations.

The cost for focus group research varies depending upon location and type of outside contractor; on the average,

[4]Henry L. Munn and William K. Opdyke, "Group Interviews Reveal Consumer Buying Behavior," *Journal of Retailing* 37 (Fall 1961), pp. 26-56.
[5]"Focus Group Interview: Consumers Rap About Today's Shopping, Buying," *Advertising Age* (March 3, 1975), pp. 37-40.
[6]James B. Higginbothom and Keith K. Cox, *Focus Group Interviews: A Reader* (Chicago, Ill.: American Marketing Association, 1979).

the cost should be in the neighborhood of $1,000 to $1,500 per group. This cost includes renting a location, recruiting participants (eight to twelve per group), conducting the discussion (three-quarters to one and one-half hours), compensating the participants ($10 to $25 per person) and reporting the results. The cost depends on the difficulty in recruiting (the more variables used to segment the target group, the more difficult to recruit), and the total number of groups to be conducted (usually six).

A Suggested Framework

The technique suggested here uses focus-group interviews as a basis for collecting qualitative, primary data, and the companion tool of content analysis for categorizing customer responses. Depending upon the degree of risk involved in following up on the analysis, the small businessperson has three alternatives: (1) take no action; (2) plan for immediate action; or (3) choose to undertake further quantitative research. This framework is illustrated in figure 1. Each of the five steps is briefly discussed, and a case history is described below.

Step 1 requires the retail strategist to define the research question or problem in order to specify the direction of the group discussion. For example, the question could focus on methods to improve customer satisfaction, or the possibility of opening a new branch store in a developing suburb. The topic for discussion should be broad enough to elicit unstructured thinking on the part of group participants, yet narrow enough to eliminate irrelevant conversation. Part of the responsibility of the moderator is to keep the discussion on the right track.

Step 2 requires the retail strategist to decide upon the target market of interest. Should it be existing customers, potential customers, women only, etc.? The research question will usually dictate the make-up of the group. Existing customers would be the natural target group for improving customer satisfaction, whereas a sample of residents in a new suburb would be the target group for the question of opening a branch store. There is often a problem as to whether the group participants should be heterogeneous or homogeneous. Homogeneous groups, such as middle-aged women in higher income brackets, are generally more comfortable and open with each other, whereas mixed sex, ethic, or socioeconomic groups make it more difficult to achieve a high degree of group interaction. One often-used approach is to run several groups, so that within each group the composition is homogeneous, but with each separate group representing a different segment of the target population.

Step 3 involves hiring a market research or consulting firm to arrange and conduct the focus group discussions. The retail strategist should plan to sit in and observe each group discussion. The author has found that "fish-bowling" (moderator and participants in the center, observers off to the side of the room) does not seem to inhibit participants once the discussion gets underway. By observing the group discussion process, the retail strategist is able to judge the intensity of the groups' feelings and the abilities of the moderator, as well as to monitor whether the discussion meets the stated objectives. As a result the retail strategist and the moderator may decide to redirect subsequent discussions to explore new areas for investigation.

Step 4 requires the retail strategist to analyze the results of the group discussions. In most cases, the research or consulting firm will provide a complete tape recording of the discussion, comments to highlight major points, and a summary report of the general findings. The retail strategist's job is to decide what factors are most important. Due to the

Figure 1
A SUGGESTED FRAMEWORK FOR FOCUS GROUP RESEARCH

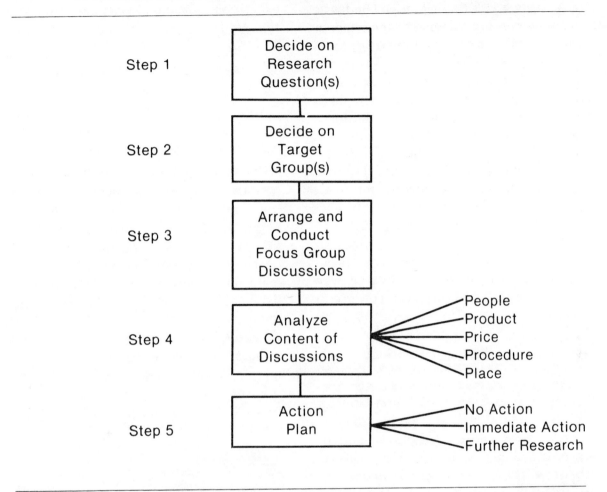

qualitative nature of focus group research, this can be a difficult task. For example, six people mention dissatisfaction with the store layout and only one person mentions cluttered displays. This does *not* mean that layout is six times more important than displays. Each comment must be thought of as the proverbial "tip-of-the-iceberg." One individual's comment may be representative of several hundred customers or may be simply a personal trait of that one participant. For this reason, content analysis of focus-group discussion purposely neglects numbers (percentages, ratios, etc.),[7] and simply reports comments by category (see the case history following).

Finally, in *Step 5*, the retail strategist can classify alternative actions into three groups. The "No Action" group includes suggestions that are not feasible; for example, lack of parking space may be impossible to remedy due to the land/lease situation. "Immediate Action" requires minimum risk or financial involvement and has good face value; for example, complaints about dirty floors and windows could be resolved easily by more frequent cleaning. "Further Research" represents a group of actions that would entail risk and/or large financial outlays; for example, suggestions that a new product line be offered. In such a case, the strategist may decide that additional *quantitative* research is required to determine the advisability of a particular course of action.

[7]A. M. Bussis, et al., *Beyond Surface Curriculum: An Interview Study of Teachers' Understandings* (Boulder, Colo.: Western Press, 1976).

The proper way to validate or quantify focus group findings is to conduct a survey, observe shoppers' behavior, or run an experiment. Frequently, one of the purposes of focus group research is to delineate a particular area requiring further study, and then develop a set of questions and response formats for a subsequent survey. For example, if focus group research seemed to indicate that shoppers disliked trading stamps, then a short questionnaire could be developed and a large number of shoppers could be interviewed. If 400 out of 500 shoppers replied that they objected to trading stamps, then the retail strategist would have validated the preliminary finding of the focus group research.

Case History

A small food retailer who wanted to develop a strategic plan for the survival of his grocery store was interested in determining customers' perceptions of the pleasant and unpleasant aspects of grocery shopping in his store. These became the focus research questions, together with customer suggestions for improvement. The target group was simply defined as individuals who shopped for groceries for their families for at least one year in the retailer's particular trading area. The participants—about ten per discussion group—were rewarded with a case of soft drinks and a case of snacks, a retail value of about $15.00. Each group discussion was moderated, tape recorded, and content-analyzed according to the 5-P method: people, product, price, procedure, and place.

The categorized list of participant comments are shown in table 1. In this particular study, "people" comments were directed principally to cashiers, "product" comments to fresh foods, "price" comments to sales items, "procedure" comments to check-out lines, and "place" comments to cleanliness.

In responding to the above comments, the retailer considered further actions according to the three-way classification scheme. Comments placed in the "no action" group included generalizations (high prices), impossibilities (larger parking lots), and complaints about cost-effective practices (placing new price stickers over old ones). The "immediate action" items included suggestions that could be acted upon right away at relatively low cost, such as more organized layouts for newspaper ads, or better enforcement of express-line conditions. The "further research" items included suggestions that would require a large financial commitment to implement. Possible topics for further research were: attitude improvement program for cashiers with measurement of its effectiveness, experimentation with new check-out procedures to reduce waiting time, and the effect of closed freezers on frozen food sales.

Conclusion

The case history outlined above illustrates how the focus group research technique provided valuable primary, qualitative market research for a small food retailer. Such qualitative research using focus groups does not replace broader-based, "hard" data obtained through surveys, but is a complementary tool that can help to identify issues for immediate action and for further research. Focus groups and the associated content analysis technique are especially appropriate when the small business strategist is confronted with very broad alternatives (expand or contract) or very general problems (sales decline or new product assortments). Once the alternatives or problems become better defined, low-risk, low-cost decisions can be made immediately, while high-risk, high-cost decisions can be delineated for subsequent study.

Table 1
CATEGORIZED COMMENTS OF FOCUS GROUP PARTICIPANTS

	PEOPLE	PRODUCTS	PRICES
Likes:	Friendly, fast efficient cashiers. Butchers on duty after 5 p.m. Bag boys to carry to car. Cashiers who call out prices.	Seeing new products first-hand. Attractive displays of fresh food. Stocking up with sale items. Last-minute gift items. Generic items (next to branded). Sampling in the store.	Coupons. Sales. Quantity discounts.
Dislikes:	Cashiers who don't know ads. Cashiers who make mistakes. Nasty cashiers. Stock boys in aisles.	Prepackaged produce. Leaky chickens; bones sticking out of meat trays. Meat packaged in large quantities. Items out of stock.	Different prices for the same item. Deceiving sales (1-2¢ difference from regular price). Running out of sale items. New sticker over old one. No prices on items. Which brand/size is actually on sale. Generic items not really cheaper. High prices.
Suggestions:	More bag boys to speed up lines. More cashiers during busy hours.	Even pounds of hamburger.	Competitive pricing on H & BA items. More unit pricing. Prices on freezer door. Coupons available as you enter store.

Table 1 (Continued)

PROCEDURES	PLACES
Express lanes. Cash with courtesy card. No hassle in returning items. Store using methods to keep energy costs down. Smooth-running, clean shopping carts.	Clean floors and products. Aisles wide enough for two carts to pass. Places to return carts in parking lot.
Trading stamps. Abuse of express lanes. Courtesy card run-around. Inaccurate scales in the produce area. Messy, hard-to-read ads. Allowing no carts in the parking lot. Not having the express lane open.	Clutter. Shopping at night. Rusty, broken-down carts. Separate liquor department. Open freezers (too cold to shop).
Large signs on how to cash checks. Carts that open up. Enforce "no smoking" regulation. Enforce express line conditions. Line-up for cashiers like in banks.	Bigger parking lots. Music. Bigger signs. Doors on freezers. Handout of store layout for new shoppers. Courtesy shopping list vis-a-vis the store layout.

Six focus group cases: 3 correct, 3 incorrect applications

BY MARTIN M. BUNCHER

CORRECT APPLICATIONS:

Case No. 1—A high-quality men's suit maker wants to explore the market for swimwear in order to take advantage of its established awareness, image, and distribution capabilities.

However, management isn't familiar with the market but would like to have a quantitative study completed outlining general trends such as brand preferences, buying habits, color implications, etc.

Lacking a basic feeling for what is happening in the market, focus groups are conducted among a few age groups to develop a better idea of what to include in a quantitative survey questionnaire.

Case No. 2—An ad agency has been handling a leading detergent account for 12 years.

Periodically the staff feels it runs out of creative ideas or becomes "stale" on the acount. The values of the detergent are known, so that the essence of what has to be communicated is established.

However, focus groups are held to generate some fresh insight as to what is going on in consumer households, particularly among buyers and non-buyers of the product. The comments given by participants are used as fresh raw material for new creative concepts.

Case No. 3—Growth was slow but steady in the panty-hose market dominated by several big brands. In spite of market growth, one major manufacturer saw his share slipping on a slight downward trend over time.

Looking for ways to boost sales, a series of focus groups was conducted oriented towards isolating current product dissatisfaction, if any, among panty-hose wearers. A second orientation was to establish what needs were unmet by existing products.

Individual ideas and opportunities from these sessions led to new product designs and current product modifications which, when built into prototypes, were ultimately tested in the marketplace. The result was a new series of panty-hose products witnessed just a few years ago, which included ventilated panels, color-complexion matching, and other market-share contributions.

INCORRECT APPLICATIONS:

Case No. 1—The marketing director of a leading manufacturer of instant desserts has data to indicate that while he is holding his share of the market, the product category is declining. Other research suggests dieting, nutrition concerns, and a weakening economy probably are forcing the marketplace down.

Some yet undiscovered product value might counteract these external forces to reverse the market trend. Several focus groups are planned to explore the possibility of such a factor.

In this situation a general hypothesis already has been formulated, based on existing marketing expertise. The appropriate first action is to test the hypothesis, to see if, in fact, the three factors are responsible for the market decline.

It might be determined, for example, that the instant dessert product is a higher-priced item purchased with discretionary income, which may be drying up in a weakening economy. Thus, a new product value probably will not solve the problem. Repackaging might help to provide smaller and less-expensive individual serving options.

This case is unusual in that it is putting the cart before the horse, but this time, the focus groups represent the cart and not the horse. While often used as initial or exploratory tools, focus groups sometimes are more appro-

priately applied as middle and even final steps in the marketing intelligence program.

Case No. 2—A firm has developed some new doughnuts with special flavoring. Before going into test market, it feels an indication of consumer acceptance could be derived from focus groups.

It also feels some guidance could be obtained if modifications are suggested by unfavorable reactions. Thus, 12 groups are planned in different locations in one state.

Assuming 12 respondents per group, the client may obtain 144 cases of performance. Unfortunately, these cases are not likely to be representative of the target population. Large numbers of respondents originating from focus groups are no more representative of target populations than are smaller ones, because of certain biases which do not disappear.

The appropriate action is to conduct some in-house studies, distributing the products and doing a callback interview. This procedure will enable product use under situations closer to normal, and the readout will be all the more valid.

Case No. 3—An automobile maker which has always stressed a sporty, luxurious, youthful appeal to the marketplace hires a new ad manager who feels the company could capture a larger share of market if it put more emphasis on performance, reliability, and low-cost maintenance.

The strategy seems to make sense. However, some focus groups will be conducted regionally to see how the appeal will affect current and potential owners.

The need here is to determine if the hypothesis concerning product values is correct, that is, if stressing those features can motivate more people to buy the car. Assuming results are positive, the new ad manager still will need to

Reprinted from *Marketing News*, XVI (September 17, 1982), Section 2-15, published by the American Marketing Association.

determine how to successfully communicate those values. Thus, the first phase of the research calls for a representative sample of the two market segments involved, accounting for regional variances.

Focus groups can neither supply this descriptive data nor generate conclusions about market trends or potential trends. They can only suggest possibilities.

If the hypothesis is shown by quantitative research to hold together, focus groups may be appropriate as an exploratory method of considering how to best convey the relevant values. But ultimately, some quantitative ad research will be essential prior to the commitment of major media expenditure.

Applications of Focus Group Interviews in Marketing

KEITH K. COX, JAMES B. HIGGINBOTHAM, AND JOHN BURTON

The focus group interview is an effective qualitative technique in marketing research. Three actual marketing applications illustrate the usefulness of this approach for marketing mix problems.

Although focus group interviews have been used by many marketing research firms since the 1950s, their role in the decision-making process is not always clearly understood by marketing management. This article describes three actual applications of the focus group interview in marketing research and management decision making, and discusses the strengths and weaknesses of the technique.

The Focus Group Interview

Basically, there are two types of group interview studies. One is nothing more than a question and answer session: the group moderator asks questions and the respondents give verbal or written answers. A second type is the *focus group interview,* where a group of people (generally eight to twelve) are led through an open, in-depth discussion by a group moderator. The moderator's objective is to focus the discussion on the relevant subject areas in a nondirective manner. Such interviews can be used to develop hypotheses in the planning or qualitative stage of the marketing research process. The interviews provide a basis in depth for the development of additional research, and they may be useful as a source of new and fresh ideas for new products and services, advertising themes, packaging evaluations, and the like.

Marketing Applications

Focus group interviews can be effective research tools in many types of marketing decision situations. The examples given here illustrate the usefulness of the technique in three distinct decision areas: (1) pricing and advertising, (2) a new product, and (3) packaging.[1]

Example 1: Alpha Power and Light

The Alpha company had requested an electricity rate increase in its trading area for the first time in 20 years and wanted to know (1) customer opinions of the rate increase, and (2) reasons for customer resistance to the rate increase, such as general service problems. Alpha company was asking for a rate increase of 6%, which it felt was reasonable and necessary. The company planned to use the research results in its negotiations about price, and for future advertising campaign ideas. Table 1 highlights the three stages of the marketing research process used in this research project.

1. Each marketing application comes from an actual marketing research project conducted in 1972 and 1973, but the company names are disguised.

> • *ABOUT THE AUTHORS.*
> Keith K. Cox is professor of marketing in the College of Business Administration, University of Houston.
> James B. Higginbotham is president and John Burton is vice president of Higginbotham Associates, Houston.

Reprinted from *Journal of Marketing,* 40 (January 1976), 77-80, published by the American Marketing Association.

TABLE 1

STAGES IN THE MARKETING RESEARCH PROCESS FOR ALPHA POWER AND LIGHT

Stage 1 (Qualitative)	Stage 2 (Qualitative)	Stage 3 (Quantitative)
Objectives 1. Identify past and current consumer complaints as to service problems and rate dissatisfaction 2. Identify perceived image of company as estimated by company employees 3. Evaluate past advertising and other materials communicated to consumers	*Objectives* 1. Evaluate consumer attitudes toward utility companies in this area generally 2. Develop hypotheses on rate and service problems of customers 3. Develop psychographic profiles of respondents' attitudes about this company and this service 4. Identify specific topics for questionnaire construction	*Objectives* 1. Quantify existing consumer attitudes toward service and rate problems 2. Quantify existing consumer images of the company 3. Evaluate hypotheses about consumer attitudes 4. Develop communication ideas for future advertising campaigns
Research Methodology 1. Personal interviews with company executives, complaint department employees, and field linemen 2. Audit of past records of consumer complaints 3. Audit of past company advertisements	*Research Methodology* 1. Focus group interviews (12 groups of 10 persons in each group), each interview session videotaped 2. Short, self-administered questionnaire for all 120 persons	*Research Methodology* 1. Random sample of 700 adult persons using telephone interviews (100 interviews in each of 7 company districts)

The first stage of the research project was qualitative in nature. It was designed to identify where the company was at the present time in terms of perceived image of the company and degree of consumer dissatisfaction with rates and services, using the internal interview and audit process described in Table 1.

The information obtained in the first stage was used in guiding the researchers in the second stage of the research, where focus group interview sessions were conducted. The focus group interviews were originally intended to obtain relevant information about the following questions:

1. Why were those consumers who opposed the rate hike really opposed?

2. What information should be communicated to those consumers opposed in order to justify a rate increase to them?

3. What reasons were given by those consumers not opposed to a rate increase?

4. How important were general service problems in influencing consumer opinions about a rate increase?

The focus group interviews uncovered a "rate bargaining" phenomenon among the groups, which could be traced back to their fear of an energy shortage and the possibility of fast-rising prices for consumer goods and services. In general, consumers wanted assurances of available utilities and were willing to pay for these services, but they felt that price changes should be negotiated within a bargaining process. In addition, valuable advertising communication themes regarding consumer resistance to the rate increase were suggested by the interviews.

In the third stage of the research process, the hypotheses developed from the first two stages were quantitatively measured. A random telephone sample of *700* people was conducted in the company's trading area. Quantitative results were obtained about consumer attitudes toward service and rate issues, and alternative communicative ideas were evaluated for future advertising campaigns.

Example 2: Johnson Car
Air Conditioning Filter

The Johnson company developed a new filter to be used in car air conditioning systems. Management wanted to find out the feasibility of the new product and develop a workable marketing plan. A two-stage research process was followed. Focus group interviews were used in stage 1 to help develop hypotheses to identify potential markets, to determine advantages and disadvantages of the product from the consumer viewpoint, and to identify specific points for questionnaire design.

The focus group interviews indicated that families in which one or more members had allergy or respiratory problems might be the best prospects for the new product. Persons seriously concerned about air pollution were also identified as good potential buyers. The major disadvantages of the product were the performance capability of the filter and the cost of replacement cartridges. Some individuals feared that the filter would cause their car's air conditioning system to malfunction. Nonallergic consumers expressed doubt about their need for the product. An unexpected resistance occurred when consumers were informed that the filter would need to be changed periodically.

After hearing the results of the focus group, the client wanted to proceed immediately with market introduction as a result of the findings that seemed favorable. On the advice of the research firm, the quantitative study in stage 2 of the research process was conducted. An analysis of 1500 respondents in five cities showed that the original marketing strategy for introducing the new product was not economically feasible. This led to the development of an alternative marketing plan.

Example 3: Harris Meat Company

The Harris meat company had declining sales of its luncheon meat wieners and franks in one region during the previous year and needed to identify and isolate reasons for the lack of sales growth. In this case, the focus group interviews exposed a serious packaging problem and minor problems in shelf space allocation and competitive pricing. The packaging problem had extensive ramifications for the product's image, the ease of using the product, the quantity and quality of the shelf space exposure it received, and the consumer's decision to buy certain sizes of the product. The interviews produced very clear hypotheses for explaining consumer behavior and brand penetration in particular market segments. Housewives in the focus groups explained clearly why the packaging was a problem to them. Therefore, the quantitative study was narrowed to specific alternatives for improving the packaging strategy, communicating brand attributes, and increasing distribution penetration.

Evaluation and Implications

Focus group interviews have several advantages for marketing management. First, they help generate hypotheses in the qualitative stage of research. They can provide a stimulus to creative people (copy writers, creative directors, new product managers, etc.), who need to have first-hand contact with how consumers think, feel, use, and talk about the product. Many times, in fact, it is good to involve these people in the evaluation of the group sessions so that they will be more receptive to the findings of the quantitative research results.

Focus group interviews can also give direction and guidelines for constructing questionnaires. Lists of relevant areas of interest of the target audience to be measured can be developed from the groups. With these lists, the risk of addressing the wrong problem is minimized.

The focus group interview can and does bridge the gap between marketing management at the manufacturing level and the end user of the product or service. Although top management should have frequent contact with the users of the product, in actual practice this contact is seldom made. The use of focus group interviews and one-way mirrors or videotape recordings is an effective and efficient means for bridging the gap from busy top executive to the ultimate consumer of the product.

There are also, however, a number of limitations in using focus group interviews. First, the moderator can bias the group results if he or she does not have adequate training and experience in conducting focus group sessions. A poorly conducted group session can be very costly if it misdirects the quantitative stage.

One serious problem that has grown in importance with increasing costs of quantitative research and tight research budgets is the use of focus groups as the only source of information in planning and decision making. For an expenditure of $3,500 to $4,000, the brand manager or advertising agency executive can point to a fat report filled with marketing jargon and page after page of verbatim comments and say—this research backs up our new advertising campaign or our product promotion. But although the advertising campaign or promotion may be great for the segment of the population represented by those in the groups who gave rise to the idea, the key question remains: How big is the segment? What is the expected dollar return?

One way of minimizing the disadvantage of the focus group interview as the only source of information is to take a sample survey. If researchers generalize from the focus group interview results without further quantitative verification, they are on very weak methodological ground. Therefore, one important rule for researchers is: "Don't generalize quantitative results from focus group interviews."

Focus group interviews are widely used by marketing researchers today in such decision areas as new product development, advertising campaigns, and evaluation of existing marketing strategies. The major advantage of this technique is in terms of developing hypotheses that can be quantitatively tested to produce further results. The focus group interview is one of a number of qualitative research techniques that can be profitably employed along with quantitative techniques to help marketing managers make better decisions.

MARKETING MEMO

Description of a Successful Executive . . .

He is a man who was usually in the upper 10 percent of his school class.

His favorite subject was probably one of the social sciences or English, even though he may have majored in engineering or business.

He reads the *New York Times*, is familiar with the Bible and prefers French impressionist paintings and Tchaikovsky's music.

His TV habits tend toward news programs and sports, with occasional mixing of such programs as "All in the Family."

His most admired leader is Winston Churchill, although Richard M. Nixon rated high with him before Watergate. Dwight D. Eisenhower and John F. Kennedy are lesser choices, but in the top four.

His average annual income is around $75,000, although his range might be as low as $25,000 or as high as $1,000,000. His age range is the mid-fifties. More often than not he is a Republican rather than an Independent or Democrat (3 to 2).

The successful executive places a high priority on moral standards and integrity, on a sense of fairness to others, and a sense of personal worthfulness. He is less interested in defeating communism or advancing capitalism than in being happy.

In his scale of values, he places power and economics at the top of the list. However, he is significantly higher than less successful executives in his concern for people.

— Henry A. Singer, "Human Values and Leadership," *Business Horizons*, Vol. 18 (August 1975), pp. 85-88, at p. 88.

Focus Groups: An Innovative Marketing Research Technique

Robert D. Hisrich, Ph.D., and Michael P. Peters, Ph.D.

CRIPPLED BY HIGHER COSTS, inflation, government red tape and a weakening of its public image, the U.S. hospital industry is faced with the difficult task of economic survival in a rapidly changing environment. In one Eastern state, for example, more than 60 percent of the hospitals are operating in the red, with many others also experiencing financial pressures. Metropolitan hospital service areas are rapidly changing with increases in elderly patients, a reduction in the number of births, ethnic influences, and more aggressive competition by area hospitals.

Hospital administrators everywhere have discovered that with limited resources, program evaluation and review must be undertaken in order to meet the needs of the community within their service area. Furthermore, to confront this challenge, hospital administrators increasingly are engaging in marketing techniques to identify needs and to allocate the hospital's limited resources in the optimal manner.

Research in hospital markets

A hospital has many markets: the community and its many agencies, regulatory bodies, third-party payors, and donors of time and money. The hospital's two principal markets, however, are the physician and the patient. Hospitals must provide quality health care services that attract the caliber of physician who, in turn, attracts patients through admissions and referrals. Patients, on the other hand, may sometimes select a physician on the basis of his/her hospital affiliation or, more often, may reject a hospital suggested by an affiliated physician. The increasing frequency of these decisions

Reprinted from *Hospital & Health Services Administration*, **27** (July/August 1982), 8-21.
Used with permission.

encourages physicians to develop contacts and affiliations with more than one hospital, thereby providing an alternative for the patient.

To monitor changes in a dynamic environment, it is important that a hospital, particularly the chief executive officer (CEO) and administrative staff, establish a market information system. Figure 1 depicts the basic components in such a system, one which enables a hospital to refine its health care delivery system to meet the needs of its primary and ancillary markets. For the system to be useful, it is essential that good information be obtained from the medical staff; affiliated physicians; non-affiliated physicians; administration; present, past, and potential patients in the service area; community agencies and regulatory bodies. Based on this information, appropriate and efficient health care services can be developed to provide quality medical care to the various markets. While much of this information can be obtained from internal documentation, hospital managers also must use marketing research and analysis.

Figure 1. The Hospital Management and Information System

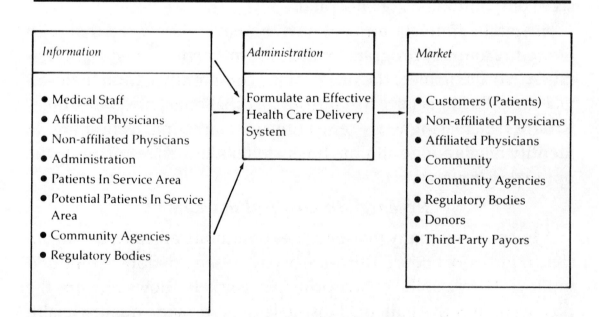

A search for relevant information

Marketing research is a formalized means of acquiring information as the basis for sound decisions. It is an objective and systematic investigation of a topic to uncover all relevant information about it. In this discovery, research usually takes one of two forms—quantitative or qualitative. Quantitative research is research which provides information to which numbers can be applied, objective information on which to base decisions. Qualitative research is identified by its lack of numbers and statistical analysis; instead, it provides an in-depth, subjective understanding of the problem being investigated.

Quantitative research is designed to generate objective information about a particular predetermined population's characteristics and behaviors. By using objective measurement and analysis, quantitative research can be used to describe a population statistically while testing hypotheses. Most hospital managers are familiar with this type of research in the form of surveys.

Survey research generally involves securing data from a sample of the total population from which relationships can be drawn and projected back to the total population. Basically, in terms of hospital research, a typical survey would involve: establishing the objectives of the research; identifying the population to be studied; determining the appropriate sampling plan; preparing the measuring instrument; collecting data; analyzing the data; and developing the final report with conclusions and recommendations. Prior hospital research has concentrated in this area, particularly on field surveys or patient attitudes.[1]

When a hospital problem warrants a subjective evaluation, qualitative research may be more appropriate. Generally, qualitative research involves determining how people think and feel. A number of techniques have been developed to elicit subjective information on people's feelings and impressions: depth interviews, projective techniques, and focus group interviews. This article describes the use of focus group interviews in the health care setting.

---

[1]See the following sources for examples of field research on patient attitudes: Roger D. Blackwell and W. Talarzyk, *Consumer Attitudes Toward Health Care and Medical Malpractice,* Columbus, Ohio: Grid, Inc., 1977; and W. Stratmann, "A Study of Consumer Attitudes About Health Care: The Delivery of Ambulatory Services," *Medical Care,* 13: 537-548, 1975; and J. Ware and M. Snyder, "Dimensions of Patient Attitudes Regarding Doctors and Medical Care Services," *Medical Care* 13: 669-682, 1975; and J. Ware, W. Wright, M. Snyder and G. Chu, "Consumer Perceptions of Health Care Services: Implications for Academic Medicine," *Journal of Medical Education,* 50: 839-848, 1975.

Focus group interviews

The focus group interview, or just focus group, is a technique evolved from group therapy methods used by psychiatrists and psychologists. It consists of a meeting of eight to twelve persons with a moderator intent on encouraging in-depth and "free-wheeling" discussion of a designated topic. Rather than using a structured questionnaire, the focus group is led through a discussion by the moderator concerning feelings, attitudes and perceptions on the topic. Although it is one of the most frequently used techniques in traditional marketing research, its applications in the health care field have only recently emerged.

A focus group generally lasts about one and one-half to two hours, thereby allowing sufficient time for the moderator to develop a good rapport with participants so that open and candid discussion can take place. Because of its flexibility and potential for in-depth analysis, focus groups can provide a different perspective to a problem under investigation, one that cannot be completely satisfied through the use of any other standard survey methodology.[2]

The physical location and atmosphere are very important to the success of the focus group. The atmosphere should be relaxed to ensure informal discussion of participants' opinions and feelings.

The importance of the moderator

The moderator also plays an important role in the focus group, since he or she must not only be able to direct the discussion, encourage participation, and develop a rapport with participants, but be skilled at probing participants without biasing their responses.

---

[2]See the following sources for information on the use of focus groups: A. Andrews, "How to Buy Productive Focus Group Research," *Advertising Age*, July 11, 1977, pp. 128 and 148; and D. Bellenger and B. Greenberg, *Marketing Research: A Management Information Approach*, (Homewood, Ill., Richard D. Irwin, Inc., 1978), pp. 171-184; and Bobby J. Calder, "Focus Groups and the Nature of Qualitative Marketing Research," *Journal of Marketing Research*, Vol. XIV August, 1977, pp. 353-64; and A. Goldman, "The Group Depth Interview," in *Marketing Research: Selected Readings*, eds. Joseph Seibert and Gordon Wills (New York: Penguin Books, 1970), pp. 266-271; B. Greenberg, J. Goldstucker and D. Bellenger, "What Techniques Are Used by Marketing Researchers in Business?," *Journal of Marketing*, April, 1977, pp. 62-68; F. D. Reynolds and D. K. Johnson, "Validity of Focus Group Findings," *Journal of Advertising Research*, June, 1978, pp. 21-24; and W. A. Flexner, C. P. Mclaughlin, and J. E. Littlefield, "Discovering What the Health Consumer Really Wants," *Health Care Management Review*, Fall, 1977, pp. 43-49.

This experience and expertise is especially important when sensitive issues are being discussed.

The composition of the focus group also is extremely important. Should the group be composed of heterogeneous or homogeneous participants? Heterogeneous groups, of course, can yield broad, diverse information. When diverse participants who generally represent both sides of the issue are present, a depth of commitment regarding not only the problems but the solution can be obtained. When one of the goals is to obtain a larger number of reasons and inputs, a homogeneous group is preferable. It has been our experience that not only do focus groups composed of homogeneous people tend to run more smoothly, they also tend to allow a more shared perspective to emerge as rapport is greatly facilitated. As a general rule of thumb, the more homogeneous the participants, the more smoothly the focus group will be conducted.

Many different technical problems occur in conducting high-quality focus groups. Therefore, a sensitive, highly-trained moderator, as self-effacing as possible, is essential to stimulate and guide group interactions.

Avoiding serial questioning

Finally, the format for each group session should be carefully developed. One universal axiom in focus groups is this: never use serial questioning (i.e., questioning routinely following an established order regardless of the discussion). Such a sequence not only minimizes the possibility of investigating all aspects of the problem, but also eliminates one of the major benefits of using focus groups to understand the problem—group interaction. In a well-conducted focus group, one member's response stimulates another member until all salient points are uncovered. While, indeed, this interaction is extremely important, information for information's sake is not the ultimate objective of a focus group.

The group and the questioning must ultimately lead to an end, which requires group direction. Obviously, it is not the group participants who will direct their own conversation to a meaningful conclusion. This direction is achieved by the moderator through implementing an interview (discussion) format.

Benefits and uses of focus groups

Many benefits can be derived from the use of focus group interviews, which provide the researcher with an opportunity to learn directly from representatives of the major segments of the market place about their needs, expectations, and dimensions of satisfaction with the product or service under examination. New procedures, products, services and techniques can be easily assessed prior to their introduction through focus group interviews.

Some of the specific uses of focus groups are to: (1) generate hypotheses that can be further tested quantitatively; (2) generate information used to design structured survey questionnaires; (3) provide background information on a product or service category; (4) provide comparative perceptions on existing providers and their products or services; (5) get impressions on new concepts, services, products, and/or procedures for which little information is available; and (6) stimulate new ideas to improve market position and penetration.

Disadvantages and misuses of focus groups

In some instances, focus groups have been used by management to support preconceived opinions. It is relatively easy to bias the participants and their responses. Because of the role of the moderator, as well as the interpretation of comments that are generated, one can find evidence to support any existing viewpoint. It is, thus, most important that extreme care be used in the interpretation of the responses gathered by a highly skilled moderator. Of course, it must be kept in mind that because of the limitations of sample size and the informality of the "measuring instrument," the data accumulated from the focus group interview is not generalizable to a large population. In other words, it may be easy to reach a conclusion that is not representative of the target population in general.

The environment in which the focus group is conducted leads to other limitations. The composition of the group and possible inexperience of the moderator may restrict the expressions to the views of only a few participants. The quiet member of the focus group may have equally important views and insights, yet say very little during the discussion.

Another disadvantage occurs in the difficulty of recruiting participants. Depending, of course, on how many focus groups are to be run, and the degree of specialty in the discussion, some difficulty and costs can occur in recruiting members. While the cost is less than most quantitative research projects, the results must always be appraised against the expected benefits.

Hospital use of the focus group

A large metropolitan teaching hospital recently was experiencing most of the market symptoms cited earlier. The patient base in its primary service area was changing, with increases in elderly and lower income residents. More Medicaid, self-pay and Medicare patients were also affecting its performance picture.

Since it was a teaching hospital, it was imperative that a strong diverse patient base be maintained; a wide range of services also had to be offered in order to accommodate its educational responsibilities. As the patient base eroded, patient days per stay declined, government regulation became more complex, and competition from HMOs and other teaching hospitals increased, this hospital was experiencing large financial losses, a deterioration of morale, and a weakened public image. The latter two factors posed a particularly threatening problem. Improving the market position of this hospital, of course, could not be accomplished without the support of its medical staff and administrators.

It was decided that focus groups could be used to identify the problems and needs of important market segments in one health care system, thereby providing insight to design an effective management plan, as well as to provide a basis for further research. Once the appropriateness of focus groups had been determined, several key issues needed to be resolved: the number of focus groups, the composition of them, the nature and role of the moderator, and the format for the focus group.

Determining the number of groups

The number of focus groups, of course, depends on the scope of the project. Given the depth and magnitude of the problem, it was possible that as many as eight focus groups would probably be needed, six with hospital personnel and two with consumers.

While the actual number remained undetermined, physicians and hospital personnel were selected and informed at the outset of the probable number and dates of meetings. The schedule is particularly important when employing a series of focus groups consisting of professional people who have many scheduled commitments.

Given the need for the solicitation of numerous opinions and the possible dominance of physicians vis-à-vis hospital personnel, it was felt that six focus groups should be appointed: two with both the doctors and administrative staff present and two with each group separately. Joint membership focus groups were held at the beginning and the end.

The focus group centered on the topics outlined in Table 1. For the medical staff focus group, representatives were selected from each of the major departments with the assistance of the Executive Director. In addition to department representation, care was taken to select a broad spectrum of age, as well as years of hospital affiliation. This was done since it was felt that the market and overall hospital problems viewed by the younger staff members probably would vary considerably from those perceived by the older, usually more established, medical staff. The final group consisted of fourteen members, although participation in the subsequent meetings varied slightly (typically ten to twelve), depending on emergency medical situations.

The administrative staff focus group followed a similar procedure as that used for the medical staff. Again, representation by functional area, as well as age and length of employment, was given top priority in the selection process. The final group consisted of nine members.

Patients and non-patients selected

The patient focus group was composed of patient and non-patient members. Hospital records were used to identify previous patients of the hospital's delivery care services. Non-patients also included in the group were randomly selected from the local community. The final patient focus group consisted of twelve members.

To ensure internal consistency, each of the independently conducted focus groups were handled by the same moderator. Drawing from the general topics listed in Table 1, a discussion format was used to identify the major market, management, and image of the hospital. For example, the session of the initial focus group began with the question: "What do you feel are the major strengths and weaknesses of this hospital compared to other hospitals in the area?" When one of the weaknesses cited was the "inability to attract new physicians," this was further pursued by asking: "If you were the hospital administrator, what would you do to attract new physicians?" It was clearly apparent after the initial sessions with medical and administrative staffs that the hospital had some problems

Table I. Major Topics Discussed By Focus Group

Medical Staff:
- Strengths and weaknesses of hospital
- Attraction of new physicians
- Role of teaching in hospital
- Hospital public relations
- Staff morale
- Specialty and sub-specialty weaknesses and strengths
- Administrative strengths and weaknesses
- Medical needs not being met
- Effects of competition
- Strategies to improve market and financial position

Administrators:
- Strengths and weaknesses of hospital
- Medical support area strengths and weaknesses
- Specialty and sub-specialty weaknesses and strengths
- Effects of competition
- Administrative needs not being met
- Role of teaching in hospital
- Staff morale
- Strategies to improve market and financial position

Patients:
- Criteria for choosing a hospital
  - Overnight admission
  - Outpatient
  - Emergency room
- Role of physician in selection process
- Image of competitive hospitals
- Importance of neighborhood health center
- Community needs not being satisfied

that needed immediate attention. The opportunity to "clear the air" also contributed to improving the morale of these important groups, a fact which was indicated in participants' comments after the last focus group meeting.

Analyzing the results

Both informal and formal procedures were used to analyze the results of the focus groups. First, information was obtained from carefully listening to the original tape-recorded feedback. Then, content analysis was used to process the data further, in a more "quantitative" fashion. This more formal research technique gives a more objective systematic appraisal of the content of communication.[3] Appropriate categories (compartments) were defined for placement of excerpts (units) from the typed transcript of the original tapes. These units were evaluated to establish themes in the focus group. A theme is a concept expressed in one or more terms. For example, it may take a physician ten words to describe a problem, strength, or weakness of the hospital, while the lab administrator would take fifteen words to explain the same problem. Both individuals would be credited with eliciting the same theme. Using a more detailed version of the general forms exemplified in Tables 2 and 3, the number of times a theme was mentioned was tabulated, with similar themes being grouped into categories derived from the focus group participant's responses to the topics discussed. The number of units in a theme category was determined by the number of responses.

Table 2. Number of Themes Per Topic Area

Topic Area	Number of Themes	Percent of Themes
(topics listed here from Table 1)	TOTAL	. . . .

[3]For more information on the technique and its application see: Bernard Berelson, *Content Analysis on Communication Research.* Glencoe: The Free Press, 1952.

Table 3. Theme Regarding the Topics of _____

Theme	Number
Nursing Care	
TOTAL	

Some of the general findings from the focus groups were as follows:

☐ While having some strong areas intermingled with some weak ones, the hospital needed to provide even better support services (i.e., billing, escort service, physical plant maintenance, and housekeeping and admitting) than more well-known "name" hospitals for the same degree of patient satisfaction to occur.

☐ In light of the increasing age of the medical staff and the small core of physicians accounting for the majority of admissions, there was a particular need to start ensuring that affiliated physicians, as well as non-affiliated physicians, in the service area start using the hospital's services.

☐ It was important for the hospital to establish a good environment (i.e., better handling of operating room bookings and complaints concerning the maintenance and housekeeping of the physical plant) for physicians so that any friction present was minimized and that harmony and referral patterns be ensured.

☐ It was necessary to initiate innovative programs (i.e., a runner's and a smoker's clinic) for the community, thereby being a trend setter, not a follower.

☐ The hospital needed to have a good sound public relations program with the necessary staff and funding in light of the extensive use of public relations by other hospitals in the service area.

☐ It was necessary to establish a sound fund-raising program so that the hospital could make the needed improvements in the physical plant, purchase the needed new equipment, and establish innovative community programs.

Since specific discussion centered on the various medical departments, medical staff and support areas, special concerns with maintenance, outpatient, admitting, billing, labs, and attitude toward patients were identified by all three groups: physicians, administrative staff, and patients. Attention was concentrated by the hospital administration on the general problems that were identified and further documented as being pervasive in order not only to alleviate them but also to provide a strong positive direction to improve the hospital's morale.

To elicit free-thinking response patterns, participants in the focus groups were also asked what they would do or need to make the hospital delivery system the best possible in its competitive environment. The responses to this general questioning format included the following, which were then systematically analyzed through follow-up research techniques:

☐ More money for technological advances.

☐ An improved attitude and surroundings among physicians and staff.

☐ More innovative health care delivery programs.

☐ Better public relations to inform patients and physicians, as well, about the quality of the hospital and its medical services.

Of course, many other problems during the course of the focus group interviews also were identified. These provided direction for further market research, which resulted in the formulation of the hospital's three- and five-year plans.

Summary and conclusions

This paper summarizes the application of focus group interviews as a means of identifying administration, market, and physician problems in the delivery of health care. Although the focus group has been widely used for marketing research purposes in industrial and consumer product firms, it has received limited use in the health care industry.

Focus group interviews were conducted with physicians, administrators and patients with the objective of determining the strengths and weaknesses of the existing health care delivery system of the hospital, as well as encouraging participation in a program to improve overall morale at the hospital.

The technique proved to be most effective in establishing a framework for further research (such as personal interviews with affiliated and non-affiliated physicians, telephone survey of the residents and previous patients in the hospital service area, and cost/benefit analysis of some proposed changes), implementing immediate changes in present strategy and satisfying existing complaints.

The physicians' focus group sessions identified their specific needs that were not being satisfied by the hospital. Scheduling for OR, poor nursing services, inconsistency in the availability of medical supplies and equipment, lack of loyalty to hospital through referrals and patient admissions, and unattractiveness of the hospital to new physicians entering the community were some of the more significant problems that emerged.

These problems were then verified; they proved to be the principal ones for the entire physician market, a determination subsequently made by a survey of this market through personal interviews which followed the focus group's conclusions.

The administrator focus group sessions identified a separate set of problems, i.e., a complicated admissions policy, poor communication of patient tests from one department to another, an inflexible billing system, inadequate maintenance service, deterioration of some of the physical plant, and a need for better data processing information. Further discussion of these problems resulted in valuable specific recommendations. Patient focus groups yielded a broad reaction, complaints and attitudes that also contributed to the formulation of an overall marketing plan. This determination of perceived community needs provided an important basis for conducting an extensive quantitative market survey through telephone interviews in order to uncover specific reactions about various services at the hospital.

Future uses of focus groups probably will center on updating management's understanding of the existing health care delivery system as well as identifying the direction for future marketing strategy and policy. It is apparent that marketing strategy will become an inherent part of the decision making of hospital management. As marketing strategy and planning needs grow, it will be helpful to employ research techniques such as the focus group to provide information on which to formulate and support hospital decisions in the short and long run. This technique will help hospitals resolve problems and enable them to maintain financial stability in a time of changing demographics.

Suggested Readings

Andrews, A. "How to Buy Productive Focus Group Research," *Advertising Age,* July 11, 1977, pp. 128 and 148.

Bellenger, D. and Greenberg, B. *Marketing Research: A Management Information Approach.* Homewood, Ill.; Richard D. Irwin, Inc., 1978, pp. 171-184.

Berelson, Bernard. *Content Analysis on Communication Research.* Glencoe: The Free Press, 1952.

Blackwell, Roger D. and Talarzyk, W. *Consumer Attitudes Toward Health Care and Medical Malpractice.* Columbus, Ohio: Grid, Inc., 1977.

Calder, Bobby J. "Focus Groups and the Nature of Qualitative Marketing Research," *Journal of Marketing Research,* Vol. XIV, August, 1977, pp. 353-64.

Flexner, W.A., Mclaughlin, C.P., and Littlefield, J.E., "Discovering What the Health Consumer Really Wants," *Health Care Management Review,* Fall, 1977, pp. 43-49.

Goldman, A. "The Group Depth Interview," in *Marketing Research: Selected Readings,* eds. Joseph Seibert and Gordon Wills. New York: Penguin Books, 1970, pp. 266-271.

Greenberg, B., Goldstucker, J., and Bellenger, D. "What Techniques Are Used by Marketing Researchers in Business?" *Journal of Marketing,* April, 1977, pp. 62-68.

Reynolds, F.D., and Johnson, D.K., "Validity of Focus Group Findings," *Journal of Advertising Research,* June, 1978, pp. 21-24.

Stratmann, W. "A Study of Consumer Attitudes About Health Care: The Delivery of Ambulatory Services," *Medical Care,* 13: 537-548, 1975.

Ware, J. and Snyder, M. "Dimensions of Patient Attitudes Regarding Doctors and Medical Care Services," *Medical Care,* 13: 669-682, 1975.

Ware, J., Wright, W., Snyder, M. and Chu, G. "Consumer Perceptions of Health Care Services: Implications for Academic Medicine," *Journal of Medical Education,* 50: 839-848, 1975.

Improving employee relations with focus groups

by J. Mitchell Elrod, Jr.

Mr. Elrod is President of Elrod Marketing Research, Inc., Atlanta.

An employee will talk about on-the-job problems and policies more openly with a third party than with an employer. This article shows how to create a neutral atmosphere that stimulates honest discussion.

What do your employees think of your benefits package—hospitalization, holidays, vacations? Are they satisfied with the training and supervision that they receive? Do they support, or will they support, current or planned marketing programs, quality-control measures, work schedules, or other changes? These and other questions important to securing employee support can be explored in depth through carefully structured discussions with small, selective groups of employees whose support is vital to the success of your business.

In marketing research terminology, such discussions are called **focus-group interviews.** They are a research technique widely used to develop qualitative data by encouraging interaction among small groups of participants. The resulting discussions produce the type of candid verbalizations often heard in normal conversation because the social setting in which they are conducted encourages complete, in-depth exploration of a topic.

Each focus group is made up of 8 to 10 preselected participants within a peer group (e.g. clerical personnel, craft workers, first- and second-level management, and so on). If interests and responsibility levels are mixed, the responses will be inconclusive, and in some cases the respondent may be reluctant to express himself or herself candidly.

Selecting the Group

For a focus-group discussion to be most fruitful, its participants need to be chosen on a random basis from a selected employee category. To ask a supervisor or manager to choose participants might result in a group composed of a nonrepresentative population (i.e. the *best* worker, the *most* cooperative, the *most* promotable, and so forth), thereby losing the objective representation that is so important. The best selection is one in which employees in a category are picked on a completely random basis—with some alternates in case of illness, prescheduled vacations, and so on—and are assigned to attend the "seminar" at a specified time and date.

To avoid complications of over-time or attendance during an employee's normal time-off period, these discussion sessions are customarily conducted during the regular workday, with transportation and meals (if any) provided by the employer. Informality and casual dress are encouraged because the setting and atmosphere are important to the free sharing of thoughts on the topics being discussed.

To avoid possible eavesdropping, which might inhibit the free interchange of ideas or concerns, employee focus-group interviews should be held in a neutral location, such as a conference room at the offices of the moderator or a centrally located hotel, motel, or restaurant meeting room.

Choosing the Moderator

The discussion is moderated by a person skilled in group dynamics and behaviorial psychology and usually lasts two hours. The moderator guides the discussion by following a carefully developed outline. The outline is produced in consultation with the employer client and is subject to his or her final approval before the discussion begins.

Vital to successful conduct of employee focus groups is the careful choice of an experienced moderator. The moderator should:

1. Work closely with the employer client to develop a suitable outline that will fulfill objectives.

2. Establish a rapport with the group.

3. Skillfully guide the discussion to keep it flowing and probe the topics of importance.

4. Prepare a useful analysis and presentation of findings.

Some firms have tried—with varying degrees of success—to conduct such group discussions using their own personnel or management people as moderators. Some pitfalls of using an in-house moderator are:

1. Too much knowledge of the way in which the firm operates; employee respondents do not have a chance to explain their ideas fully.

2. The strong tendency to become defensive about, or to apologize for, policies and procedures that are criticized by respondents.

3. A lack of objectivity in the analysis and presentation of findings.

4. Difficulty in establishing good rapport and developing an open interchange with discussion participants who may regard the in-house moderator as a "company spy."

The session is audiotaped to enable the moderator to prepare a formal analysis and interpretation of the findings. In the case of focus groups composed of employees of one company, the participants are assured of the confidentiality of their remarks and protection of their identities as related in specific statements, though their words and ideas are used in the final report. To date, the moderators from our firm have had no known problem establishing an atmosphere of mutual confidence with employee groups. In fact, the overwhelming reaction has been one of gratification that "someone up there really does care what I think."

Reprinted with permission from *BUSINESS Magazine,* **November-December 1981, 36-38.**

Leadership is the Key

Knowing when to conclude discussion of one topic and move on to the next or (of great importance) when to pursue a point of concern that may not appear in the discussion outline are invaluable skills in group leadership. The moderator's expertise in evaluating and following up on expression (body language), tone of voice, and indications of tension are key factors in the conduct and interpretation of the discussion session. The moderator must also be skillful in bringing "quiet ones" into the discussion and in suppressing dominant participants without destroying the mood and cooperative spirit of the group.

Respondents are not told in advance the details of the topics to be discussed. This is to keep participants from developing preconceptions or discussing the topics with others. Opinions expressed in the group discussion must be spontaneous and be the product of the respondent's own thoughts and feelings.

Putting Results to Work

The results of focus-group interviews are not projectable to all employees. Rather, they are designed to develop hypotheses that can be tested by interviewing a suitable sample of all employees in subsequent phases, if needed. Quite often, such hypotheses can be examined in a modest deeper investigation.

How are such groups used by the employer? In one recent instance, an employer was concerned about certain aspects of his company's benefits package, in particular which of several benefits might be candidates for expensive modification in future negotiations. A series of discussion groups revealed that employees were generally well satisfied with the benefits package as it existed but were greatly concerned about another administrative item that had not been considered. This item of concern turned out to be readily modified at little cost.

Another employer was considering the adoption of a new corporate service slogan and needed to know how this slogan would be regarded by employees and to what degree they would support the slogan to make it meaningful to customers. It was found that employees at all levels vigorously supported the new slogan and the added responsibility that it placed on all of them. However, they were deeply concerned about the need for improved orientation and training that would prepare them and fellow employees to uphold their responsibilities in meeting the promises of service made by the new slogan. These needed procedures are being set up.

Communications are an ever-important facet of employee relations. A great deal of money is spent by American business on meetings, pamphlets, notices, magazines, and many other means of keeping the employee informed. One client, in an effort to evaluate the effectiveness of his company's very expensive efforts to communicate with employees, commissioned a series of discussion groups to review coporate media.

The discussions revealed that employees in the widely scattered, small offices of this firm were feeling sorely neglected and thought that "no one cared particularly about them." These people received some, but not all, of the employee information pamphlets and almost never had a chance to see or talk with management people beyond the level of their own office. These factors seriously affected their morale.

After determining which publications were most valuable to employees, it was recommended that the employer start mailing copies to each employee's home. It was further recommended that corporate management people visiting branch offices should make a special effort to have a brief meeting with all employees and give a short informal talk about "what's going on in the company."

Any business with 50 or more employees that is having problems with employee morale or productivity or is planning to make changes that will have a marked effect on the way employees do their jobs can use the focus-group discussions with excellent results, *provided the information developed in the groups is put into practice.* Like any other tool, this technique is valuable only if used.

No matter how well any of us know our employees or believe we know how they feel about their jobs and job-related issues, there is always a lack of employee candor or understanding on some matters. Years of experience have proved that, even though they may be on the best of terms with supervisors and management, employees will talk much more frankly to a third party not directly affiliated with their employer. This extends even to simple suggestions about procedural matters that should be natural candidates for the suggestion box.

The finding derived from each discussion group, including appropriate direct quotations, are prepared for the client in an analysis report. If a series of discussion groups is completed in various cities or with different segments of employees, a composite synopsis or overview of the series is prepared, as well as a report for each group. The composite report is presented as an executive summary with appropriate conclusions and recommendations for management consideration.

A critical factor affecting the value of focus-group interviews is the employer's use of the information secured from the groups. Suitable dissemination of information about the conclusions derived from the discussion and any present or planned action is necessary to let employees know they have been heard.

Firms that have used this employee-relations communication techique have been unanimously high in their praise for its morale-building effectiveness and early-warning signals for potential trouble spots. The focus-group interview technique could be an effective personnel-management tool for you. Why not try it?

Are Focus Groups a Viable Tool for PR Practitioners to Help Their Companies Establish Corporate Responsibility?

By Robert L. Heath

The title of this article highlights one of the major tasks facing PR practitioners today. For two decades companies have struggled mightily to clarify the ground rules of corporate responsibility. And this effort will continue. Recent scandals created by brokers on Wall Street have renewed the outcry for corporate ethics. Publications such as *Rating America's Corporate Conscience,* by the Council on Economic Priorities (Lydenberg, 1986) show that activist groups will employ many strategies to pressure companies to comply with the activists' standards of ethics and responsibility. The House of Representatives Public Works & Transportation Committee began hearings in June 1987 to investigate operations of the airline industry that had generated substantial lists of passenger complaints. Public standards and values have changed to such an extent that smoking is not only unfashionable but condemned, and drinking of alcohol beverages may receive similar criticism.

These examples highlight the need companies have to monitor constantly the opinions of key groups to determine whether they favor, frown upon, or understand the quality of products, services, and ethical operating standards. External surveillance is needed most when environmental uncertainty and demands for ethical accountability are highest (Dutton & Ottenmeyer, 1987, p. 362).

Executive managements of some companies that have adopted standards of ethical behavior have turned to their PR specialists for assistance in defining and implementing appropriate guidelines, but many PR practitioners have been, and continue to be, left out of this process for a variety of reasons. As R. Edward Freeman (1984) observes, PR managers must "demonstrate the ability to ADD VALUE. It is only by adding value on an issue that credibility can be established with management" (p. 226). The guiding model for this approach to public relations depends heavily upon the ideal established by Grunig and Hunt (1984), who see organizations and their publics as interpenetrating entities that affect one another in various ways. The balance between internal and external interests, they contend, can be modeled as a two-way symmetric arrangement where information and influence flow freely.

One of the major tasks in this coming decade will be to develop increasingly sophisticated methods for determining the standards of corporate responsibility. It is likely that more and more companies will use this tactic proactively to prevent outbursts of public (activist group) criticism that can lead to embarrassing publicity, even if the company is correct, and to additional legislation and regulation. To participate in this future, PR practitioners will need as many tools as possible to satisfy their current mandate or earn the credibility needed to advise executives on matters of corporate responsibility.

Robert L. Heath

Reprinted from *Public Relations Quarterly,* 324 (Winter 1987-88), 24-28. Used with permission.

Solving the problem of achieving acceptable standards of corporate responsibility is not easy. (Note that I omit the term *social* from the standard concept, corporate *social* responsibility. A company is not only concerned by social responsibility. It is also confronted with economic and political responsibility. *Social* responsibility can be too narrowly interpreted as philanthropy.) Hundreds of books and articles have been written on the merits and liabilites of companies' seeking or not striving for corporate responsibility. A recent major addition to this discussion is by William C. Frederick (1986) who argues that the best standard is what he calls corporate social *rectitude*. He challenges "corporations to act with rectitude, to refer their policies and plans to a culture of ethics that embraces the most fundamental moral principles of humankind" (p. 136). This stance is not without merit, but it poses enormous problems regarding what constitutes ethics and rectitude. The key question always is "whose ethics?"

Scouting the Terrain

Freeman (1984) has argued that each company must be sensitive to and take into account the fit between its values and those of its many stakeholders. He lists examples of the obvious stakeholders: customers, neighbors, regulators, legislators, competitors, courts, activist groups, employees (including labor unions), and companies in other industries. The prospect of building harmonious relationships with each of these stakeholders is enormous. Such an effort requires several ingredients: monitoring and analyzing their values and their perception of the compatibility between their values and the company's; communicating to help stakeholders understand the company's values and operating philosophy and procedures; and establishing a strong sense of ethics on the part of the company along with well defined and thoroughly implemented internal controls and climate that encourage employees to plan and perform in an ethical way.

Any effort to achieve and assure corporate responsibility should begin with a firm understanding of the political dynamics of the ethical battle ground. Ethical incompatibility can produce emerging issues that can lead through the normal cycle of public policy issues development: emerging issues (public discussion of consumer and public policy issues), pre-legislative interest, development of legislation or regulation, passing of legislation or regulation, and litigation.

To cope with the goal of maximizing the company's ethical fit with its stakeholders, some inter-

nal person or group should be responsible for conducting surveillance at each point of interface between the company and each stakeholder group. For instance, key persons who have contact with lending institutions should monitor that stakeholder relationship. Similarly, all stakeholder relationships should be monitored, including management-labor, company-legislator, company-competitor, and company-neighbor. Personnel in key positions in each company should intuitively come to mind as the appropriate persons to oversee whether the company enjoys the needed degree of harmony or fit with each group of stakeholders vis-a-vis standards of corporate responsibility. (Freeman sees PR playing a crucial role in this monitoring and management of key issues in support of and conjunction with other departments.)

Each company must be sensitive to and take into account the fit between its values and those of its many stakeholders.

The public relations group seems particularly fitted to monitor the relationship with several stakeholders; for instance: activists, media, neighbors, customers, and that nebulous stakeholder called the public. The past two decades have impressed upon us the fact that any of these stakeholders can make an explosive combination leading companies to realize too late that their standards of corporate ethics (and the accompanying operating procedures) are at odds with those of stakeholders. Networking and personal contact seem to be reasonable ways of monitoring the fit with activists, the media, and any other group where persons have visible and vocal representatives (Bergner, 1986; Gorney, 1987). If the stakeholder monitors know who the players are, they can talk to and listen to them to determine where there is a harmony or friction.

But what about groups which are ill-defined and do not have visible spokespersons? Some issues managers might ask, who cares about the faceless and voiceless masses, such as neighbors, customers, and the public. The key to unlocking the answer is understanding the role these stakeholders can play in the public policy battleground. Some critics of those PR practitioners who would be attentive to the faceless and voiceless groups argue that "public opinion" is what activists, media, or pollsters want it to be. (We could even throw into the matrix the legislators and regulators who either make public opinion or follow it closely.)

A very good argument for including the faceless and voiceless publics in the surveillance system is to know how explosive some issues of ethics and performance is before it is broadcast by the media and activists. PR practitioners can help ther executives win public policy battles if they can accurately estimate the likelihood an issue will catch on in public discussion and calculate what its impact will be in the public policy arena. One of the ironies of activism and media scoops is this: If there is likely to be no public outcry about company operations or ethics, there is likely to be no story. Public outrage is fertility ground to be used by the media and activists who seek to make corporations act "responsibly." If a company can take away the potential for outburst, it has helped to defend itself in public policy contests.

Selecting the Tools

What tools are available for the PR practitioner who sets out to monitor the degree of harmony between the values of the company and those of the stakeholders who lack visibility and vocal leadership? Public opinion surveys immediately come to mind. They offer some help, but often are flawed by the predispositions of a company to find out good news and the myopia of not knowing what questions to ask. Sometimes companies cannot sense their own vulnerability, especially during the emergence stage of consumer and public policy issues.

One worthwhile alternative to surveys is focus groups. They offer a viable means for replacing or augmenting surveys. For years, several standard public relations texts (Dunn, 1986; Newsom & Scott, 1985; Cutlip, Center, & Broom, 1985; & Agee, 1986) have recommended using focus groups in a marketing sense to determine key publics' opinions toward company images, products, services, and commercial messages. A few PR texts mention focus groups as devices for pre-testing public relations and advertising messages. However, it is ironic that many PR texts do not discuss focus groups for any non-marketing purpose, let alone testing public sensibilities to ethics. And Coates and his associates (1986) in *Issues Management,* a premier text on issues monitoring, do not mention focus groups as tools for monitoring issues.

But some companies have utilized focus groups or a version of this tool to sense public sentiments. In this vein, AT&T has used consumer advisory panels to determine whether rate increases or other changes will be opposed or accepted. Elmendorf (forthcoming) believes that groups were crucial to discovering that public sentiment was favorable for a massive grass roots effort in the American

---

It is ironic that many PR texts do not discuss focus groups for any non-marketing purpose, let alone testing public sensibilities to ethics.

Bankers Association campaign against President Reagan's 1982 10% withholding proposal. When two focus groups were presented with the content and apprised of the implications of the tax proposal, their reaction was so hostile that the ABA believed that it could mount a successful grass roots campaign against this tax proposal despite the extreme popularity of President Reagan.

Focus groups seem to be a useful means for determining what some public thinks about the ethics involved in company operating philosophies and product or service quality. Focus groups can be used to aid efforts to clarify the latitudes and limitations of corporate responsibility and can help assess the four dimensions of a public policy issue: likelihood, impact, timing, and potential for resolution. They can be used to estimate the *likelihood* that an issue will gain popular support. Focus groups can be used to calculate the *impact* the issue might have on marketing strategies, operations, and public policy. *Timing* refers to where the issue is in its development; the earlier issues are spotted the easier they may be to deal with. An estimate of timing is the degree of awareness and hostility exhibited toward the topics presented by the focus group moderator. The *potential for resolution* is an estimate of whether the public will be receptive to the company's explanation of some operating standard or other issue of ethics.

The procedure for using focus groups can take many approaches.

•The moderator of the focus group can assume the role played by activist groups or media reporters who would present a corporate activity and then contend that the activity should be interpreted as having negative consequences. The moderator might briefly state the activist group point of view and then elicit the focus group's reaction. (Depending upon the circumstances, one focus group session might consider several corporate activities.) The session is devoted to eliciting responses from focus group members to assess the kind of reaction and its degree, whether favorable, unconcerned, or negative.

• A focus group might be exposed to typical company activities and potential activist group criticism. But this time the focus group might be asked to go one step further. The moderator could offer the company's explanation of the activity. This effort would be intended to estimate the likelihood that the issue could be defused by issues communication.

• A focus group might be asked to describe what it feels constitutes an ethically *and* unethically operated company. The group could be encouraged to describe specific operations or attitudes that are particularly good or bad. This kind of discussion can help establish brackets or latitudes that can serve as guidelines for determining corporate responsibility. If the company wants to determine the extent (including degrees of concern or support) to which publics at large share the focus group's sentiments, a survey could be constructed using key findings generated by the focus group. This "good company-bad company" approach can reveal sentiments that are held by various publics but which have not yet surfaced into public dialogue.

> ## This "good company-bad company" approach can reveal sentiments that are held by various publics but which have not yet surfaced into public dialogue.

• As well as using external focus groups, a company can use internal groups of employees. This tactic has several advantages. It helps inculcate a sensitivity for corporate ethics and responsibility into the climate of management philosophies and operations. It can surface feelings about ethical

standards which employees feel but are afraid to voice outside of the protection of a focus group. This tactic can help employees indicate the kinds of arguments and concerns about the company which they encounter during stakeholder contact and while visiting with people in the community. Employees offer a vast reservoir of ethical opinion.

> ## The most serious limitation of focus groups is the difficulty of extrapolating how widely held any opinion is.

Once the information is generated by the focus groups, the key is to manage it candidly and use it constructively to increase the likelihood that the company complies with prevailing standards of corporate responsibility. The information can be helpful in understanding stakeholders' reservations sufficiently well that an effective communication campaign can be created and executed.

The Limitations

Focus groups have several obvious limitations, the most serious of which is the difficulty of extrapolating how widely held any opinion is. Findings from focus groups have limited generalizability to the total population from which they are drawn. But if surveys are used to follow up focus group findings, this shortcoming can partially be mitigated. And additional focus groups can be used to increase the representativeness of the breadth and depth of opinions discovered.

Another liability is that the dynamics of each focus group can depend heavily upon the mix of persons selected. If members of the focus group happen to belong or subscribe to any relevant activist group, the dialogue could have a negative bias. If the persons selected for the focus group are particularly apolitical, the results could lead the company to be less cautious than would be desirable. These reservations should serve as cautions in the selection and handling of the focus group. But they are not compelling reasons to avoid using focus groups as another window through which public relations practitioners can view the worlds of various stakeholders whose opinions can be fueled by critics of the company's activities.

Companies put themselves into peril by being inattentive to the opinons of the voiceless and faceless stakeholders in their operating environments. One of the hardest tasks of issues monitoring is to identify emerging issues in their earliest stages and to assess the likelihood an issue will mature and the degree of hostility that it is capable of generating. The company also needs to know the extent to which publics—the grist of public policy power tactics—are willing to respond to activist or media arguments regarding the seriousness of an issue. Savvy issues managers should be interested in estimating the degree to which their arguments could allay public apprehensions. And finally, if the company finds that some of its operations would be met with public hostility, those operations and the accompanying standards of ethics could be changed as a vital part of the company's strategic planning. If the focus groups disclose that stakeholders misunderstand the company's ethics or can be more effectively informed regarding why a set of ethics is followed, the PR specialists have a better sense of what needs to be said to the stakeholders. Companies are learning that they need to foster a supportive public opinion environment. Focus groups appear to be a vital means by which PR practitioners can develop data to use when attempting to influence corporate strategic planning and operations and while developing and refining the company's public policy and communication plans.□

References

Bergner, Douglas J. (1986) "The Maturing of Public Interest Groups," *Public Relations Quarterly, 31, 3, 14-16.*

Coates, Joseph F.; Vary T. Coates; Jennifer Jarratt; and Lisa Heinz (1986) *Issues Management,* Mt. Airy, MD: Lomond.

Cutlip, Scott M.; Allen H. Center; and Glen M. Broom (1985) *Effective Public Relations* 6th ed. Englewood Cliffs: Prentice-Hall.

Dunn, S. Watson (1986) *Public Relations: A Contemporary Approach,* Homewood, IL: Irwin.

Dutton, Jane E. and Edward Ottensmeyer (1987) "Strategic Issue Management Systems: Forms, Functions, and Contexts," *Academy of Management Review, 12, 355-365.*

Elmendorf, Fritz, M. (forthcoming) "Campaign to Repeal 10 Percent Withholding of Interest and Dividends," in *Issues Management and Strategic Planning for Corporate Survival,* ed. by Robert L. Heath, San Francisco: Jossey-Bass.

Frederick, William C. (1986) "Toward CSR3: Why Ethical Analysis is Indispensable and Unavoidable in Corporate Affairs," *California Management California Management Review, 27, 126-141.*

Freeman, R. Edward (1984) *Strategic Management: A Stakeholder Approach,* Boston: Pitman.

Gorney, Carole (1987) "How to Use Public-Participation Groups Successfully," *Public Relations Journal, 43, 6, 29-30.*

Grunig, James E. and Todd Hunt (1984) *Managing Public Relations,* New York: Holt, Rinehart and Winston.

Lydenberg, Steve D.; Alice Tepper Marlin; Sean O'Brien Strub; and the Council on Economic Priorities (1986) *Rating America's Corporate Conscience,* Reading, MA: Addison-Wesley.

Newsom, Doug, and Alan Scott (1985) *This Is PR/The Realities of Public Relations,* 3rd ed. Belmont: Wadsworth Publishing Co.

Wilcox, Dennis L.; Phillip H. Ault; and Warren K. Agee (1986) *Public Relations: Strategies and Tactics,* New York: Harper & Row.

SECTION IV

Advantages And Limitations

While a number of articles in previous sections have offered suggestions and cautions about using focus groups, the four articles in this section concentrate on the appropriate role of focus group research.

Margaret Roller in "Mental Image of Groups is Out of Focus" suggests that often focus groups are not perceived as a serious research technique. She emphasizes that groups have an important role in total research programs and offers a number of guidelines for approaching this research in a more professional manner.

"Validity of Focus Group Findings", another "classic" from the first edition presents a systematic look at the question of "should qualitative reports be regarded as purely speculative." Reynolds and Johnson offer reassurance to users of qualitative research but also note the vulnerability of such studies.

Ted Karger in "Focus Groups are for Focusing and for Little Else" presents a set of admonitions about the use and administration of focus groups. He makes the point that proper application of the focus group technique starts with a clear understanding of its essential reason-for-being.

"More Truth and More Consequences" emphasizes the value and dangers of using focus groups. Crimmons, like some of the other authors, cautions the reader against misusing the techniques of relying solely on qualitative research.

Mental image of groups is out of focus

BY MARGARET R. ROLLER
President
Roller Marketing Research
Atlanta

SOMEWHERE ALONG THE LINE some clients have lost—or they never had—a true research perspective when it comes to focus-group technique.

While quantitative research never has been questioned as the methodology from which strategies are formed and executed, focus groups are often thought of as some lesser, therefore weak, animal in the research arena.

This attitude tends to pervade marketing. It has important implications not only to the client-researcher relationship but also to the marketer's ability to understand fully how each aspect of the research process relates and works together to provide strategically sound directions.

Numerous pieces of evidence suggest that marketers have failed to perceive focus groups as a serious research technique:

● The viewing room often overflows with clients, many of whom have been brought along for a variety of inappropriate reasons, the most popular one being, "We thought we'd bring Joe and Tom along since they've never seen a focus group."

● With the room filled with clients, a party atmosphere quickly develops, spurred by plenty of food and drink. Hostesses become "watchdogs" and have to cut off liquor to some clients if the drinking gets out of hand. As the party ensues, two critical problems occur: the client misses important information during the group discussion, and the moderator loses faith in the client and interest in the project.

● The moderator often is asked to cover *too much* material in a discussion, causing confusion or generating little information on variety of topics.

● Clients often see focus-group recruiting as a telemarketing effort, in which the salesperson is really target-ing participants as his next sales call.

● Marketers tend to overemphasize ideas emerging from focus groups that confirm preconceived notions.

● Marketing executives often make decisions, strategic and otherwise, on the basis of focus groups, rather than use the technique as a preliminary research step.

ALTHOUGH FOCUS GROUPS are not quantitative research, they are an important research tool. Yet, they have a unique place in research. The difference that sets focus groups apart from the other techniques is the human behavior and psychological element, which is fundamental to understanding the important role focus groups play in connection with qualitative and quantitative methodologies.

Yet it is the social or group dynamic aspect of focus groups that often make them suspect, and as a result misused by marketing managers.

Much has been written about the limitations of focus groups, and, possibly as a result, confusion, distrust, and even irreverence have grown for the technique.

What can or should be done? An obvious answer is to make marketers and in-house research staff more aware of the proper ways to look on focus groups as a technique.

Hopefully, this awarenes will lead to better appreciation for and use of group discussions.

MARKETING MANAGERS can begin to overcome "focus group smart" by incorporating the following suggestions:

1. **Avoid the party atmosphere.** People who are invited to focus-group sessions simply because they have never attended one are a big expense, in time and money, to the sponsor. For substantially less cost, the groups can be videotaped, in color, limiting attendance to two or three essential people.

Later, the tapes can be presented to other key staff members in a forum conducive to interpretation and open discussion. Videotaping has the added advantage of allowing the client to gain a proper perspective of a group discussion, from the time the group was conducted until viewing the group again on videotape.

2. **Do not place too many, very specific quotas on the recruiting process.** Doing so strongly implies that focus groups are too often thought of in quantitative terms. Filling a group with any number of consumer types is inappropriate, assumes the research is projectable, and by meeting certain quotas will provide a well-rounded basis on which to draw definite conclusions.

Such an attitude is false and misguided.

Many focus-group sessions have become a waste of time because of too many variables interacting, leaving the moderator and the client no smarter than they were.

3. **The moderator should not be asked to cover a multitude of material.** When this happens, the moderator and the client are left confused, not having learned anything meaningful on any one subject.

Remember, focus groups are meant to be just that: focused, concentrating on one respondent-type and a limited range of topics. The group dynamic process can work for or against you and is most likely to work in your favor if the group is as homogenous as possible.

4. **Do not expect the moderator to provide all the answers immediately upon concluding a couple of group discussions so that you can develop strategies overnight.** A good moderator will hesitate to make quick interpretations at a time when emotions and the stimulation resulting from information overload are running high.

THE FINAL, but possibly the most important, suggestion for marketing managers is this: Focus groups are a legitimate form of research that live

Reprinted from *Marketing News,* **19** (November 8, 1985), 21, published by the American Marketing Associaton.

by the same research ethics employed in quantitative studies, particularly the ethics concerning respondent confidentiality.

As in survey research, successful group recruiting is contingent on gaining the trust and confidence of the interviewees, with the certainty that their responses will not be divulged or that the research is not a sales effort.

It is hoped that if marketers change their thinking about what focus groups are and what they are not, they will realize that the rules of research are not confined to quantitative studies, but cross into all forms of well-designed techniques—including the focus group.

Validity of Focus-Group Findings

Fred D. Reynolds and Deborah K. Johnson

Focus-group reports often start with a disclaimer: "Qualitative research is exploratory in nature. Findings should not be considered conclusive or projectable." This disclaimer deserves close examination because it sums up a self-contradictory attitude toward the validity of focus-group research: "Believe me, but don't believe me" or perhaps "Believe me, but not too much." Indeed, the warning has become the marketing equivalent of the surgeon general's warning about the hazards of cigarettes. Like committed smokers, users of focus groups ignore the warning on the package and find great delight in practicing what is warned against. Is this prudent behavior? Or should qualitative reports be regarded as purely speculative?

Such questions become fundamental when the consequences of focus-group addiction are considered. It is generally accepted that quantitative studies are needed to make definitive inferences, and that "only in emergencies" are groups to be used in lieu of quantitative studies. But emergencies are the daily facts of marketing life, and qualitative studies frequently do indeed substitute for quantitative studies as the basis for making decisions—especially "no go" decisions. Marketing practice, if not marketing theory, holds that group interviews, even with their acknowledged limitations, are better than no research at all.

But are they?

An affirmative answer suggests that the results of a group study have predictive and/or convergent validity. A negative answer suggests hazards ahead for the brand manager and the researcher.

This article presents a tentative answer by offering a point-by-point comparison of some qualitative and quantitative research.

Two Studies

Two studies conducted at Needham, Harper & Steers Advertising, Inc., provide the basis for comparing findings. The first, the qualitative study, was a large-scale focus-group study conducted for the benefit of Needham, Harper & Steers's food clients. The report, called "The Shopping Crisis," was based on an analysis of 20 group interviews conducted in 10 U.S. cities during December 1974 and January 1975. The discussion focused on food shopping and food preparation, on reactions to inflation and concerns about nutrition, and on what was different then from the way it was the year before. Respondents were homemakers responsible for food shopping and food preparation, selected so as to vary in age, family size, and social class.

The second study was a nationwide life-style survey conducted in spring 1975. It employed a 19-page questionnaire mailed to 2,000 female members of Market Facts' Consumer Mail Panel. Usable questionnaires were returned by approximately 90 per cent of the initial sample. Demographic checks indicated that the obtained sample matched the U.S. homemaker population on age, education, income, and area of residence.

The questionnaire included sections on interests and opinions, activities, product use, media use, and perceived changes in behavior. The section on changes is of particular interest here because it provided opportunities for many comparisons between the trends it indicated and the trends set forth in the qualitative "Shopping Crisis" report. The quantitative-change question read:

As times and circumstances change, people do less of some things and more of others. Below is a list of activities. For each activity, please indicate, compared to this time last year, whether you yourself are engaging in the activity a lot more, a little more, about the same amount, a little less or a lot less. Remember the comparison is with what you yourself were doing *this time last year*.

There followed a list of activities, many of which had been covered in the "Shopping Crisis" interviews.

In addition to the perceived changes, several of the interest and opinion statements in the life-style survey touched on matters that had been discussed in the "Shopping Crisis" groups. These statements are presented along with the percentages of respondents reporting agreement to them.

Our way of addressing the supportability of the focus-group findings is straightforward: comparisons are based on direction rather than magnitude. This approach fits the notion that group interview findings, including those reported in the "Shopping Crisis," are not—and should not be—reported in statistical form. The comparisons between the qualitative results and the quantitative results are presented in Table 1.

Table 1
Consumer Changes and Opinions

Qualitative (Groups)	*Quantitative (Life Style)*

Price Conscious

Check prices
Pay more attention to food prices
Pay more attention to food prices

1. I find myself checking prices even on small items—90% agree.
2. I pay a lot more attention to food prices now than I ever did before—90% agree.

Nutrition

Concerned about nutrition

3. I am very concerned about nutrition—87% agree.

Concerned about cholesterol—especially older women

4. I try to avoid foods that are high in cholesterol—total, 62% agree; 55 and older, 79% agree.

And worrying about cholesterol a little more

5. Worrying about cholesterol—total, 35% change, 22% more; 55 and older, 52% change, 35% more.

Try to avoid additives, but

6. I try to avoid foods that have additives in them—56% agree.

Concerned about salt—especialy older women

7. I am concerned about how much salt I eat—total, 56% agree; 55 and older, 66% agree.

How They Shop

Specials

8. Shop a lot for specials—84% agree.

Comparison shopping

9. Shopping around for the lowest prices on food—68% change; 65% more.

Coupons

10. Saving and using "price off" coupons—56% change; 52% more.

Labels

11. Looking at labels in the grocery store—64% change; 62% more.

Quantity

12. Purchasing larger-size packages of food products—52% change; 41% more.

Eliminate runs to store

13. Going to the grocery store—30% change; 19% less.

No fun to shop

14. Shopping is no fun anymore—54% agree.

What They Buy/Do Less

Snacks

15. Buying snack foods—67% change; 58% less.

Snack cakes

16. Buying snack cakes—% change; 59% less.

Cookies

17. Buying cookies—59% change; 51% less.

Sugar

18. Buying sugar—70% change; 67% less.

Candy

19. Buying candy—70% change; 48% less.

Soft drinks

20. Buying soft drinks—58% change; 48% less.

Jam or jelly

21. Buying jam or jelly—50% change; 42% less.

Entertaining at home

22. Entertaining in my home—51% change; 28% less.

Dining

23. Going out to dinner—60% change; 35% less.

Movies

24. Going to the movies—52% change; 43% less.

Cutting down on hard goods such as a house

25. Thinking about buying a new house—78% change; 63% less.

Cutting down on hard goods such as a car

26. Thinking about buying a new car—78% change; 56% less.

Cutting down on hard goods such as an appliance

27. Thinking about buying a new appliance—61% change; 40%

What They Buy/Do More

Fruit

28. Buying fruit—48% change; 40% more.

Do-it-yourself gardening

29. Gardening—61% change; 44% more.

Canning

30. Canning things at home—59% change; 32% more.

Discussion

In only one comparable instance—baking—were qualitative and quantitative findings not in accord. In this one instance later sales data showed the qualitative finding to be the more accurate reading of the market.

With a confirmation rate of 97 per cent, brand managers, copy writers, and other users of group interviews should rest a bit easier about the validity of focus-group findings. Even with their acknowledged methodological limitations, a set of focus groups produced much the same information as a large-scale quantitative survey.

This conclusion is tempered by two "Yes, buts." Yes, but "Shopping Crisis" was not a typical group study. It was based on 20 groups conducted over a period of two months in various parts of the country instead of the more typical two to four groups conducted at one site. Would it have been possible to have arrived at the same conclusions within the typical two-to-four-group format?

Our experience with the "Shopping Crisis" findings suggests that it would have been possible to obtain similar results from a much smaller number of groups. Certainly, the most salient points were apparent early. But our understanding of some important details did change as the groups accumulated, and we do not have a firm conviction on when it would have been safe to stop. Certainly this issue merits empirical investigation.

The other "Yes, but" concerns the rather broad descriptors focus-group reports employ—"some women," "they say," "most women," "women agree." The range of meaning implied by such descriptors leaves room for much doubt. For instance, if a group study reports that "women agree they are concerned about salt," does this mean a general consensus or a simple majority? Clearly, where quantitative rather than directional conclusions are required, quantitative data are necessary.

We do not mean to imply that quanti-tative data are always preferable or even always right. Quantitative findings depend on respondents' ability to make sensible replies on issues that are often difficult to frame as simple, straightforward interview questions, and the circumstances of the normal questionnaire survey do not permit the flexible give and take between interviewer and respondent that assures the question was correctly understood. In this connection, it should be remembered that in the present comparison, in the one flat contradiction between qualitative and quantitative, the qualitative data later proved to be correct. We believe this occurred because the respondents in the quantitative survey did not understand the question the way it was intended.

Conclusions

The comparison presented in this article should prove reassuring to users of group interviews. We think it shows that if interest is in detecting the direction of changes in the behavior of consumers—in getting the drift of the market—the group study has a viable position as a research tool for decision making as well as for hypothesis generation.

We do not deny that quantitative studies are often necessary. But we do contend that qualitative information is important as a double check, because quantitative studies have their own set of vulnerabilities. In fact, we believe that it would not be unreasonable to insist that reports of questionnaire surveys begin with the disclaimer "Warning: This study was purely quantitative. Findings should not be considered conclusive without confirmation from focus groups."

Focus groups are for focusing, and for little else

BY TED KARGER

CONSUMER FOCUS GROUP studies evoke polar opinions among executives.

Some like observing "real customers" in action, quickly and conveniently, and think of conducting such studies whenever qualitative information is sought. Others have been deeply disappointed with group studies, or consider them spurious research and resist them for any purpose.

These divided opinions curtail professional considerations of how to apply them.

Groups are excellent for a limited range of marketing requirements. When group studies are appropriate, there are not one but many different ways to conduct them.

Moreover, such studies should be conceived of as researchers' and not moderators' work.

Proper applications of this format start with clear understandings of its essential reason-for-being. Here are seven observations to suggest when and when not to use focus groups:

1. Groups are but one of many qualitative field methods. This format is qualitative in character but should not be equated with "qualitative research."

It is one data-gathering approach in a large toolkit of exploratory, clinical and phenomenological research approaches, which apply qualitative analyses to discursive data.

As such, the group format should be used only when it is deemed the most effective investigative method for the qualitative purpose at hand.

2. Groups are for examining "group dynamics" not personal behavior or thinking. This format's special reason-for-being is to provide the means for examining what normally takes place when a set of consumers engage in collective activities or dialogue.

This interactive vehicle is misapplied if viewed as a convenient device

Ted Karger is president of The Nowland Organization Inc., a Greenwich, Conn., strategy research firm.

to conduct a bunch of separate mini-interviews all at one time and place (for example, where the group leader structures the proceedings to ask each person the same questions).

A two-hour group session consisting of 10 consumers (after subtracting moderator talk, preliminary and digressive chit-chat and lulls) typically allows each person about eight minutes of personal talking time (a 90-minute session permits fewer than six minutes each).

To audit and understand personal behavior, interviewing 10 people separately and more fully will produce far better information, and at less cost per consumer.

3. Groups are for learning, not testing. A format designed to study an assemblage of people constitutes a poor arena for assessing reaction to new concepts, products, packaging, advertising, names, etc.

The nature of group dynamics erects serious obstacles not only to obtaining individual reactions to concepts or executions, but also to amplifying or refining the underlying comprehensions, feelings, or reasons for these reactions.

As the group members listen to others' comments, they subtly separate themselves from their own thinking. Moreover, when a group is asked to appraise some stimulus, the collective discourse is unlikely to reflect a balanced explication of the whole group's true reactions.

There often is a self-reinforcing dynamic toward extreme views. For example, there may be some individuals whose vociferous views dominate those of less assertive members. Finally, even if these problems could be surmounted, there are some fundamental risks in generalizing small-sample test findings to the mass market.

Hence, this vehicle's use for testing has raised criticisms that it produces directions way off the mark.

An example of inappropriate conclusions occurred when a leading electronics producer used the group format to prescreen 12 new equipment ideas. This meant that each idea only could be briefly depicted and theoretically was limited to only 40 seconds of discussion time per person.

The overall appraisals were further distorted because the discourse focused on those ideas suggesting only minor modifications in current products. The more innovative ideas were not clearly understood and largely ignored in consumer discussions, leading to lower scores than those for the minor change ideas.

Ironically, some of the overlooked innovative ideas subsequently became winning introductions for competitors. Thus, what was intended to be fast and inexpensive testing proved quick but very costly to the company, as well as to personal careers.

4. Groups are for selective, not general-purpose, learning. The group format not only severely handicaps each participant's capacity to react to test stimuli, but also imposes severe constraints on its ability to provide dynamic case histories along with causal explanations.

If one truly wishes to obtain comprehensive consumer understandings about an important subject, and if one wishes to learn the deeper causes of consumer attitudes and behavior, then the vehicle of choice would be probing one-on-one interviews.

On the other hand, the group dynamics format provides the best means for observing actual consumer behavior which normally is collective in character.

The ideal way to use groups, then, is to have aggregates of people engage in a discrete activity and then to observe them as they behave and share their experiences.

Another way to use groups is to have participants describe and share

---

Reprinted from *Marketing News*, 21 (August 28, 1987), 52-55, published by the American Marketing Association.

their experiences, but focused only on selected topics because the collective discourse tends to be rearward-oriented and anecdotal.

This can produce a thin veneer of unsystematically derived understandings if the attempt is to cover a broad spectrum of issues.

Therefore, focus group discussions must be centered on learning about particular topics if they are to produce their most useful results.

5. Groups are for learning about particular brand marketing issues, not for developing fundamental innovative, repositioning or expansionary strategies.

Establishing the market-based understandings for generating ideas for new or diversified products or fundamental restagings in brand strategy demands lengthier, more reflective interrogation and conceptual thought processes than is possible from a group's limited speaking time per person.

It demands more dynamic, forward diagnostic thinking than is possible in an experimental and anecdotal-oriented setting.

Researchers certainly have difficulties in obtaining appropriate understandings to generate novel strategies even if personally interviewing consumers for hours at end.

Focus groups exacerbate these difficulties and thus generate only limited and superficial content for strategic speculations. Similarly, attempts to obtain brand extension guidance in a group context face the obstacles of addressing abstract perceptions of brand imagery and prospective trademark leveraging in a severely limited time-span, and subject to the group dynamics influence.

Consequently, such efforts are apt to produce and reinforce stereotyped understandings and shallow, uninsightful directions for extension.

On the other hand, focusing on existing product offerings or presentation treatments permits group members to quickly orient themselves to pertinent issues, and to expeditiously draw upon and share their recent experiences to illuminate their specific requirements.

6. Groups are most helpful for obtaining insights to refine existing product/marketing/communications approaches as well as to guide follow-up research studies for established brand franchises.

The group format can be a useful marketing focusing tool when product managements will benefit from learning what happens as people engage in activities usually conducted collectively or when the interactive sharing of separate experiences facilitates synergistic contributions from the assembled members.

In all cases, the key is to never use consumers as "test subjects" or "guinea pigs"—rather as enactors or describers of their real-life patterns.

Experience in using groups since the 1940s suggests that such examinations can help product managers and researchers in four main ways:

● To refine follow-up diagnostic, descriptive, or test-research studies.

● To improve existing product characteristics.

● To strengthen existing communications.

● To intensify a sense of consumer realities.

Here it is important to recognize that groups do not compose a single method. There are various ways to conduct them, each serving different informational purposes, yet all still bound to a limited array of proper applications.

7. Group methods and techniques must be carefully matched with the specified market knowledge requirements.

Each method offers its own particular capacities to provide requisite information; none is best for all purposes. Designing such studies requires clarifying both the purpose to be served and the attendant way to serve it.

● Research refining. Initially, groups came into use as a preliminary exploratory way to improve follow-up studies (qualitative or measurement), especially when marketers knew very little about their customers or when the marketplace was experiencing massive change.

They can be as helpful as a pilot research approach for refining the substance or operational procedures of larger-scale studies because they provide a facile means for consumers to share and jog pertinent comprehensions and thoughts, and to depict what is important to them.

Occasionally, and with due caution, groups also can be useful for generating or selecting some preliminary hypotheses to be verified via future research.

● Product improvement. Over the decades, groups also have been found useful for some product improvement purposes.

They can produce directions for refining existing product offerings, lines, features, packaging, and pricing when they multiply and sharpen consumer contributions.

Such behavior-oriented groups stimulate more crystallized individual consumer thinking while accommodating diverse viewpoints. Handled sensitively, the group synergy generates practical product refining directions.

● Communications strengthening. In recent years, groups have been used to learn how consumers interpret marketing realities in their own everyday terms.

When used to increase one's understanding of those consumer buying behaviors which typically are collective in nature, groups can help marketers to strengthen existing brand or corporate communications, promotions, merchandising, public relations programs, sales literature, store displays, warranties, and instruction booklets.

Such groups permit examinations of the actual learning processes people engage in during collective planning or shopping activities—what they are thinking about (dimensions, criteria); how they trade information and spark one another's thinking; the ways they formulate consensual attitudes and come to judgments and compromises; and how and why they alter their purchasing actions.

● Market sensitizing. A newer way to use groups is to have marketers experience consumers directly, either to enrich their basic marketing know-how or to demonstrate the veracity of startling findings uncovered in previous research.

Here, marketers and researchers involve themselves in the lives of consumers within the latter's milieu, not as aloof observers, but as fellow participants in the consumers' actual behaviors.

By experiencing the end users' perspectives as well as digesting the ensuing research report, managers can detach themselves from any idiosyncratic market preconceptions and be better equipped to make empathetic week-to-week marketing decisions.

THE PROPER administration of group studies is as important as the appropriate uses of this format's intrinsic strengths. Seven suggestions:

1. Company researchers must take complete charge of focus group studies.

Having observed that strong polar opinions have developed about the worth of groups, researchers must inject themselves centrally into determinations of when and how to apply them. This is particularly important because the format is highly seductive, especially to the less experienced marketer.

Also, there now are vested-interest voices who proselytize groups for many purposes. Beyond advertising agency executives and some fast-moving marketers who feel that such studies are an expedient and pleasant way to do research, we must recognize that groups are the single most lucrative service a research supplier can offer.

These studies seem inexpensive because their total costs are small. But, the group doer will earn far more income on an hourly basis by selling groups than by handling any other kind of study.

This tempting situation has attracted into the business numerous entrepreneurs, not always trained in marketing research or group dynamics techniques, who aggressively promote group studies for a wide and mostly inappropriate range of purposes.

Company marketing researchers, who themselves may be uncertain about qualitative research, find it difficult to resist the pressures favoring such projects. The way to exert professional control is for researchers to apply the same discipline to the conduct of these studies as to any other kind.

This discipline must be grounded in a clear understanding of the appropriate correspondences between various planning informational purposes and the special capabilities and limitations of specific focus group methods.

2. Group studies require much more than moderating. Study planning always must commence with marketing informational requirements and not with stipulations of the field method.

As with other investigations, the ultimate value of this collective format is a function of what happens before and after the actual fieldwork.

The first research task is to carefully set forth the marketing planning purposes and questions which need to be addressed. Then, care must be devoted to preparing the full range of specific market issues that will be covered to answer those questions and to determine who in the marketplace can best answer them.

This sets the stage for ascertaining whether those issues can be covered appropriately by the group format and, if so, which particular kind. The issues then must be converted into a consumer-oriented procedural and discussion guide ensuring the most relevant participant contributions.

After the group discussions are concluded, the crucial task is to translate the answers into recommendations for company decisions and actions. Penetrating analysis of the results is especially important because groups produce broad-ranging unstructured observations, which are susceptible to cursory and conflicting interpretations by those unskilled in analyzing such data.

In addition, the analysis should be conducted by a team of marketing researchers, not a single analyst, to avoid the idiosyncratic biases which so easily creep into small-sample investigations.

Researchers certainly should discourage instantaneous interpretations, which really are impossible to do well even by the most experienced analyst, and must never passively permit informal behind-the-scenes conclusions or session transcripts to constitute the final output.

Premature interpretations by action-prone marketers are hard to stymie. Nonetheless, the work at hand constitutes "research," not an informal "happening." Researchers must thoughtfully convert the information into guidance directions to help company talents integrate company capabilities.

Analyze the often messy and confusing raw consumer nonverbal and verbal content into a repository of meaningful findings.

Distill the organized findings for their strategic implications.

Synthesize the implications into basic market diagnoses which prescribe directions.

Report the results in work meetings, which stimulate appropriate applications and confidence in using the results.

3. Discussion leaders should be chosen for their facilitating characteristics vs. their consultative capabilities.

Performing as a group leader requires talents different from those involved in planning the research and analyzing the study results.

In essence, focus groups use the participants to modify company marketing behavior. The group leader must foster full and natural group involvement on the part of participants. Moreover, this must be done subtly so as not to externally contaminate the group dynamics.

Accordingly, the leader is not there to be a dominant or intrusive presence, but rather should be a gentle facilitator vs. an assertive moderator or mediator.

Attempts to befriend the participants or impress the clients with verbal adroitness or intellectual brilliance are to be strenuously avoided. Doing so shifts the focus of attention away from the contributions of the consumers and onto the behavior of the leader.

This can only distort the group process and undermine the forthright applicability of the results to the central questions being addressed.

Essentially, the facilitator is responsible for ensuring coverage of the predetermined issues. During the session, the facilitator must resist temptations to materially alter the issues coverage by chasing tantalizing thoughts which may occur to him based on offhanded, on-site interpretations.

Client observers must avoid sending notes to the facilitator, likewise altering the issues. It is reasonable to explore some unexpected and obviously pertinent issue which may arise, but the facilitator is responsible for following up on answers, not creating a new set of questions.

In short, the facilitator must devote his main efforts to helping the group participants behave realistically, and amplify, refine, and further explain their contributions relative to the issues at hand.

The facilitator should concentrate on nurturing an ambiance that focuses entirely on the participants and permits them to be themselves.

The best facilitator has unobtrusive chameleon-like qualities; gently draws consumers into the process; deftly encourages them to interact with one another for optimum synergy; lets the intercourse flow naturally with a minimum of intervention; listens openly and deeply; uses silence well; plays back consumer statements in a distilling way which brings out more refined thoughts or explanations; and remains completely nonauthoritarian and nonjudgmental.

Yet the facilitator will subtly guide the proceedings when necessary and intervene to cope with various kinds of troublesome participants who may impair the productive group process.

All this requires professional techniques and intense involvement. To have the facilitator simultaneously stand outside the proceedings to perform analytic tasks is to ask for flawed results.

4. Consumer participants can be enlisted to offset deficiencies in the group facilitators.

Consumers will become more involved in the proceedings and be exceedingly forthcoming if they understand the purpose of the meeting, believe the investigators are truly interested in their activities, and trust that their contributions would never be abused or misused.

The simple act of opening a session with such encouraging content itself will galvanize the audience to produce richer information, and it is imperative that the facilitator reinforce such encouragements through his own empathetic demeanor throughout the proceedings.

5. Groups should not be conducted in formal facilities unless required for special reasons. Formal group suites hinder more than help.

Consumers behave most meaningfully and feel emotionally comfortable in sharing their views when they are operating in their own real-life settings. Artificial environments separate people from their normal behavior, thinking, and feelings.

Sterile office buildings, conference room furnishings, fancy or high-tech decor, impressive sound and video systems, gracious serving platters, and judgmental or social babble filtering from a viewing room can have invidious effects on normal consumer behavior.

Moreover, a sense that one is being herded through a survey center and scrutinized by hidden observers or is being watched in a ''school atmosphere'' evokes feelings of depersonalization and insecurity which likewise inhibit open and honest portrayals.

Formal facilities also have the unfortunate effect of creating ''meetings'' in the viewing room.

Observers engage in discussions during the session that shift the focus of attention from truly listening to consumers, to reviewing and debating the action implications of what they have heard.

This often regresses to ''vote counting,'' selective listening and nonlistening as clients strenuously argue or explain any unwelcome consumer attitudes. It degenerates further into making disdainful judgments about the consumers whose demeanor contradicts their position.

A noteworthy example: a food marketer was so upset by the views of one particular consumer that he afterwards pursued her to the parking lot and excoriated this woman for her ''wrongful thinking.'' So that formal facilities not only can impair the consumers' ability to present themselves realistically. They also subtly cause the consumers to disappear from sight.

In contrast, some of the best groups have been conducted in average neighborhood living rooms, kitchens, or stores. Company persons can attend such naturalistic sessions if they blend themselves informally into the context, for instance by acting as ''assistant facilitators.''

If formal facilities with observers behind one-way mirrors are required, it then is the responsibility of the group facilitator to frankly inform the audience of this and to ameliorate the intimidating ''fish bowl'' atmosphere through his open and trust-inducing demeanor.

The viewers should be asked to concentrate fully on hearing the consumers themselves.

6. One facilitator must not be permitted to conduct all the study groups. Frequently observed phenomena are that a group leader stops listening after, say, three or four sessions on a given topic or gives greater subsequent interviewing attention to the most striking insights derived from prior sessions.

This is a prescription for using different facilitators for a study.

In some cases, more than one group doer will be required in a session: one to run the proceedings and the other to record observations of nonverbal behavior.

These respective roles should be clearly assigned and followed, though it also is possible to have the multiple doers trade roles from session to session.

It can be useful to debrief facilitators and observers on their top-of-mind thoughts following each session. But these thoughts should be used to further direct the ensuing work procedures, not as the final informational output.

7. Research analysts should concentrate on answering the questions which spawned the study in the first place.

Efforts to analyze and synthesize consumer contributions would follow the information collection using a team of trained research analysts.

Analysts may be tempted to report on additional consumer information just because it spontaneously came up in the discourse. As one company researcher observed with irritation: ''We did three major studies to find the best new advertising campaign, and a high-powered moderator then raised unsettling questions about all our efforts because of a few random consumer remarks in a study which had nothing to do with the advertising.''

Obviously, serendipitous findings can be worth reporting, but they are to be included with due care and qualification.

FOCUS GROUPS are better than field methods for a restricted range of marketing management purposes: to find effective ways to improve existing offerings, communications and marketing, and also as pilot studies.

When used, they must be approached with the same professionalism applied to all other research. This will ensure that they are adopted only when appropriate, that the right interactive method among many possible ones is used, and that the results are systematically analyzed.

Then their ability to gain unique consumer-based guidance will be realized, and this format will constitute an integral set of special-purpose qualitative learning tools in a complete marketing research toolkit.

More Truth and More Consequences

Jim Crimmons

Although qualitative research is quite valuable in developing marketing strategies, this article also suggests that it is dangerous to base decisions on qualitative data alone. Illustrated herein are the merits of using combined methodologies, both qualitative and quantitative, in gaining a deeper understanding of marketing issues.

Jim Crimmins is senior vice president, director of strategic planning and research, DDB Needham Worldwide in Chicago. Crimmins joined DDB Needham in 1978, and has held his current position since October 1986. Crimmins holds both a masters degree in statistics and a doctorate in sociology.

In the article "Truth and Consequences," Dr. William Wells (1986) compared the role of qualitative research and quantitative research in marketing. He observed that qualitative research has become heavily used in marketing, even though qualitative research is not good at enumeration or sampling and does not permit multivariate analysis. Dr. Wells attributed his frequent use of qualitative research to certain distinct advantages that qualitative research enjoys over quantitative research:

- **Time** - A useful set of qualitative interviews and analysis can be put together in a week or so. The typical survey takes much longer.

- **Money** - Qualitative studies tend to be relatively cheap, and surveys tend to be relatively expensive.

- **Form** - The typical survey report is a low-involvement medium, but the typical qualitative report is high involvement. A qualitative report is "full of people and emotions, events and conversation." It invites participation. Marketing managers want to participate.

- **Distance** - Qualitative research is more likely to remove the middle men who come between the marketer and his customers. Marketers can, and often do, sit behind the one-way mirror and watch and listen to their customers first hand.

- **Cognitive connections** - Qualitative data are encoded in words and images, whereas quantitative data are encoded in numbers. Words and images more easily hook into our broader experience, both inside and outside of marketing, and are more likely to lead to a fresh perspective, a creative insight or a new understanding.

With these advantages, qualitative research has indeed come to play a very large role in marketing. For many marketers and their advertising agencies, qualitative research is often the first response to a question about consumers and, for some, is often the only response to a question about consumers.

Reprinted from *Applied Marketing Research*, 28 (Spring 1988), 44-49. Used with permission of the Marketing Research Association, Chicago, IL.

This article acknowledges the unique strengths of qualitative research, but cautions against drawing marketing direction exclusively from this methodology. Following are three "real-life" illustrations of marketing strategies developed through use of qualitative *and* quantitative research.

Case 1: Grocery Chain A Versus Grocery Chain B

Our agency was interested in winning the advertising account of Grocery Chain A. Together, Grocery Chain A and Grocery Chain B dominate a large metropolitan market. Stores from Chain A and Chain B compete head-to-head in most neighborhoods of that market.

We found that the tentative direction developed from the qualitative research was backwards.

We needed to know how consumers think and talk about grocery stores in general, and the stores of these two chains in particular. With that information, we hoped to design an advertising strategy that would draw consumers into Chain A rather than Chain B.

We also needed a fresh perspective, and creative insights. Because of the superior cognitive connections of qualitative research, we conducted focus groups with women who lived in neighborhoods near stores from both chains. We learned a good deal from the research.

During and after the qualitative research, a tentative strategic direction began to take shape. In the discussions, women seemed to feel the two grocery chains were roughly comparable on basic grocery store attributes such as "quality of meat," and "freshness of produce." We began to feel that the way to draw customers to Chain A instead of Chain B was to advertise the fine points of the shopping experience at Chain A. Those fine points might include wheels that work on shopping carts and courteous employees.

Direction Following Qualitative

• Chains roughly comparable on basics.
• Emphasize the fine points of the shopping experience.

Because of the advantages of quantitative research in enumeration and sampling, we also conducted a telephone survey of 365 women in neighborhoods with stores from both chains. In the survey, women were asked to rate the stores of the two chains on a variety of attributes, including both the basics and elements of the shopping experience.

We found that the tentative direction developed from the qualitative research was backwards.

Direction Following Quantitative

• Chain A is well behind Chain B in consumer perceptions of the basics.
• Advertising should correct this consumer misperception.

From the consumers' perspective, Chain A is well behind Chain B in the basics, such as quality of meat and fresh produce. The first and most important job for advertising was, therefore, to correct this consumer misperception. Thus, the quantitative survey revealed that our preliminary marketing plan, based on qualitative research alone, was poor.

Case 2: Two Frequently Purchased Packaged Goods Brands

We were pursuing a prospective client who had two major brands in the same packaged goods category. The client's first brand, Brand X, is somewhat superior and somewhat higher priced than the client's second brand, Brand Y.

We wanted research results in a form which invited the participation of everyone working to win the new business assignment for the agency. We also wanted to get our creative team in direct contact with consumers. Because of the advantages of qualitative research in form and distance, and because of all the other advantages of qualitative research, we conducted several groups with a range of consumers who bought this type of product.

Again, we learned a great deal from the research, and again, strategic direction began to take shape as the qualitative results become known and discussed. One element of the tentative strategic direction had to do with the target audience.

Since almost everyone we talked to in our focus groups bought both brands occasionally, our best target seemed to be the general heavy user of this product category. Further, we felt that to differentiate Brand X from Brand Y we could not rely on customer differences. We would have to emphasize the different needs or occasions appropriate for each brand.

Direction Following Qualitative

• Most people seem to buy both Brand X and Brand Y.
• Therefore, we should not emphasize customer differences. We should emphasize the different needs or occasions appropriate for each brand.

We wanted to know who these heavy users of the product category were. The large syndicated data bases, such as Mediamark Research Inc., or Simmons Market Research Bureau, did not contain data on purchases in this product category. To get this data, we recontacted a nationally representative sample of our Life Style data base. (We have conducted a 4,000 person Life Style survey every year for the past 13 years. The survey contains over 900 questions on attitudes, interests and opinions, activities, product use and media habits.)

We recontacted about 600 members of the Life Style sample and asked them questions about purchase frequency and perceptions in Brand X and Brand Y's product category. We then merged the new data from the recontact survey with the original life style data for each respondent.

But, in each case, one major marketing idea emerging from the qualitative research proved to be wrong, and not just a little off, but 180 degrees off.

We were surprised by our quantitative results. While most people reported buying both Brand X and Brand Y occasionally, the frequent purchasers of each brand are quite different. Figures 1 and 2 describe purchase frequency by age and income. The frequent purchases of Brand X are younger and have a slightly higher income than frequent purchasers of Brand Y. The frequency of purchase of Brand Y is concentrated in a more mid-range income and age group. Their demographics are different and their life styles are, in some ways, dramatically different. Both products, however, are put to the same basic types of uses.

FIGURE 1
PURCHASE FREQUENCY

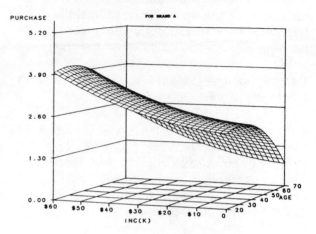

FIGURE 2
PURCHASE FREQUENCY

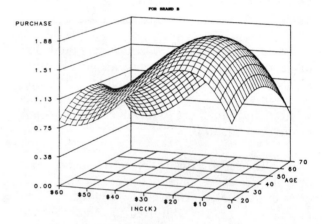

Direction Following Quantitative Research

• There are large differences in the frequent customers for Brand X and Brand Y, and minor differences in the way the brands are used.

• Create two distinct brand images to appeal to two different sets of customers.

Rather than emphasizing different uses or occasions for the two brands, we needed to build two different brand images to appeal to two different sets of customers.

Case 3 : Life or Death of an Animated Character

We created an animated character to promote Chee-tos from Frito-Lay. Chee-tos are primarily eaten by kids whose moms serve as gatekeepers. The animated character was Chester Chee-tah. Chester is cool, very cool, except when he sees Chee-tos. At the sight of Chee-tos, he loses his cool.

We developed some rough commercials using Chester Chee-tah. Working together with our client, we wanted to see first hand how moms and kids reacted to Chester. We took advantage of the immediacy of qualitative research and showed our rough commercials to a couple of groups comprised of moms and a couple of groups comprised of kids.

We learned a lot from the groups. But, if we had assumed that the reaction Chester got in the groups would be typical, Chester would have died a quick and untimely death. The respondents, particularly the moms, felt that Chester might be too cool, too hip, almost threatening.

The understanding we gain by looking at a problem from these two very different approaches will be deeper, richer and more reliable than the partial understanding gained from just one approach.

Quantitative research was also conducted with the rough Chester Chee-tah commercials. The same rough commercials, with very little change, were shown to a larger group of moms in a number of cities, using a relatively standard communication test format. From this research we learned that Chester is cool, indeed, but also funny, cute, goofy and friendly. Together with the client, we decided Chester should live. Chester Chee-tah has been a wonderful success for Chee-tos.

In the three cases we have just reviewed, we gained valuable information from qualitative research. But, in each case, one major marketing idea emerging from the qualitative research proved to be wrong, and not just a little off, but 180 degrees off.

We do not recommend avoiding qualitative research. We are heavy users of qualitative research, and intend to go on being heavy users of qualitative research. Likewise, we do not suggest the marketers stop drawing ideas from qualitative research. The advantages that qualitative research offers in time, money, form, distance and cognitive

connections make it a wonderful tool for generating marketing ideas. But whenever you set about generating ideas, some of them will be wrong. The point is simply that qualitative research, like quantitative research or any powerful tool, can be very dangerous if not used carefully.

Following are four suggestions toward more prudent use of qualitative research in marketing.

Suggestion 1: Remember that qualitative research is wonderful at generating marketing ideas, but very poor at telling us whether a marketing idea is good or bad.

This advice is nothing new but is often disregarded. We avoided a serious marketing mistake in each of the three cases described because we coupled the qualitative research with quantitative research, and learned that some of our marketing ideas were dead wrong. I'm glad we avoided those mistakes, but I'm worried about those times when we or our clients did not have the chance to do both qualitative and quantitative research.

The two certainties of research are "not enough time" and "not enough money." Our research plan will always be more limited than we would like it to be. We will often be tempted to limit our research to either qualitative or quantitative. This leads to my second suggestion.

Suggestion 2: Take the position that a lot of qualitative research, or a lot of quantitative research, is much less valuable than a little bit of both.

No matter how much qualitative research we do, we will never overcome its weaknesses in enumeration, sampling and multivariate analysis. No matter how much quantitative research we do, we will never overcome its weaknesses in form, distance and cognitive connections. The understanding we gain by looking at a problem from these two very different approaches will be deeper, richer and more reliable than the partial understanding gained from just one approach.

The documentary quality of qualitative research lends itself to dramatic presentations. Few presentation devices are as compelling as the consumer quote that coloquially, but unerringly, cuts to the heart of the problem. The right quote can sound so true it becomes almost irrefutable. In fact, the request for qualitative research sometimes comes in the form of "Let's do some groups and get some 'verbatims' to help sell this idea," or more recently,

"Let's do some groups and get some video-taped comments to help sell this idea."

Suggestion 3: Be careful to use the riveting power of a qualitative research exerpt to illustrate an idea, and not to justify an idea.

The fourth suggestion asks for a basic improvement in the method itself. The focus of this suggestion is not on data collection but on data summary.

First, let's think about the way that quantitative data are summarized. Quantitative research made great strides once we developed good techniques for summarizing a bunch of numbers. The discovery of measures of central tendency (mean, median, etc.), dispersion (standard deviation, interquartile range, etc.), and association (correlation coefficient, chi square, etc.) made quantitative information much more understandable and useful than it had ever been before. After these discoveries, demand for quantitative data exploded.

Judges, given a small sample of data, will be all too quick to form firm conclusions, even when firm conclusions may not be warranted.

What techniques do we have to summarize and make sense out of the rich and voluminous qualitative data that qualitative interviews produce? We really have only one technique, idiosyncratic expert judgment.

Over the last twenty years, expert judgment has itself been the subject of a great deal of research. Every type of expert judgment has been examined from a doctor's diagnosis to a personnel manager's guess as to the future success of an applicant. The results form one of the most consistent bodies of data in all of social science and demonstrate that experts are good at gathering information but are poor and inconsistent at subjectively combining information to make summary judgments. (See Slovic, Fischoff and Lechtenstein, 1977.)

One well documented example of judgment bias seems particularly appropriate to a discussion of qualitative research. Tversky and Kahneman (1971) demonstrated a bias they called "the law of small numbers." Judges, whether laymen or statistically trained experts, tend to underestimate the error and unreliability that are inherent in small samples of data. Judges, given a small sample of data, will be all too quick to form firm conclusions, even when firm conclusions may not be warranted.

In applying qualitative research, judgments are often required. If a particular package design did poorly in some quantitative test of appeal, a marketer may conduct some qualitative research to better understand why. The marketer may observe in the qualitative interviews that several people don't think much of the shape, others find the color unappealing, some say the product photo is not appropriate, and a few have difficulty reading the text on the front. There will be no shortage of ideas for package improvements coming out of the qualitative research. The marketer has to use the qualitative data, along with any other information he or she has, to make judgments about how to proceed. What in the qualitative data will raise the probability that the changes considered will be those most beneficial to the brand? Our only technique relies on idiosyncratic expert judgment, a technique which has been repeatedly demonstrated to be inaedquate.

In many of the studies on expert judgment, the researchers found that the experts could improve their judgment by applying a rather simple set of decision rules. (For example, see Kahneman and Tversky, 1979.) The rules helped the experts organize the qualitative data at their disposal and to apply the data consistently. There may be a simple set of decision rules that can help all of us get more out of our qualitative research. Hence, my fourth suggestion.

Suggestion 4: Search for better tools to summarize what we have learned in qualitative research, and translate qualitative insight into marketing judgment.

The purpose of this article has not been to criticize qualitative research, but rather attempts to make a valuable marketing tool even more valuable.

Qualitative research will be much more valuable if we can:

• Use qualitative research to stimulate rather then evaluate marketing ideas;

• Combine qualitative research with quantitative research to increase the power of both;

- Use qualitative exerpts to illustrate ideas not to sell them;
- Find tools to interpret qualitative data which improve on idiosyncratic expert judgment.

References

Kahneman, D., and Tversky, A. "Intuitive Prediction: Biases and Corrective Procedures," *Forecasting,* Makridakis, S.G. (Ed.). JIMS Studies in the Management Sciences 12 (1979(313-327. North Holland Publishing Company.

Slovic, P., Fischoff, B., and Lichtenstein, S. "Behavioral Decision Theory," *Annual Review of Psychology,.* 28 (1977) 1-39.

Tversky, A., Kahneman, D. "The Belief in the 'Law of Small Numbers.' *Psychological Bulletin.* 76 (1971) 105-110.

Wells, W.D. "Truth and Consequences." *Journal of Advertising Research,* June, July (1986) RC-13 to RC-16.

SECTION V

Variations On A Theme

The articles in this section are presented to give the reader some exposure to some innovative techniques which may be used in qualitative research. In each case the authors have offered techniques which they have found useful, without giving a critical review of their strengths and limitations. Thus, one should be aware that the inclusion of such articles does not constitute an endorsement but offers these possible techniques for the critical review of the reader.

"Projective Techniques Uncover Real Consumer Attitudes" presents a definition and some examples of projective procedures used in groups.

In the second article, "Two-Way Focus Groups can Provide Startling Information," Silverstein discusses a technique in which the observers of one focus group become the respondents in a second stage set of focus groups.

Lederhause and Decker describe and advocate the use of Nominal Group Techniques for certain problems in their article, "Nominal Groups Help Identify Issues and Develop Effective Surveys" while Anastas advocates the use of one-to-one interviews when dealing with sensitive subjects.

Finally, Simon suggests the use of new telecommunications technologies for conducting focus groups in his article "Focus Groups by Phone: Better Way to Research Health Care."

Projective techniques uncover *real* consumer attitudes

BY SHARON L. HOLLANDER

DURING A RECENT airline flight I sat beside a manager who told me about his involvement in a series of brainstorming sessions for a client's floundering paper-matchbook business.

In the middle of one such session, the manager's mind wandered to the home gardening he'd been doing the day before. When he refocused on the meeting, he astutely linked the topic of discussion and his daydream about gardening and came up with the ingenius idea for creating seed sticks, packaged and delivered in convenient "matchbooks," a product that has since become popular in England and extremely profitable for the company.

The manager was surprised that I did not consider his "solution in a daydream" merely a fortunate accident, but an excellent example of a legitimate problem-solving technique.

Increasingly, market researchers are using "projective techniques" that deliberately stimulate a relaxed freeflow of associations that can uncover and identify deep, normally unacknowledged feelings to a degree not usually achieved in a standard focus group.

This kind of research bypasses our logical minds and critical faculties and plumbs the depths of emotions that have a crucial effect on consumers' purchasing decisions and brand loyalty.

Because these techniques are specifically designed to bypass people's built-in censoring mechanisms, they are particularly useful in eliciting honest information about sensitive or embarassing topics and products.

The experience of the individual conducting this type of research is critical if projective techniques are to be used effectively. Equally important are the subjects themselves.

Although it is true that given sufficient time virtually anyone can be drawn out, it is most cost-effective to screen for "creative-articulate" con-

Sharon L. Hollander is president of Solutions Marketing Research and director of Sharpen the Focus, Moderator Training Workshops, in Locust Valley, N.Y.

sumers, who see themselves as spontaneous, willing to take risks, flexible, imaginative, nonconforming to strict rules and structure, able to get along with different people, and uncomfortable with routine activity and wasting time.

In contrast, those people who are screened out before the research are likely to describe themselves as quiet, peacemakers, neutral group members, most comfortable with structure, and committed to tried and true solutions.

In selecting natually expressive and creative individuals, is the research biased at the outset? Experience says that's not the case.

Deeply personal emotions are usually the emotions shared by human beings across the board, no matter what their personality type. Moreover, although researchers screen for creativity and a willingness to recognize and verbalize deep emotions, they must be careful to include representatives from a variety of appropriate socioeconomic and educational populations.

In general terms, a projective technique is the use of any vague stimulus that an individual subject is asked to describe, expand on, or build a structure around. Market researchers sometimes employ the "modified TAT," an adaptation of the Thematic Apperception Test (TAT) used by psychologists, in developing print ads and billboards.

The participants are first shown an unbranded visual that is under consideration for the ad and asked to create a story around it. The moderator or interviewer encourages participants to go beyond the literal and release some of the more elusive feelings and associations that the imagination stirs up.

What is happening in this picture? What are the characters doing, thinking, feeling? What happens next? What will the outcome be?

Participants do not directly address their feelings about a product or brand, but reveal them indirectly through their responses to visuals and changes in the visuals. Even a slight change in presentation—a tilt of the model's head in a photograph, for example—can evoke a significantly different response.

The picture might be shown a second time with a brand name and a tagline. The participant is asked whether he or she sees the same scenario and how well the picture and the brand match. Sometimes an appealing story loses its intrigue when a less than popular brand is added.

On the other hand, a neutral visual can become more exciting when a well-liked product or tagline is added. The interplay of brand and visual can then be explored.

Because most people view these exercises as fun, they take the opportunity to express themselves more fully and openly. One interesting finding is that people from different segments of the population tell similar stories about the same photos or images.

Another approach is "guided imagery." Instead of asking participants to appraise a product or brand directly, they are asked to concentrate on creating and experiencing an associated image. This technique takes pressure off the respondents because they do not have to come up with a rational or "right" response.

For example, in using "The Looking Glass"—our own registered brand of guided imagery—we ask participants to imagine the kind of door that would bear the imprint of a particular brand name. Subjects are then asked to walk through their imagined door and experience what's behind it.

People tend to forget themselves in their involvement with the process, allowing them to be more creative in their images and ultimately more hon-

---

Reprinted from *Marketing News,* **22 (January 4, 1988), 34, published by the American Marketing Association.**

est in revealing their inner thoughts and feelings.

Here, too, common responses are found. Positive feelings about a brand name usually generate a solid or carved oak door, with a brass lever handle. Negative feelings usually conjure up a plain or shabbier door that lacks a handle and simply pushes open.

The "benefit chain," also called "laddering," is most often used in a one-on-one interview. It generally begins with a practical benefit statement from which respondents are asked to provide or name two new benefits. For each benefit identified, they are asked for two more, until as many as 16 possible benefits are developed. The progression is normally from the practical to the more emotional, motivational factors.

The advantage of the benefit chain is that it is relatively easy to administer without a highly sophisticated interviewer. The only key decision is when to stop probing. In our training classes, instructors tell moderators to listen for references to self-esteem, because the ultimate benefit is always one of feeling good about oneself.

Using a technique called "category sculpting" allows for greater projection than the benefit chain, but requires more guidance on the part of the moderator.

In this exercise an entire category of brands in considered as a family. Each brand within the family is assigned a role and characteristics, such as the cute child, the irresponsible uncle, the domineering mother, the needy cousin. The relationship of one brand to the other is clarified, as is the specific niche that has been carved out for each. Participants also discuss what traits all the family members have in common.

Other useful projective techniques include "sentence completion," "synesthesia," and "Scent-sations." With sentence completion ("Mother always said toothpaste...") participants are encouraged to fill in the sentence several times, rather than just once.

In synesthesia, participants are asked to deliberately fuse their senses and answer questions such as: What does a smooth shave sound, smell, look, and taste like? The registered Scent-sations technique is based on the fact that the perception of scent and emotion both reside in the temporal lobe, accounting for the finding that scent can be used to trigger feelings about a particular aromatic product such as coffee, cologne, soap, or pizza.

During all sessions involving projective techniques, the moderator and backroom staff are key participants. While listening to the material presented by the respondents, they must remain alert to their own images and associations.

Very often moderators and observers are able to find innovative solutions or draw insightful conclusions by paying attention to their own random thoughts. "Listening with the third ear" is a vital function in completing one's research.

Like the manager who was "distracted" by his garden, an enormously valuable idea may be hidden among our most unfocused reveries.

Two-way focus groups can provide startling information

BY MICHAEL SILVERSTEIN

"TWO-WAY FOCUS" is the name of a research technique developed by Bozell, Jacobs, Kenyon & Eckhardt. It allows one target group to listen to and learn from a related group.

Two-Way Focus emerged from work the agency was doing with physicians and patients related to the management of arthritis.

The new technique would seem to be just the medicine the pharmaceutical industry, as well as others, needs. It gets at the inner workings of the relationship between providers of a service or product and customers.

There is often a huge gap between reality and perception. Often, what patients think they are accomplishing by taking a medicine is different from the actual result.

And physicians often do not know what their patients are thinking; how they feel about the medicine they are taking and what their emotional needs are, as opposed to physiological needs.

To close this gap, we first held a series of focus groups with arthritis patients. We heard over and over that their physicians didn't talk to them enough and didn't take the time to listen.

THEN WE HELD groups with physicians to learn how they managed their arthritis patients. These groups made it obvious to us that many physicians don't appreciate how much their patients really need to talk with them.

This more or less traditional approach to qualitative exploration provided interesting insight into the physician-patient relationship. But it

Michael Silverstein is the marketing director at Bozell, Jacobs, Kenyon & Eckhardt, New York.

didn't seem to be enough, and we decided to go further.

We had the physicians observe a focus group of arthritis patients talking about their physicians and medications. We immediately followed the patient group with a focus group of the physicians who had observed the patients.

The effect of the patient group on the physicians was startling. They emerged from behind the viewing room's one-way glass flushed and glassy-eyed. As they talked in their own group, with us observing, it became apparent they had little idea that patients would be taking as many as 10-15 medications at one time.

Nor, it seems, had they really known the desperation their patients felt when their physicians didn't take the time to really talk with them; didn't take the time for them to feel they were being taken seriously.

We knew we had a breakthrough technique when, observing the physician's group, we saw the transforming effect the patient group had on the physicians.

WHAT WERE SOME of the more important hypotheses that came from this first application of Two-Way Focus?

One was that physicians seem to assume patients put control of their pain into their hands; in fact, the patients don't willingly relinquish control over their discomfort. Instead, they want to

feel that they, too, can take control.

Second, physicians may not adequately cover everything relevant in their patients' case histories, and certainly they need to update their patients' histories periodically.

They sometimes miss the over-the-counter medications their patients take in combination with prescribed products, the combination of which can seriously affect the efficacy of the medication and symptomology of the patient.

SINCE THIS FIRST application of our technique, we've successfully used it in the analgesic category: we had mothers watch their daughters talk about headache pain remedies, and we learned that one generation can influence another.

We've also employed the technique to learn which products and services used by "sophisticated" users of telephone systems seem to most impress "casual" users of telephone systems.

Members of our account and creative teams are now working closely with our market research director and other members of the agency's strategic planning and research team to make full use of information learned from the groups.

They are also developing ways to further apply the technique to more categories.

Two-Way Focus would seem to be especially useful for creative development whenever advertising is directed at multiple constituencies. Some of these other situations might include closing the gap between financial consultants and investors, retail store managers and shoppers, and franchisees and customers.

Reprinted from *Marketing News*, 22 (January 4, 1988), 31, published by the American Marketing Association.

Nominal groups help identify issues and develop effective surveys

BY MARY ANN LEDERHAUS
and JANE E. DECKER

A RELATIVELY NEW dimension has been added to our Center for Local Government through adaptations of the Delbecq, VandeVen, Gustafson Nominal Group Technique (NGT), named for the three professors who developed it.

We have found that the NGT enables us to not only identify public issues and problems, but also develop relevant suggestions for survey instruments.

The technique is highly recommended for marketing researchers and new-product planners.

For us, a major advantage is the forced participation, interaction, and responsiveness of diverse individuals to issues and problems the center is studying.

The center regularly conducts nominal groups with employees of government agencies. We use our successes with previous nominal-group procedures to design current programs.

The NGT is structured as a day's session and works as follows:

1. Problem statement: To identify issues and problem areas or develop ideas for survey instruments, a question to be answered by the group is written.

We carefully preselect a group of nine to 12 persons, usually practitioners, who have expertise in the topic and present them with the question.

The question is printed on a flip chart and on sheets of paper placed on a table in front of each participant. A group leader reads the question aloud before the technique begins.

2. Idea generation: Each individual receives 20-30 minutes to generate and write down as many ideas or answers to the question as possible.

Participants are asked to be specific. Although no maximum number

Mary Ann Lederhaus is a faculty associate and associate professor of marketing at the University of North Florida, Jacksonville. Jane E. Decker is an associate professor of political science and director of the university's Center for Local Government.

of answers is required, usually some minimum per person, such as six to eight, is encouraged.

This is mainly to stimulate individual thinking. We emphasize that each person's responses are important and will be considered.

In a recent study to develop ideas for a questionnaire, 11 persons generated an almost burdensome 95 answers. The results proved invaluable in developing a questionnaire on the use of public facilities, which has been sent to a stratified random sample.

3. Round-robin feedback: When the idea-generation time is up, the group leader asks each person to share one idea with the group.

The idea is written on flip-chart sized pieces of paper, which are displayed on the walls of the room. The process continues until all ideas have been exhausted.

No criticisms are permitted, and no comments are allowed until all answers are displayed. A person may pass a chance in the round-robin and enter later on, if desired.

4. Editing: When the group has presented all ideas or answers to the question, answers are clarified and similar responses are grouped.

Every participant must endorse this editing process. Grouping must be approved by those who originally gave the responses.

5. Rating: This occurs in two stages. After the final editing, the group members rate the answers by

pulling out their 10 or 15 favorite.

The members receive index cards and place the numbers of their favorite responses on them, one number per card. They are asked to throw away five (two if using 10 favorite responses) of their least favorite answers.

6. Ranking: Participants rank the remaining 10 cards in numerical order, 10 being their most favorite. Duplication of numbers is not allowed.

7. Tabulating: Participants usually are dismissed from the nominal group while tabulators summate responses to the questions.

If several group sessions are taking place at once, they are timed carefully so all sessions finish at about the same time.

Tabulators do the following: sum the total points accrued to each response; sum the number of people voting for a particular response; and tally the distribution of points for the response.

It is interesting, from an analysis perspective, to know whether 20 points were accrued by two persons, four persons, or more.

Also, the distribution of points gives us the deviation of responses.

8. Break: Group members break for lunch and meet again afterward to conclude the process. Potential solutions to the problem areas generated earlier are discussed.

(The process for the public-facilities questionnaire, however, ended at this point. These group members were invited to a reception, and tabulations were presented. Because ideas for a questionnaire were the goal of this nominal group, it was not necessary to generate potential solutions.)

If a reception is not held, answers and rankings are typed and sent to each nominal-group participant.

9. Potential solutions: Don Ungrait, of Florida State University,

Reprinted from *Marketing News,* 21 (August 28, 1987), 44, published by the American Marketing Association.

helped us develop a technique that made it possible to ask for solutions to more than one of the winning problem areas generated in the morning session.

It is possible, for example, to take the top four or five, or more, problems and develop solutions in a relatively short time.

In only one instance we divided a group of 20 persons into four groups and gave each a question written on a pad of paper. Each group was given a number to put on the pad above their answers.

They were asked to write down as many answers to the problem as possible, numbering each answer. We asked that each member of the group contribute responses, but that only one write them on the pad.

In the first round, each group was given 15 minutes, after which the pads were rotated to the next table. The new groups were asked to read the question and the responses that the previous group had made, add more responses or solutions, and number their group and solutions.

Twelve minutes were allowed for the second round. The pads were rotated two more times, first with 10 minutes allowed and then with eight minutes.

At this point, each group should have responded to each problem. The round-robin, editing, rating, and ranking procedure were not used. Instead, pads were rotated again, and the participants rated their favorite solutions on index cards and ranked them, five being the most favorite and one the least favorite.

SPECIAL EMPHASIS must be given to grouping like-minded people to generate uniform output. This occurs if the NGT facilitator or leader has substantive knowledge about the topic and the participants' personalities.

The output is presented to the contracting business to help it make decisions.

For sensitive research subjects, one to one interviews work best

by Michael Anastas, President
Focus Probe Inc., New York

Banks need not—and should not—wait for new consumer research. On a regular basis, banks should use qualitative research as part of a continuing education process.

Bankers have to reach out and touch the hearts, mind, breath, and shape of the consumer.

The qualitative people can take the form of focus groups or one-to-one interviews. Focus groups are fine for open-ended exploration. However, to find the deeper attitudes about specific issues, you need the privacy of the one-to-one—particularly when the subject is money and personal finance. People don't like to talk about their money in a group.

Trust is Essential

The ability of the qualitative researcher to gain the trust of respondents frees them to be candid, encourages them to elaborate, and allows them to reveal their true feelings in the privacy of the one-to-one interview.

Usually, the first few minutes of the interview are crucial. This is when a bond must be created between the interviewer and respondent. The respondent enters confused, not knowing where he or she is, and having only a vague notion about what is to happen and why. It is essential that a respondent be drawn in and trusting, almost immediately.

The setting for a one-to-one interview is usually a conference table where the interviewer and respondent sit across from one another, creating an intimate, direct eye contact situation. A typical interview begins with a welcome and small talk from the interviewer until both are seated. Once seated, it's helpful if the interviewer makes an outright request for candor. Sometimes I will half-joke, "I only make money on this if you speak frankly." The respondent should be assured that all information is absolutely confidential.

Typically, the initial questions relate to the general research subject. Since the respondent has been prescreened, he or she should have some familiarity or expertise in the subject. Calling on this expertise and asking opinions not only makes the respondent feel confident, but also gets him or her thinking in the right groove.

Several psychological techniques can keep the respondent

Consumers who shy away from focus groups generally prefer to talk privately about their money matters.

feeling confident and expressive. People are afraid of being put on the spot, so encouraging comments ("interesting," "Yes, go on"), understanding comments ("Yes, that's the downside of big business"), gestures (nods), and a sense of humor are essential.

To encourage stream of consciousness, the interviewer should also use colloquialisms ("What's the deal with the price range?"... "Do you feel cool about what we're doing?"), provide transitions ("and...," "therefore..."), and paraphrase questions so the respondent doesn't get stuck.

Keeping an interview moving at a good clip is one way to insure gut-level answers.

Of course, these techniques must be employed according to the interviewer's assessment of the respondent's personality. For example, a reserved executive might clam up at the first sign of irreverent humor.

I usually note responses on paper, sometimes asking the respondent to repeat observations so I can get every nuance. This makes the respondents feel that their words are important and taken seriously. Because they sense the interviewer's confidence in their opinions, they feel they owe candid, honest answers, and are forthcoming.

Qualitative research can peel away layers of response like the layers of an onion to get to the real emotional attitudes. For example, take the questions: Why do you bank at North Bank? Here are some predictable answers:

■ "It's convenient to my home."

■ "It's big."

■ "It's where my payroll comes from."

■ "They offer a good rate on IRAs."

A qualitative researcher doesn't stop there. He seeks the gut responses that are elusive and fragile. Digging deeper in one-to-one interviews, we find that customers want to believe that the bank is their friend. They really wish they had a friend at First National. While they know it's not really true, they wish to believe there is some human link.

Individuals often are loyal to a bank because of some little anecdote, some small favor that made that human link with

Reprinted from *Bank Marketing*, 20 (July 1988), 18-22. Used with permission of Bank Marketing Association.

the bank come alive. For example, a middle-aged executive rewards the bank with his continued business because, years previously, when he had no credit, the bank extended him trust.

Often the human factor is the real reason behind customer loyalty, even though initial repsonses tend to be much more superficial (''close to my home,'' etc.).

To illustrate how a qualitative researcher probes for the gut-level response, here's an example of the method:

Question: Why do you bank at North Bank?

Answer: ''Because it's close to home.''

Question: Why do you choose North Bank instead of the other banks close to your home?

Answer: ''Because I've had an account at North Bank for years.''

Question: What's kept you at North Bank all these years?

Answer: ''It was the first bank where I opened an account.''

Question: How long ago was that?

Answer: ''When I was 19 years old and away at college, they were the only bank that made it easy for me to open an account.''

After peeling away the layers of response, the researchers discovered that the man was loyal to ''North Bank'' because it did him a favor when he was 19. Twenty years later, he's depositing $75,000 a year and transacting other profitable business.

After discovering the critical human link behind a customer's loyalty, the question for the bank is: What is the organization doing to support, maintain, and protect his essentially fragile relationship?

The vaulted cathedral architecture of banks may be a thing of the past, but people still want bankers to represent solidity and responsibility. They may be banking out of a kiosk window or at an outlet that resembles a Fotomat store, but they want bankers to convey a serious, conservative attitude toward money.

Qualitative one-to-one interviews for a home equity loan concept study revealed that respondents were repelled by the idea of ''quick and easy'' money based on using their home as collateral. The most acceptable concept took a more responsible tone, and gave serious examples of how the loan might be used, such as college tuition, home improvement, or business expansion.

In this same concept study, the term ''instant cash'' prompted one respondent to equate the term with ''Satan.''

As a result of this research, the bank stayed away from words such as ''instant,'' ''easy,'' and ''quick.'' Instead, it developed communication strategies that stressed a warm yet professional, responsible approach. Afterwards, applications for equity loans increased by 300%.

Underlying Objectives

The face-to-face closeness in qualitative research may seem unusual to some, but by tuning into attitudes and needs, bankers can reach their objectives.

For a bank interested in pursuing small businesses of $45-50 million, open-ended exploratory research revealed what these businesses look for in a bank. The initial question put to respondents was: How do you pick a bank?

Through probing their answers, an underlying factor emerged. These companies were interested in continuing contact with an officer who they felt knew them, understood their business, and with whom they were accumulating a history. They wanted to do business, not with a bank, but with a banker. ''I'm dealing with Harry, not with Empire Bank.''

Access to a decision-making officer wasn't enough. The access needed to continue over time so that the company could depend on the relationship. Thus the bank learned that when a ''personal banker'' is promoted, it could be a mistake to drop the small business customer. Moving personnel up or to other branches could disrupt the continuing that is the key to their bond with this customer.

Qualitative research helped a bank become sensitized to the mortgage market. Worried about losing share to commercial banks and mortgage brokers, it commissioned research among real estate agents. The bank discovered that, uppermost in the agent's mind at the moment he was recommending a bank to a prospective buyer, was how fast the bank approved a loan, rather than the actual rate or percentage.

The real estate agent would say to the buyer, ''it might take you longer at this bank than at that bank.'' While there is nothing exactly new about this insight, it made a tremendous impression on my client. The next morning he rushed to the real estate department to initiate new emphasis on speedy approvals.

Qualitative research should not be taken as the final word. It is only a directional guide. But as a way for banks to stay in touch with their customers, it is invaluable.

Focus groups by phone: better way to research health care

BY MURRAY SIMON

FOCUS GROUPS with physicians and dentists are substantially different from all other types of groups.

When you weigh the underlying factors that are unique to the average focus group with health care providers, it's enough to make you decide not to do them. Consider the following:

● Focus groups with health care practitioners are generally conducted in or near major cities, primarily to ensure a large enough recruitment pool.

Within any sizable metropolitan area, there will invariably be a heavy concentration of graduates from nearby professional schools. This can easily lead to philosophical biases in focus groups based on the teaching philosophies in these institutions.

In addition to regional similarities in educational background, recent research has shown that treatment methods and types of treatment rendered have definite regional consistencies.

● There are noticeable similarities in the office environment and work ethic of practitioners from any given area. The dentist practicing in New York City tends to work differently than the dentist from Roanoke, Va. It can therefore be expected that focus groups with providers in any given location will be similar in attitude by virtue of geographic professional "inbreeding."

● It is very difficult to convene groups of professionals without having some respondents who know each other or know of each other within the group. All too often the people in the viewing room sit and watch groups of practitioners file into the conference room carrying on friendly conversations with each other as they take their seats.

Screening out colleague familiarity isn't easy, particularly when specialists have to be recruited, and often leads to the establishment of an immediate pecking order based on seniority and/or standing within the professional community.

Murray Simon, DDS, is president of D/R/S Consultants, New Fairfield, Conn.

● After a day at the office or hospital, it is quite difficult to get practitioners to give up an evening to attend a focus group. The old concern about how typical is the "typical" respondent is especially apt with these groups. The problem becomes particularly acute when there is the need to recruit small-incidence specialties or people with highly specialized knowledge.

● It is frequently important in health care marketing research to get feedback from a variety of specialists or a mix of general practitioners and specialists on the same product or subject. Researchers tend to avoid developing mixed groups, often for good reason. Some general practitioners will be reluctant to offer opinions in the presence of specialists.

Some specialists will defer to the training or experience of other specialists. And lately there seems to be a rash of groups wherein general practitioners will take verbal pot shots at the specialists present, or one type of specialist will try to do a character assassination on another type of specialist.

The result is that if a number of specialties and/or general practitioners must be heard, there will be the tendency to run a larger series of groups to avoid mixing.

● Recruitment costs and incentive payments are getting high for these groups. In part this is due to the extraordinary amount of time that must be spent in recruitment, and it is based partially on the belief that it takes a bigger carrot dangled in front of a doctor to get participation.

If you add the standard focus group problems to the above list—inclement weather, geographic sampling limited by facility location, reluctant participants, travel costs, the increasing difficulty of getting "virgin" respondents, and trying to extract information from a sea of cross-conversations on tape—what we wind up with is a problem very much in need of a solution.

Despite all the difficulties, focus groups with health care practitioners are necessary to keep up with the rapid changes taking place in medicine and dentistry.

Searching for a better way, D/R/S HealthCare Consultants has explored the telephone focus group, using teleconferencing techniques to link respondents, moderator, and client in a focus group format. Initially our thought was that it might prove to be an acceptable substitute for some face-to-face group situations, particularly when time, convenience, and/or budget are a factor.

But in the time spent working with this technology, our thinking has changed dramatically. This is a strong, solid marketing research tool that can stand on its own and deliver a high quality of information when used properly. Not only that, there are distinct advantages of the telephone over the face-to-face group:

1. Groups can have tremendous geographic diversity.

It is possible to reach every nook and cranny in the country. A great number of respondents who would not have been heard from are now available to the researcher.

Respondents find it quite interesting to conference with colleagues from other parts of the country. The variation in thought and attitudes can be quite refreshing. In addition, groups can be held in South America, Europe, the Far East, and Australia with the researchers and client never having to leave the U.S.

2. Travel costs can be virtually eliminated.

All participants—respondents, moderator, and clients—can particpate from their homes or offices.

3. Recruitment is easier because you are not asking a respondent to spend the better part of an evening

Reprinted from *Marketing News*, 22 (August 29, 1988), 47-48, published by the American Marketing Association.

traveling to, sitting in, and returning from a facility.

Many practitioners not only appreciate the convenience, but they are intrigued by the idea of participating in a research conference over the telephone. It is often possible to get them for a lower remuneration than that customarily paid for attending a face-to-face group.

4. Mixed groups are no problem.

Because of the tremendous geographic diversity, none of the respondents in a group knows each other—they don't run into each other the next day at the hospital or at local meetings and have to defend something they said at a focus group meeting.

We also feel that allowing the respondent to participate while seated in comfortable and familiar surroundings tends to make them less defensive and protective of what they are saying. There is no one present who might pass judgment.

5. Any moderator who has had to do midwinter focus groups in the Northeast or Midwest knows what it's like to get on a plane with a prayer for good weather.

With the possible exception of blizzards, hurricanes, or tornadoes, weather will not knock out a telephone group. As long as phone lines are intact, the group can go on as planned.

6. The information that comes out of a telephone group is clean, concise, and to the point.

The problem with cross-conversations and wandering minds that often afflicts the face-to-face situation is virtually eliminated. Extracting information from the tapes for report writing is a moderator's dream; everything is clear, nothing is lost.

7. The overbearing respondent can put in an appearance at virtually any kind of focus group, but this character can be a rather special problem in groups of physicians or dentists.

The respondents in a provider group feel they were recruited because of their knowledge and experience, and Dr. Tellitall is determined to see to it that the moderator gets an earful.

Assuming all moderator attempts at neutralization fail, the final solution is to politely ask the good doctor to leave. While this is not commonly done, there are many times when a moderator is tempted.

Removing a health care practitioner from a roomful of colleagues can eas-

---

Telephone focus raises questions

BY MURRAY SIMON

IN DISCUSSING TELEPHONE GROUPS with clients who are unfamiliar with them, similar questions or comments arise:

● "I have to see their faces to know what they're really thinking."

As a moderator, I've seen this work both ways. There are times when the slender respondent in the custom-tailored suit is given more credence than the chubby one in the jeans. Once a moderator is familiar with the telephone technique and with health care providers, it is relatively easy to judge the mood of the respondents by the sound of their voices and the way they phrase their comments.

● "How can you get client interaction with the moderator during the group session?"

There are two ways to handle this. A second telephone line can link the client to the moderator. This line is manned by an associate who relays questions or comments to the moderator.

The second method is to have a representative of the company, perhaps the product manager or someone from R&D, on the line with the group. This individual is introduced at the start of the session as a research associate and can make comments and ask or answer questions as the need arises.

● "How can you get group interaction over the telephone?"

Two types of telephone "bridges" can be used. One is the voice-activated bridge that allows only one person to speak at any given time. While this would seem to preclude interaction, it has been our experience that in a well-moderated group this is not the case.

Respondents frequently comment on previous statements and will often address their remarks to others in the group. It is not uncommon for one respondent to ask a question directly of another.

The second bridge is an interactive one that allows two or three voices to be transmitted simultaneously. Interaction is alive and well in the telephone focus group.

● "Isn't it difficult to identify who's speaking during the conference?"

At the beginning of each conference the respondents are asked to identify themselves as they come on. Should anyone forget to do so, it's a simple matter to interrupt (even with the voice-activated bridge) and ask for identification.

● "Are tapes of the groups available?"

All telephone groups are taped. The moderator's copy is available immediately after the meeting. Clients can have tapes in hand within 36 hours. If the client requires transcripts of the proceedings, it is much easier to transcribe telephone-group tapes—and with far greater accuracy than it is in working with conventional focus group tapes.

---

ily lead to a "circling of the wagons" on the part of those who remain, with the result being the loss of any further relevance from the group.

On the other hand, leaving this character in place can prove to be a turnoff for the other respondents.

This particular problem is much easier to handle in the telephone setting with far fewer potentially disturbing results. The moderator's assistant can call the operator/facilitator who is supervising the bridging equipment and have him or her switch the problem respondent to the assistant's line.

This can be done immediately and allows the assistant to have a heart-to-heart talk with this individual without anyone else in the group knowing about it. If this person refuses to cooperate, the operator/facilitator can be instructed to arrange for a "problem with one of the lines" to occur.

8. Concept testing is easy.

Materials can be sent to the respondents in sealed envelopes to be opened at the meeting. This technique has been used quite successfully to test advertising concepts, packaging, product design, etc. We have even discovered a method to deal with many of the problems of security and secrecy.

9. Researchers and clients do not have to chase all over the country to put together a sufficient number of representative groups from among the smaller sub-specialties.

10. Health care providers enjoy participating in these groups.

It gives them an opportunity to tap into the thinking of their colleagues in other parts of the country. We have received many notes from respondents asking to be included in future groups.

There are additional applications for this technology that are either being used now or suggest themselves

for future use. It can serve as an effective vehicle for the dissemination of information, particularly in terms of developing an awareness among practitioners of new products, current research on well-established products, or repositioning products.

Many health care manufacturers find the use of professional panels helpful in developing marketing strategies. Unfortunately, too often these panels are expensive, difficult to recruit, regionalized in their thinking, often affected by absenteeism, and difficult to manage.

The telephone technology would appear to be the answer to many of these problems. Panels can be convened on a regular basis, generally in the evening, with each of the panel members participating from the convenience of home or office.

The panel can easily consist of practitioners from all parts of the country. In addition, practitioners representing smaller subsegments become more readily available to participate. Hard copy, ad, product design, or packaging concepts can be sent in advance for evaluation at the time of the meeting.

The telephone group isn't meant to be a replacement for the face-to-face group. D/R/S does face-to-face as well as phone groups because there are times when it is necessary to go out and run videos or show concepts and observe the reaction. It is important to realize, however, that qualitative marketing research with health care providers presents some serious obstacles.

Anyone who is a health care moderator or a marketer involved in research with physicians, dentists, or other providers is fully aware of how problematic these projects can be. Unfortunately, compromises are often the rule rather than the exception, particularly in the areas of recruitment, controlling group dynamics, and obtaining information that is truly representative of the thinking of the profession.

The telephone group isn't to be considered a panacea, but it does offer advantages and opportunities that should be given serious consideration by health care marketers and researchers.

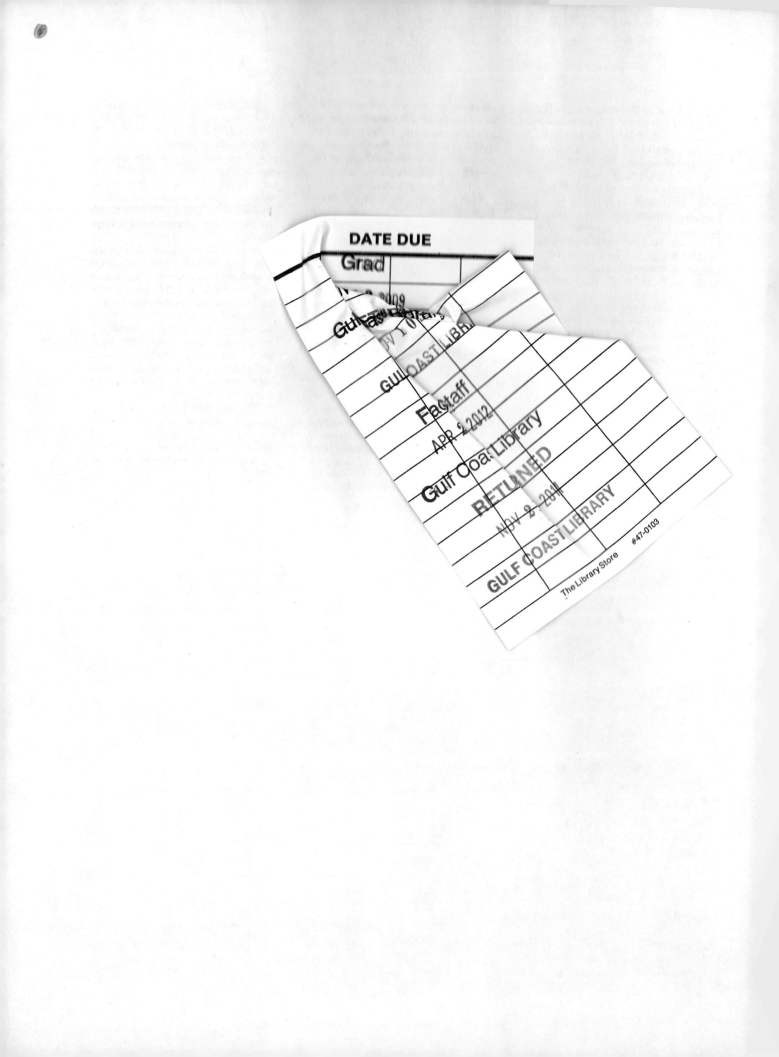